WHAT'S WRONG WITH ETHNOGRAPHY?

Ethnography is today widely used and accepted as an approach to social research, yet it remains controversial. In this stimulating critique, Martyn Hammersley concentrates on the major methodological issues currently facing ethnography. How valid is its claim to represent an independent social reality? What is the link between ethnography and social and political practice? What is its proper relationship to quantitative method? *What's Wrong with Ethnography?* provides novel answers to these questions.

Neither endorsing traditional ethnographic thinking nor simply accepting the views of its critics, the author argues that traditional ethnography involves a naïve realism that is indefensible but at the same time he rejects the appeal of relativism. Similarly, while insisting that ethnographic findings must be relevant to practical and political issues, he rejects the arguments of advocates of critical and practitioner ethnography. He questions the idea that ethnography represents a distinct epistemological, or even methodological, paradigm, and suggests instead that ethnography should be integrated into the mainstream of social research methodology.

Martyn Hammersley's conclusions have radical implications for ethnography and will challenge and provoke both practitioners of ethnography and their critics. His book is essential reading for anyone with an interest in qualitative research, or indeed in social research methodology generally.

Martyn Hammersley is Senior Lecturer in the School of Education, Open University.

WHAT'S WRONG WITH ETHNOGRAPHY?

Methodological explorations

Martyn Hammersley

London and New York

First published in 1992
by Routledge
11 New Fetter Lane, London EC4P 4EE

Simultaneously published in the USA and Canada
by Routledge
29 West 35th Street, New York, NY 10001

Reprinted 1993

Typeset by LaserScript, Mitcham, Surrey.
Printed and bound in Great Britain by
Biddles Ltd, Guildford and King's Lynn

British Library Cataloguing in Publication Data
Hammersley, Martyn
What's wrong with ethnography?
1. Ethnography
I. Title
306.072

Library of Congress Cataloging in Publication Data
Hammersley, Martyn.
What's wrong with ethnography?/Martyn Hammersley.
p. cm.
Includes bibliographical references and index.
1. Ethnology–Methodology. 2. Ethnology–Research.
3. Ethnology–Philosophy. I. Title.
GN345.H36 1992
305.8–dc20   91-10212
                                              CIP

ISBN 0–415–05476-1
ISBN 0–415–05477-X (pbk)

CONTENTS

CONTENTS

FIGURES

ACKNOWLEDGEMENTS

Thanks to Barry Cooper, Peter Foster, Roger Gomm, Colin Lacey, Donald Mackinnon, John Scarth, Thomas Schwandt and John K. Smith for comments on or discussions about various of the essays included in this book. Thanks also to Joan, Rachel and Paul, just for being there.

Chapter 1 was previously published in a slightly different version in *Sociology*, 24, 3, pp. 597–617.

Chapter 2 is a substantially modified version of 'Making a Vice of our Virtues', which appeared in I.F. Goodson and S.J. Ball (eds) *Defining the Curriculum*, Lewes, Falmer, 1984.

The author is much obliged to the British Sociological Association and to Falmer Press respectively for permission to reprint these articles.

INTRODUCTION

The title of this collection of essays is ambiguous. Read in one way it might be taken to imply a defiant defence of ethnography (what's wrong with it?). Alternatively, the title may be interpreted as promising the discussion of some serious problems facing this approach to social research.[1] This ambiguity is intentional. It captures what I take to be ethnography's ambivalent status at the present time. On the one hand, it has come to be widely accepted as a legitimate approach to social research. The proportion of social researchers who use qualitative method has increased considerably in recent years. Criticisms that it is unscientific, or at best can only serve as a preliminary to the 'real' (that is, quantitative) work of social science, have declined sharply in many quarters. Even many quantitative researchers now accept that qualitative research has its own logic and criteria of validity. This reflects a movement from a situation of methodological conflict to one of *détente*, or at least of peaceful coexistence, between different approaches to social research (Rist 1977; Smith and Heshusius 1986; Eisner and Peshkin 1990).[2] At the same time, criticism of ethnographic practice has arisen from new directions; indeed, from among ethnographers themselves. One reason for this is that the widespread acceptance of ethnography has led to considerable internal diversification of approach (Jacob 1987; Atkinson *et al.* 1988), which has generated internal criticism of various kinds (see, for example, Wolcott 1980; Lutz 1981; McDermott 1982; Atkinson and Delamont 1985). Political and philosophical trends outside of ethnography, notably a growth in questioning of the value of scientific ways of thinking and increased demand for knowledge that is practically relevant, have also had their effects. These developments have led to criticism centring on rather different

1

issues from those that were at the focus of the earlier debates between quantitative and qualitative researchers; though there remains some continuity since a prominent argument in recent criticism is that much ethnography has retained elements of positivism, rather than making a sufficiently radical break with it.

There are two especially salient areas of current criticism. First, there is the issue of representation. To what degree can ethnographic accounts legitimately claim to represent an independent social reality? In the past, much of the argument supporting the value of ethnography in comparison with quantitative method was couched in terms of its greater ability to capture the nature of social phenomena. However, in recent years many have come to question this realist conception of validity, arguing that the data which ethnographers use is a product of their participation in the field rather than a mere reflection of the phenomenon studied, and/or is constructed in and through the process of analysis and the writing of ethnographic accounts. The most obvious example of this anti-realist trend is the growing interest in the rhetorical strategies used by ethnographers, these often being treated as constituting rather than merely representing what they describe (see, for example, Tyler 1985; Clifford and Marcus 1986; Clifford 1988).

Another area where traditional ideas about ethnography are being challenged concerns the relationship between research and practice. In a variety of fields conventional ethnography (along with other forms of social research) has come to be criticised for failing to contribute to practice; whether to political activity, narrowly defined, or to various relevant forms of occupational practice (such as that of policy-makers, administrators of various kinds, social workers and schoolteachers). Examples of such criticism are to be found in the writings of advocates of critical and action ethnography (see, for example, Carr and Kemmis 1986). In arguing that ethnography should have a more direct relationship with practice, perhaps even being integrated with it, such critics raise queries about what the purpose of ethnography is and should be, and how well current ethnographic research serves that purpose. Also arising here are questions about the relationship between facts and values, and between researchers and practitioners. As with anti-realism, this type of criticism has often been presented, not as a rejection of ethnography in favour of some other approach, but rather as capitalising on its strengths or even purging it of extraneous positivist elements. In the course of such

2

arguments the distinctive capacity of ethnography to contribute to practice has often been emphasised, the criticism being that this potential has not been maximised in previous work.[3]

It should be clear that these two areas are not peripheral to ethnographic methodology. If it were to be concluded that ethnographic accounts do not represent reality but rather constitute one (or more than one) 'reality' amongst others, and/or that ethnography should be a form of applied or even action research, this would have profound implications for ethnographic practice. The first seems to lead to 'experimentation' with rhetorical devices, including the use of fiction (see Krieger 1984 and van Maanen 1988). The second is often taken to imply the abolition of specialist inquiry in favour of research carried out by practitioners themselves.

The ambiguity of my title, then, indicates what seems to me to be the currently ambivalent state of ethnography. On the one hand, in many fields it has achieved recognition so that the question of what is wrong with it may be interpreted rhetorically as implying its acceptance as one legitimate approach to social research amongst others. On the other hand, the emergence of some fundamental criticisms of ethnographic method suggests that the question ought to be interpreted in a more literal way. In this book I shall give emphasis to the second of these interpretations. I accept the value of ethnographic research and of the methodological ideas associated with it. At the same time, I think it faces serious problems. I believe that the challenge of anti-realism and of those who advocate a more direct relationship between ethnography and practice must be addressed. While I regard many of the arguments of these critics as mistaken, I think that they point to important and neglected methodological questions. On top of this, I believe that the issues involved in the earlier dispute between quantitative and qualitative researchers have not yet been satisfactorily resolved. The debate simply subsided, and, ironically, the present climate of *détente* seems to discourage rational discussion of these issues almost as much as did the earlier period of cold war. Today, disagreements seem often to be put down to the incommensurability of paradigms or are dealt with by means of pragmatic compromise. In my view these issues still require sustained attention, and the conclusions I draw about them have some radical implications for ethnography.

So, the chapters in this book constitute my answer to the some-what ambiguous question posed in its title. They range across the three areas of debate I have identified; and they offer what I hope are coherent and effective responses to the key issues involved. I must emphasise, though, that they *are* separate essays. Even taken as a whole they do not constitute a systematic treatment. They are the best response I can give at the moment to what seem to me to be the most pressing concerns in ethnographic methodology.

The first section of the book is concerned with the purposes of ethnographic research, the nature of the theory and descriptions it produces and draws on, and the question of how the validity of ethnographic accounts is to be assessed, including whether they can reasonably claim to depict an independent social reality. In the article from which the book takes its title, I examine the concept of theoretical description, which is often treated as the intended product of ethnographic research. I consider the differ-ent meanings of the term 'theory' that seem to be used by ethnographers, and look at what is implied by the concept of ethnographic description. I show that none of the current interpretations of the concept of theory is without problems, and that the common tendency to treat ethnographic description as involving reproduction of the phenomena described is mis-leading. I argue that such description is always selective and that for this reason the relevances and values that structure any ethnographic description ought to be made explicit.

Chapter 2 takes a little further the issue of the nature of theory in ethnographic research. It seeks to show the parallels between ethnography and historical research, particularly in the sorts of explanation they employ. While there has been rather little attention given to the form of explanation used by ethnographers, there is a considerable literature dealing with historical explan-ation. I draw on that literature to illuminate what seem to me to be the two central problems of ethnographic explanation: the neces-sarily pragmatic and value-based character of the selection of explanatory factors; and the question of the nature of the general assumptions employed in such explanations.

Chapter 3 discusses the realist assumptions that seem to be built into ethnography, and the mounting challenge to them. I try to show that there is an ambivalence towards realism within ethno-graphic thinking. On the one hand, justifications offered for ethnography often involve the argument that it enables us to capture social reality more accurately than other approaches. On the other hand, it is intrinsic to ethnography that the people studied are viewed as constructing distinct social worlds. And if that idea is applied to ethnographers themselves it may seem that, rather than representing reality, ethnographic accounts simply construct versions of reality. I argue that we can recognise the fact that accounts are selective constructions without abandoning the idea that they may represent phenomena independent of themselves, and of the researcher, more or less accurately. And I sketch some of the implications of this 'subtle realism' for ethnographic practice.

The issue of the assessment of ethnographic research, and especially of the criteria on which such assessment should be based, is the area where many of the issues dealt with in the first section of this book become of most obvious significance. This is the topic of Chapter 4. Here I look at the two main strategies for specifying assessment criteria appropriate to ethnographic accounts that are to be found in the literature: those derived from quantitative methodology; and those presented as distinctive to ethnography. I argue that neither of these approaches is satisfactory, and present my own assessment framework centred on the concepts of validity and relevance. In discussing this framework I seek to show how validity can be conceptualised in such a way as to avoid naïve realism, and also to establish that emphasising the importance of relevance does not imply that all research must be directly related to practice.

The second section of the book concerns the relevance of ethnographic research; that is, its relationship to other forms of practice. Chapter 5 deals with the problem of how an ethnographic study of a single, small-scale setting (or of a small number of such settings), at a particular point in time can have relevance for a wide audience of the kind that ethnographers typically address in their publications. In other words, how ethnographic findings can have general relevance. Occasionally, the settings studied by ethnographers have intrinsic interest to a large audience. In general, though, they do not. There are two ways in which ethnographers typically seek to deal with this problem, though they do not always distinguish between these. One is to treat the case(s) studied as representative of a larger population of cases that *is* of wider relevance; the other is to use the case to exemplify and/or establish a theory.[4] The two strategies face different problems and require different sorts of evidence, and these are examined in this chapter. My conclusion is that the first strategy (empirical generalisation) is rather more straightforward than the second (theoretical inference), but that neither is pursued very successfully by ethnographers at present.

One of the most influential bases for the argument that there should be a more direct relationship between ethnography and practice is critical theory, and a number of authors have drawn on this approach to advocate what is sometimes called 'critical ethnography'. In Chapter 6 I outline the rationale for this approach and the criticisms that its advocates make of conventional ethnography. I then assess its viability. My conclusion is that critical theory is not a convincing basis for an alternative approach to social research since it suffers from a number of serious problems of its own, as well as inheriting most of those that face conventional researchers.

Advocates of critical ethnography and others who argue for a closer relationship between ethnographic research and practice often make strong claims for the potential practical contribution of ethnography as compared with quantitative method. In Chapter 7 I argue that we must take care not to exaggerate either the likely validity of current ethnographic research or its possible contribution to practice. I suggest that there is no general reason to believe that the findings of ethnography are any more valid than those of quantitative research, and I suggest that the contribution of any form of research to practice is necessarily rather small. Also, I question the argument that ethnographic research should be multi-purpose, designed simultaneously to serve the needs of practitioners directly and to contribute to the cumulative knowledge of the research community. I argue for different forms of research designed to serve different functions and audiences, rather than the adoption of a single all-purpose model; and that the relevance of ethnography to practice is most likely to be general and indirect, rather than providing solutions to immediate practical problems.

This theme of the nature of the contribution that ethnography can make to practice is taken up again in Chapter 8. I examine the case for practitioner ethnography, the proposal that ethnographic work should no longer be the domain of specialised researchers but should be open to all. The criticisms of conventional ethnography advanced by advocates of this approach – that it is irrelevant to practice, that it is invalid because the product of outsiders, and that it is exploitative – are considered. I conclude that they are not convincing, and that while conventional research is not the only legitimate form of inquiry, its function cannot be served by practitioner ethnography.

The final section of the book is composed of chapters that deal with the relationship between quantitative and qualitative method. In 'Deconstructing the quantitative–qualitative divide' I identify a variety of issues on which quantitative and qualitative researchers are often taken to hold contrasting views. In each case I argue that we are not faced simply with two options, but rather with a range of different possibilities. Furthermore, adopting one of these views on one issue does not automatically commit us to particular views on the others. In short, there is scope for far more than just two positions overall. Moreover, I suggest that addressing method-ological issues in terms of the precepts of contrasting paradigms provides an inadequate basis for deciding among the various methodological options that social researchers face.

Chapter 10 addresses the idea that quantitative and qualitative research involve different kinds of inference. In an influential article Clyde Mitchell has claimed that ethnography relies on theoretical inference, where quantitative research depends on both this and statistical inference (Mitchell 1983). In my view, however, both types of research involve the same forms of infer-ence and therefore face the same basic methodological problems; though they often adopt different strategies to deal with them. Furthermore, I suggest that there are misconceptions on the part of both qualitative and quantitative researchers about the nature of these types of inference. On the one hand there is the tendency to regard empirical generalisation from sample to population as necessarily statistical. On the other there is the idea that valid theoretical inferences can be based on intensive study of a single case in which causal or functional relationships are effectively visible. I argue that both these assumptions are mistaken.

The final chapter, entitled 'So, what are case studies?', sketches some of the implications of my rejection of the quantitative–qualitative divide. I take one aspect of social research method, the selection of cases for study, and compare different strategies for dealing with it: case study, survey and experiment. I argue that the choice of one or other of these strategies involves trade-offs whose significance must be judged in terms of the purposes and circumstances of particular studies. And while the weaknesses of case study can be ameliorated in various ways, they should not be ignored. Once again, the point is to show that the problems that social researchers face are more complex than is sometimes suggested, and cannot usefully be conceptualised in terms of competing paradigms.

There is a brief *Postscript* which summarises my diagnosis of the problems currently facing ethnographic methodology. It makes clear that what is offered in this book is not some final solution to these problems. The possibility of any such solution is a myth. However, here, as in other fields, we can improve the adequacy of our knowledge. These essays are offered as a contribution to that process.

NOTES

1 Throughout this book I use the term 'ethnography' in a general sense that is broadly equivalent to 'qualitative method'.
2 Though, of course, this coexistence takes a variety of forms, from advocacy of the combination of quantitative and qualitative methods – each being regarded as having its own strengths and weaknesses – to treatment of the two approaches as incommensurable paradigms that are valid in their own terms.
3 The two sorts of criticism I have identified are sometimes found together: see Gitlin *et al.* 1989.
4 By their very nature theories apply in many different situations, and therefore probably have general relevance.

Part I

ETHNOGRAPHY, THEORY AND REALITY

1

WHAT'S WRONG WITH ETHNOGRAPHY?

The myth of theoretical description

In the past thirty years, ethnography and other forms of qualitative method have moved from a marginal position in many social science disciplines towards a much more central place. Of course, in the case of social and cultural anthropology ethnography has always been the predominant method; but it now has a strong presence in sociology and social psychology, as well as in applied areas like education and health. While this shift in methodological opinion among social researchers is to be welcomed in some respects, it is important to emphasise that ethnography offers no immediate solution to the problems that currently face social research. Indeed, I shall argue in this chapter that it suffers from a disabling defect itself: it is guided by an incoherent conception of its own goals.[1]

The rationale for ethnography is based on a critique of quantitative, notably survey and experimental, research. The validity of this research is challenged on a number of grounds:

1 That the structured character of the data collection process involves the imposition of the researcher's assumptions about the social world and consequently reduces the chances of discovering evidence discrepant with those assumptions.

2 That making claims about what happens in 'natural' settings on the basis of data produced in settings that have been specially set up by the researcher – whether experiment or formal interview – is to engage in a largely implicit and highly questionable form of generalisation.

3 That to rely on what people *say* about what they believe and do, without also observing what they do, is to neglect the complex relationship between attitudes and behaviour; just as to rely on

observation without also talking with people in order to understand their perspectives is to risk misinterpreting their actions.

4 That quantitative analysis reifies social phenomena by treating them as more clearly defined and distinct than they are, and by neglecting the processes by which they develop and change.

5 That quantitative analysis assumes that people's actions are the mechanical products of psychological and social factors, thereby neglecting the creative role of individual cognition and group interaction.

This is not an exhaustive list of the criticisms directed at quantitative research by ethnographers, but it reveals the main assumptions underlying advocacy of qualitative method: that the nature of the social world must be *discovered*; that this can only be achieved by first-hand observation and participation in 'natural' settings, guided by an exploratory orientation; that research reports must capture the social processes observed and the social meanings that generate them. On the basis of these assumptions, ethnography is directed towards producing what are referred to as 'theoretical', 'analytical' or 'thick' descriptions (whether of societies, small communities, organisations, spatial locations or 'social worlds'). These descriptions must remain close to the concrete reality of particular events, but at the same time reveal general features of human social life.

The claim to integrate description with theory is one of the most distinctive characteristics of ethnography. In this chapter I shall argue that this concept of theoretical description is problematic. It can be interpreted in several ways, all of which raise difficult questions. Furthermore, I believe that ethnographers' adoption of the goal of theoretical description has led to a fundamental misconception about the nature of the descriptions and explanations they produce. I will examine each aspect of this dual goal of ethnography in turn.

ETHNOGRAPHY AS THEORY

While ethnography places great emphasis on description, it claims to offer a distinctive kind of description: *theoretical* description. But the nature of this distinctiveness is not very clear. On the one hand, descriptions cannot *be* theories. Descriptions are about particulars (objects and events in specific time–place locations),

whereas theories are about universals (relations between categories of phenomena that apply wherever those phenomena
occur). On the other hand, *all* descriptions use concepts which
refer to an infinite number of phenomena (past, present, future
and possible). And *all* descriptions are structured by theoretical
assumptions: what we include in descriptions is determined in part
by what we think causes what. In short, descriptions cannot be
theories, but all descriptions are theoretical in the sense that they
rely on concepts and theories.

Given this, what sense can we give to ethnographers' claims that
their descriptions are distinctive in being theoretical? There seem
to be several interpretations of this idea to be found in the
ethnographic literature. I shall examine the following possible
rationales, treating theoretical descriptions as:

   i   *insightful* descriptions;
   ii descriptions of *social microcosms*;
   iii *applications* of theories;
   iv *developments of theory* through the study of crucial cases.

These rationales are often not clearly distinguished in the ethnographic literature, nor are they necessarily mutually exclusive.

i Insightful descriptions

The title of Everett Hughes's collection of papers *The Sociological
Eye* nicely captures the dual emphasis of ethnography. The analogy
with vision indicates the priority given to description, while the
adjective 'sociological' signals (though does not specify unambiguously) the distinctive character of the view offered. For many,
the value of Hughes's work lies in the provision of insights coming
from the use of analogies and metaphors embodied in sociological
concepts. In his introduction to the book, Hughes comments:

> when people say of my work ... that it shows insight, I cannot
> think what they could mean other than whatever quality may
> have been produced by intensity of observation and a
> turning of the wheels to find a new combination of the old
> concepts, or even a new concept.

> (Hughes 1971: vi)

From this point of view, the aim of ethnographic description is to
present phenomena in new and revealing ways. Much of Hughes's

work in the sociology of occupations, for example, involves analogies between high and low status occupations that are designed to display the similar concerns, problems and strategies of people who are conventionally thought to be very different: the doctor and the prostitute, the SS guard and the social worker etc. Analogies also play a central role in the writings of Erving Goffman: for example, social life as drama or as a compendium of games. In addition, he deluges his readers with less comprehensive concepts that cast new light on familiar features of our everyday social world. One of the most strikingly effective, of course, is the concept of 'total institution', by which Goffman draws parallels between life in such diverse institutions as mental hospitals, prisons, monasteries and ships (Goffman 1961).

There is no doubt about the suggestiveness of the work of Hughes and Goffman. Their writings lead us to see things differently, to see possible parallels and links that we had not noticed; and, perhaps most important of all, they enable us to free ourselves from those frameworks that we employ so routinely that we have come to take them for reality. But we must ask: on what basis are we to assess candidate insights? Are insights simply of value in themselves, or are they valuable because they are useful for other purposes? More precisely, are insights the end products of social research or does their value derive, for example, from their role as potential hypotheses that can be developed and tested by more systematic and rigorous research?

If the insights are intended as end products with their own intrinsic value, then this represents adherence to a conception of social research that is discrepant not only with that of quantitative researchers, but also with that expressed by many ethnographers.[2] At the very least it seems that such a view would abandon the idea that the representational validity of candidate descriptions, explanations and theories needs to be tested. Instead, the value of accounts is taken to depend on their novelty, aesthetic appeal or political appropriateness. Ethnographers sometimes seek to justify their work on the grounds that it challenges taken-for-granted assumptions. But are all novelties to be valued? Should all taken-for-granted assumptions be questioned? Surely not.[3]

Lofland (1988) has suggested that interactionist ethnography is wedded to a kind of political anarchism, a green philosophy and politics that is at odds with its blue and red competitors. And it is true that a strong theme in much ethnographic research is what we

14

might call an urbane romanticism that celebrates the diverse forms of rationality, skill and morality to be found among ordinary people, including (indeed especially) those who are conventionally regarded as irrational and/or immoral. But if political advocacy is the function of ethnography, why is the politics so rarely made explicit? And on what basis are we to distinguish between ethnographic insight and political prejudice? Furthermore, what distinctive role can ethnography play in political advocacy? Is it anything more than an effective rhetorical device?

Of course, ethnographic insights need not be tied to any particular political view; they may simply be offered for others to use however they wish. The rationale here might take something like the following form:

> The purpose of ethnographic analysis is to produce sensitising concepts and models that allow people to see events in new ways. The value of these models is to be judged by others in terms of how useful they find them: they are not intended to be theories in the conventional sense of the term, allowing prediction and control; or to represent privileged information of any kind. Rather, they are simply contributions to a public dialogue that should compete on equal terms with those from other sources. The task of the ethnographer is to add to our general store of sensitising concepts and models. Perhaps we might argue that additions or modifications to this stock are necessary as social conditions change, since such changes modify the appeal or usefulness of the models. There is no idea here of theories and concepts being progressively developed to approximate correspondence with reality. Models are used as and when they are found to be appropriate. And, indeed, aesthetic criteria might be as important if not more important than cognitive ones.

There are problems with this rationale. Does it assume that theories of a conventional kind are not viable in the domain of human social life, and that both factual and value claims must be judged solely in terms of their pragmatic utility or their market appeal? If so, on what grounds? And on what basis is it believed that consumers will, and should, evaluate the products of research favourably? We must also note that it is not at all clear that ethnographic research bears any necessary relationship to the production of insights. Might these not be produced on the basis of experience, or even armchair reflection, rather than research? And, indeed, is not this rationale very close to that of literature? If so, what is distinctive about ethnography, and why do we need it?

There are then, many questions surrounding the idea that theoretical descriptions are *insightful* descriptions. These need to be answered if this version of ethnography as theory is to be convincing.[4]

ii Theory as the description of social microcosms

A related argument for the theoreticity of ethnographic descriptions is the claim that the phenomena described, though apparently particular and unique, exemplify universal social processes. The aim of ethnographic investigation, then, is to find the general in the particular; a world in a grain of sand. General features of human social life are to be illuminated *through* the description of particular events. Indeed, it is sometimes argued that it is only by means of this inductive, or discovery-based, approach that generic social processes can be understood. This strategy is contrasted with the hypothesis-testing character of much social research.

This is an idea that can be traced back to nineteenth-century historicism, and beyond to German romanticism. The historicist movement emphasised the diversity and particularity of human social life, and opposed those tendencies in philosophical and social scientific thinking that sought to understand particular social phenomena by applying abstract ideas about universals. Thus, they rejected both positivist attempts to develop natural sciences of human society, whose findings were universal laws parallel to the laws of nature, and Hegelian interpretations of history in terms of the progressive realisation of a universal rational spirit (Hammersley 1989a).

The historian Ranke was a particularly influential exponent of historicism. The overwhelming emphasis in his work is on the careful description of historical events, relying on the interpretation of written documents, 'to show only what actually happened' (Krieger 1977: 4–5). But at the same time Ranke distanced himself from history as mere antiquarianism. Ultimately, for him the goal of history was to detect 'the hand of God' behind or within particular historical events (Krieger 1977: 26–7, 137). Ranke believed that intuition, and perhaps even a certain genius, were required to discover the historically universal. Furthermore, the truths discovered might not be expressible in abstract form: at one point he comments that the universal is 'to be narrated not proved' (Ranke, quoted in Krieger 1977: 137). None the less, for Ranke the study of historical events only gained its value from its discoveries about the universal, and the spiritual and practical value that these had.

These ideas were developed further in Dilthey's attempt to discover the methodological foundations of the human studies. For example, he believed that through the study of 'representative individuals' we could discover general types of human individual. He regards this identification of the essential within the particular as characteristic of great art and literature:

> The characters and situations presented to us in a poem, and the feeling-responses evoked by them in us, are *typical* of a segment of possible human experience, and of its value or significance to us. By contemplation of the type, our acquaintance with what it represents is widened, and our power to see its true significance is heightened. Art therefore, no less than science, but in a very different way, is a vehicle of truth.
>
> (Hodges 1952: 113)

For Dilthey, the human studies partake of aspects of both science and art. They share art's goal of evoking the typical, but pursue it more systematically, seeking factual as well as symbolic truth. Furthermore, they are concerned not just with the study of individuals, but also with investigating cultural and social systems. Here too, though, the general is to be discovered through the study of the particular.

Something like this approach, the study of particular cases as social microcosms, is present in ethnographic thinking today. Ethnographic work often seems to amount to a celebration of the richness and diversity of human social life, but at the same time seeks to identify generic features. Ethnographers' commitment to the urbane romanticism that I mentioned above often serves an important function here. They trade on the significance that this perspective gives to descriptions of what otherwise might be regarded as fleeting and trivial events occurring in unimportant places. But even apart from this, the value of ethnographic work often depends on showing that the particular events described instantiate something of general significance about the social world.[5] Furthermore, as with Ranke's conception of historical work, the aim is to do this through narration, rather than abstract demonstration. Thus, Krieger (1983: 179) comments approvingly on *Street Corner Society*:

> Whyte's stories ... create his theory and are not just evidence for it. We understand his explanation of racketeering and, more basically, his theory of social organization, not because we are told its tenets in abstract or 'theoretical' terms (although we are told some of it in these terms in the end), but because we are led through a world in which we can develop an experiential sense of the way that individual actions relate to each other and to a larger whole.

Atkinson argues that this discursiveness is a characteristic feature of ethnographic writing. He suggests that the instances that ethnographers describe can be taken to stand for general cultural themes or social types, and that this process of representation is semiotic rather than statistical (Atkinson 1990: 83–4). Like Krieger, he takes *Street Corner Society* as a key example, commenting that while some may believe that Whyte 'sidesteps a great many sociologically important questions', it is reasonable for a reader to conclude that the aspects of everyday life in Cornerville described in the book are 'microcosmic' of the life of young Italian-American men in the 1930s. Whyte achieves this by inviting 'the reader's sympathetic engagement with the text through a close marriage of description and narration', rather than relying on a 'detailed propositional form of argument' (Atkinson 1990: 136, 138).

However, despite its long history and widespread influence, this idea of particular phenomena exemplifying general social types has never received a convincing presentation. Some, for example Atkinson, simply avoid the epistemological problem by restricting themselves to a description of what ethnographers actually do and the persuasive success of their accounts. This leaves entirely on one side the question of whether the interpretative and textual strategies used by ethnographers are legitimate ones. The crucial question remains unanswered: on what basis can ethnographers reasonably make a link between data and theory?[6]

While any universal processes that are operative in human social life are necessarily realised in particular events, and while we can only discover and validate them through study of particulars, the character of most events seems likely to be the product of multiple processes and perhaps also of accident and creative activity on the part of human beings. Indeed, most ethnographers, like the historicists before them, emphasise the diversity, complexity and creativity of human social life. But to the extent that this emphasis is correct, it seems that the task of distinguishing universal principles from one another and from their contexts is very difficult, if not impossible, when studying a single case or a small number of cases. Ethnographers sometimes talk of theory 'emerging' from the data, but the process remains as mysterious as it did for Ranke. The crucial question, it seems to me, is: how can the fact that a theory has 'emerged' from data justify our belief that the processes it describes were operative in the case investigated, and (more important still) that they represent universal principles? Unfortunately, today, as in the days of Ranke, we are often left with an appeal to intuition (Hammersley 1989a).[7]

iii Ethnographic descriptions as applications of theory

Another view underlies McCall and Simmons's discussion of 'analytic description', which they regard as the goal of participant observation. The authors argue that 'an analytic description is primarily an empirical application and modification of scientific theory' (McCall and Simmons 1969: 3).

In terms of social science methodology today, this is a much more conventional position than the previous two. It trades on the idea that theories are clearly formulated claims about the relationships between categories of phenomena (rather than analogical insights) and that they are analytically distinct from (not simply narrated in) descriptions.

But there are some questions that must be answered about this interpretation of theory application. Most notably, there is the issue of the validity of the theory that is to be applied. Clifford Geertz provides one solution to this problem in his discussion of 'thick description'. He argues that ethnographers test theories in the very process of using them:

> Theoretical ideas are not created wholly anew in each study;
> ... they are adopted from other, related studies, and, refined
> in the process, applied to new interpretive problems. If they
> cease being useful with respect to such problems, they tend
> to stop being used and are more or less abandoned. If they

19

continue being useful, throwing up new understandings, they are further elaborated and go on being used.

(Geertz 1975: 27)[8]

By contrast, McCall and Simmons argue that the application of theory in ethnographic studies does not represent 'an efficient and powerful test' because only one case is involved. Instead, they recommend the systematic comparison of cases. They claim that: '[The] test of theory comes in *comparing* ... analytic descriptions of complex cases when these are available in sufficient number and variety' (McCall and Simmons 1969: 3).

McCall and Simmons's criticism of the idea of testing theory through its application seems sound. Testing requires comparison, along with a record of the conclusions drawn in each of the cases compared. However, there are also serious problems with their own proposal to apply the comparative method to cases that have been described 'in their own terms', rather than in terms structured by the theory being tested. Herbert Blumer remarks that the comparison of unique cases 'is scarcely calculated to yield "laws" or "generalizations" like those which mark physical science' (Blumer 1928: 357). This is because it does not enable us to distinguish essential from accidental features, or differences that arise from variations in description from those that reflect real differences between the cases.[9] This suggests that what is required is the strategic selection of cases that are critical for testing the theory in relation to its competitors. And, in fact, this points to a fourth interpretation of the theoretical character of ethnographic descriptions.

iv Ethnography as developing theory through the study of critical cases

There are two well-known approaches to ethnographic research that move beyond the comparison of unique cases to claim that inferences may be made about the validity of a theory through the study of cases selected on strategic grounds. These approaches are 'grounded theorising' and 'analytic induction'. Both are attempts to apply the hypothetico-deductive method to ethnography. Thus, Strauss (1987: 11–12) describes grounded theorising as involving processes of induction, deduction and verification. Similarly, analytic induction was advocated by both Znaniecki and

20

Lindesmith as the method of the natural sciences, and as involving the systematic testing of hypotheses (Znaniecki 1934; Lindesmith 1968).

In fact, though, neither of these ethnographic approaches to theory development involves an effective implementation of the hypothetico-deductive method. Grounded theorising seeks both to represent concrete situations in their complexity *and* to produce abstract theory. It thus operates under conflicting requirements. Furthermore, there is considerable ambiguity in the writings of Glaser and Strauss (Glaser and Strauss 1967; Glaser 1978; Strauss 1987) about whether grounded theorising is designed to test theory as well as to develop it, and what it recommends in practice does not conform closely to the features of the hypothetico-deductive method (Hammersley 1989a).

Analytic induction is closer to the hypothetico-deductive method, though it gives inadequate attention to sufficiency of conditions (Robinson 1951). But, while analytic induction is often appealed to by ethnographers as a model for ethnographic analysis, there are very few examples of its full and explicit implementation. Only Lindesmith (1968) and Cressey (1950 and 1953) provide clear examples.[10] Furthermore, the form of their research, with its investigation of a large number of cases and exclusive reliance on interviews, is discrepant with that of most ethnographic studies. This fact highlights a considerable practical problem in applying the hypothetico-deductive method to ethnographic research. Finding and gaining access to cases that vary the independent variable and control relevant extraneous variables is by no means easy. To my knowledge, the only example of a series of participant observation studies that remotely approximates to this is the work of Hargreaves (1967), Lacey (1970) and Ball (1981) in the sociology of education (Hammersley 1985a).[11] If ethnographers are to pursue the development and testing of theory they will need, at the very least, to coordinate their studies in a systematic way to focus on the testing of particular theories, and they may also need to modify their data collection and analytic procedures substantially (Hammersley 1987a. See also Woods 1987 and Hammersley 1987b).

However, there is a serious question about whether theoretical inference of this kind is possible even in principle. It is worth noting that analytic induction presupposes that there are scientific laws of human social life (and deterministic rather than proba-

21

bilistic ones at that). It is only on this assumption that reconstruction of the theory in the face of conflicting evidence makes any sense.[12] Yet, few ethnographers today believe that there are such laws, on the grounds that this conflicts with what we know about the nature of human behaviour from our experience of the social world. And they argue that the idea of sociological laws amounts to the imposition of an inappropriate model drawn from the natural sciences. But if there are no sociological laws, then we have no basis for making the kind of theoretical inferences from the study of particular cases for which the hypothetico-deductive method provides.

In my view, the most reasonable interpretation of the concept of theoretical description is that it refers to the *application* of theories. However, I think we must leave open the question of whether these theories are of the sort that require testing by means of the hypothetico-deductive method or whether they are teleological models or ideal types of the kind identified and developed by Max Weber (Weber 1949). Either way, the 'theoretical descriptions' that ethnographers produce are little different from the descriptions and explanations employed by us all in everyday life. What distinctiveness they ought to have concerns not their *theoretical* character but the explicitness and coherence of the models employed, and the rigour of the data collection and analysis on which they are based.

ETHNOGRAPHY AS DESCRIPTION

There are at least three reasons for the ethnographic emphasis on description:

1 As we have seen, most views of theorising that have informed ethnographic methodology are inductivist, in the sense that they treat theory as emerging out of the description of particular events. Such an approach views description as (at least) the first stage in the development of theory.[13]

2 There is the fact that much of the interest of ethnographic research comes from description of events in types of setting of which the reader probably has no experience. Sometimes the information provided concerns simply what happens: who does what, when and how. More often, though, what is offered and enjoyed is vicarious experience of what it is like to be in this type

of place, allowing us to see the world from the point of view of the people involved. This is most obvious in the case of anthropology, but it is also true of studies in sociology, whether the focus be inmates in mental hospitals (Goffman 1961), occupational groups like schoolteachers (Becker 1952) or drug dealers (Adler 1985).

3 There is an emphasis within ethnographic methodology on the importance of understanding events *in context*. *Out* of context the nature of what occurred may be misunderstood. Indeed, it has been argued that placing events in context is a form of explanation that is particularly suited to ethnographic research (Williams 1976). From this point of view description *is* explanation.

The most common conception of the descriptive character of ethnographic accounts is that they map the morphology of some area of the social world. Indeed, this is often a key feature that advocates emphasise about ethnography in contrast to other approaches to social research. Practitioners of these other approaches are criticised for failing to investigate 'naturally occurring' phenomena in a sufficiently direct and detailed manner, failing to get beyond the 'veil' of their own common-sense assumptions (Blumer 1969: 39). This conception of ethnographic research is central to Matza's influential characterisation of a naturalist approach, where the aim is to 'render the phenomenon cogently in a manner that maintains its integrity' (Matza 1969: 6. See also Lofland 1967). And this concern is reflected in the realistic or naturalistic mode of writing that ethnographers typically adopt, in which the *production* of understanding and *construction* of the text are hidden by a form of account that purports to present what is described simply 'as it appeared'; this being treated, with more or less conviction, as 'how it is' (Carey 1975; Atkinson 1982; Marcus and Cushman 1982).[14]

This represents a commitment to what I shall call the reproduction model of research, the aim being to investigate and describe the social realm as it really is, beyond all presumptions and prejudices. Cultures, social systems or social worlds are assumed to be objectively existing phenomena present in the world and awaiting description. Of course, ethnographers recognise the existence of diverse perspectives or 'multiple realities', but very often only in the sense that they regard it as obligatory for ethnographic accounts to document the multiple perspectives as part of the field being described. Such a view still relies on the notion that the ethnographer's aim is to construct descriptions that *reproduce* some portion of the world.[15]

Ethnographers' commitment to the reproduction model is signalled by the fact that the coherence of ethnographic accounts often lies primarily in their focus on the particular community, group or situation that they study; rather than in any substantive or theoretical issue. Thus, the titles of some ethnographic studies refer solely to the phenomena described: *The Andaman Islanders* (Radcliffe-Brown 1922); *The Gold Coast and the Slum* (Zorbaugh 1929); *Middletown* (Lynd and Lynd 1929); *Street Corner Society* (Whyte 1943); *Boys in White* (Becker *et al.* 1961); *Hightown Grammar* (Lacey 1970); *The Mountain People* (Turnbull 1973); *The Nude Beach* (Douglas *et al.* 1977). Even where the title includes reference to some issue, the account is still often constructed as a description of the community, group or setting in which the research took place, with the substantive and/or theoretical issues arising out of that. The task of ethnography is frequently formulated as the description of a culture, social system or social world, conceived as bounded and internally structured. The phenomenon being described is generally the anchor of ethnographic accounts.

Implicit in the reproduction model is the idea that there is one true description that the ethnographer's account seeks to approximate, albeit one that incorporates the multiple accounts of participants. Yet the idea that the goal of ethnography is to describe some empirical phenomenon in a way that is uniquely appropriate to that phenomenon is misconceived. Empirical phenomena are descriptively inexhaustible: we can provide multiple true descriptions of any scene. How one describes an object on any particular occasion depends on what one takes to be relevant. Given that the value of truth underdetermines descriptions, other values and concerns *must* play a constitutive role in their production.

This is where the concept of theoretical description is especially misleading. The concept of theory, whether in its historicist or more conventional scientific forms, necessarily carries with it the idea of capturing some universal feature of the world. As a result, the label 'theoretical' applied to a description may be taken to indicate the general relevance and value of the account. But I have argued that ethnographic descriptions are theoretical only in the sense that they *apply* theories to the understanding of particular phenomena. Different theories can be applied to produce different, but equally valid, accounts of the same phenomenon. The question of why one description is provided rather than another remains.

In framing descriptions, then, we cannot be concerned solely with truth: what is to be included in the description must also be determined by assumptions about what is relevant. These assumptions are based partly on theoretical ideas about the relationships among different types of phenomena, but ultimately on purposes and the values that ground these purposes. The idea that ethnographic accounts are simply descriptions of reality 'as it is' is just as misleading as the notion that historical accounts simply represent past events.[16]

This has some radical implications for ethnographic description. To the extent that it has been conceived as naturalistic discovery and its findings presented simply as realistic portrayal, the relevances that have shaped the data collection, the analysis and the resulting account are unlikely to have been given much attention by the researcher, and may as a result be less coherent and less justifiable than they should be. Certainly, they will not have been made explicit for the reader. Yet if descriptions are always from a particular, value-based point of view, ethnographers need to make rational decisions about the value and factual assumptions that are to structure their descriptions, to make these decisions explicit, and to justify them where necessary.[17]

Of course, the influence of values upon ethnographic research has long been recognised. For example, in social anthropology Asad and others have pointed to the selective descriptions of African societies provided by British social anthropologists, and in particular their neglect of the British colonial apparatus and its effects (Asad 1973: 108–9. See also Rosaldo 1986). Within sociology, in the area of education, Marxist ethnographies have been criticised for interpreting data within a rigid framework of assumptions about what *must* occur under certain circumstances, the validity of Marxist theory being assumed (Hargreaves 1984; West 1984). In the field of deviance the compliment has been returned, with criticisms of interactionist ethnographers' preoccupations with 'nuts, sluts, and perverts', and the distorted picture of crime that this has produced. Liazos, for example, points to the bias implicit in the very use of the term 'deviant': that despite the arguments of sociologists of deviance they regard deviants as no different from ordinary people, the fact that there is a sub-discipline concerned with them implies difference. Furthermore, he charges that interactionist ethnographers' accounts of deviants neglect the role of the power structure of society and the crimes of the powerful (Liazos 1972).

However, in these critiques the grounds for criticism are not always clear. There are at least two forms that criticism of the role of values in shaping ethnographic descriptions can take. First, what may be at issue is the role of values in illicitly influencing the construction of the description. The critic may believe that because of the researcher's value assumptions the concepts used have been misapplied so that the phenomenon has been mis-described. Much more common, though, is that the critic does not accept the values on which the purposes and relevances that have shaped the description are based. Here the argument is not about the accuracy or validity of the description but about its rationale. It is the value assumptions on which it is based that are being criticised, not the description itself. Furthermore, the critic is not challenging the fact that values have played a role, but the *particular* values that have shaped the account; or the ways in which these have been combined with theoretical and factual assumptions to create the relevances that structure the description. Thus, it is not enough here for the critic to show that values have played a role, any more than to show that things have been left out of account. He or she must argue either that things have been left out *that should have been included given the researcher's relevances* or *that those relevances are themselves unjustifiable.* Very often, in criticisms of ethnographic and other research on grounds of value bias, these different types of criticism are not distinguished, and the relevant supporting argument is not presented.

It is important to emphasise that in arguing that ethnographic accounts are value-based, I do not mean to imply that ethnography is mere propaganda or even that it must be explicitly evaluative. Once the relevances that are to frame the description have been decided upon, work on it can be guided primarily by a concern with truth.[18] Thus, while I am arguing that the relevances structuring any description must, in large part, reflect a commitment to values other than truth, this does not imply that these or other practical values should determine which of the range of findings possible within the framework set by the relevances are taken to be true.[19]

Up to now I have written about ethnographic descriptions and not given any attention to explanations. Often ethnographers do not draw a sharp line between description and explanation, as I noted above. However, it seems to me that there is an important functional distinction. Descriptions tell us about the features of some phenomenon; explanations tell us why it has those features. But, like descriptions, explanations are also structured by practical values. For any phenomenon there is an infinity of factors that played a role in its production. We select from that range those factors that are relevant to the purposes that our explanation is intended to serve (Collingwood 1940; Hart and Honoré 1985). Here again we see how values other than truth play a role in inquiry. But, once again, they do not entirely determine the outcome: we must still decide whether or not it is true that particular factors did contribute to producing the phenomenon of interest. And to do that our investigation must be guided by a concern with truth, in which we guard against the illegitimate influence of other values.

At present most ethnographic research does not make explicit the values, purposes and relevances on which it is based; and even where it does, supporting argument is rarely provided. One reason for this, I suggest, is ethnographers' commitment to the confused goal of producing theoretical descriptions. Not only does the resulting lack of explicitness sometimes make it difficult to assess the validity and value of ethnographic studies, but it also has the potential to turn ethnographic description into an ideological device in which an account shaped by particular values is presented as if it were the only description or explanation possible. Clearly, this is unacceptable.

CONCLUSION

In this chapter I have questioned the commitment of ethnography to the goal of producing theoretical descriptions. The concept of theoretical description is problematic. On the one hand, descriptions cannot be theories since they represent objects and events in particular space-time locations; whereas theories are about types of phenomena, wherever their instances occur. On the other hand, all descriptions are theoretical in the sense that they involve concepts and are structured by theoretical assumptions. I have examined a number of possible interpretations of the concept of 'theoretical description', all of which raise difficult issues. My suggestion was that ethnographic descriptions are theoretical in the sense that they involve the application of theories, but that at present it is unclear whether these theories are of a conventional scientific sort or are teleological models of an ideal typical kind. More importantly, the fact that ethnographic descriptions apply theories does not make them at all distinctive: common-sense descriptions do the same. Their distinctiveness should lie in the explicitness and coherence of the models employed and the rigour of the analysis.

In the second half of the chapter I argued that commitment to the goal of theoretical description on the part of ethnographers had led them to adopt what I called the reproduction model. From this point of view ethnographic descriptions must simply portray the phenomenon of interest 'in its own terms'. However, this presumes that there is a single, objective description of each phenomenon, and this is not the case: there are multiple, non-contradictory, true descriptions of any phenomenon. How we describe an object depends not just on decisions about what we believe to be true, but also on judgements about relevance. The latter rely, in turn, on the purposes which the description is to serve. Much the same is true of explanations: what we take to explain a phenomenon depends not just on our ideas about what causes what, but also on the purposes for which the explanation is being developed. Ethnographers' commitment to the repro-duction model obscures, from readers and perhaps even from ethnographers themselves, the relevances that structure their accounts. As a result, the rationales for those accounts may be incoherent; and, wittingly or unwittingly, ethnography may become a vehicle for ideology. What is required is that the relevances and the factual and value assumptions that underlie ethnographic descriptions and explanations are made explicit and justified where necessary. Overall, the conclusions of this discus-sion are that the goals of ethnographic analysis need rethinking, and that some major changes may be required in the precepts and practices of ethnographic researchers. Above all, we need to answer the question of what purposes ethnography should be designed to serve.[20]

NOTES

1 'Ethnography', and cognate terms like 'qualitative method', 'case study', 'participant observation' etc. are not well-defined in their usage. However, for the purposes of my argument here this is not a serious problem. I am concerned with those kinds of qualitative research, whether based on observational or interview data, that aim both at accurate portrayal of particular phenomena *and* at more general conclusions about types of phenomena that are founded on such description. Much anthropological and sociological ethnography falls into this category.

2 I am not suggesting that either Hughes or Goffman adopted this view. It is very difficult to identify their positions on the nature of theory. For the argument that Goffman's work is guided by a rather unconventional view of social research, see Anderson *et al.* (1985). See also Williams (1988).

3 See Chapter 4 for discussion of the criteria for assessing ethnographic research, and for an account of when the questioning of assumptions should stop.

4 Some of these questions are touched on in recent discussions of sociological and ethnographic rhetoric, but in my view they are not dealt with very effectively. See, for example, Brown (1977); Clifford and Marcus (1986); and Marcus and Fischer (1986). For relevant criticisms of this work, see Sangren (1988) and Polier and Roseberry (1989).

5 See, for example, Glaser and Strauss's (1967), Lofland and Lofland's (1984) and Prus's (1987) emphasis on formal theory and generic social processes. For further discussion of the issue of relevance in ethnographic descriptions, see Chapters 4 and 5.

6 For a discussion of Atkinson's treatment of this issue, see Hammersley (1991d).

7 There is also the problem of how universals can be part of the particular; and whether, once recognised, knowledge of them can be 'applied' to understand other particulars.

8 Geertz qualifies this claim in a footnote, discussing the problems of eliminating 'exhausted' ideas because theories are 'seldom if ever decisively disproved ... but merely grow increasingly awkward, unproductive, strained, vacuous ...'.

9 Later in his career Blumer seems to recommend precisely this type of comparison as the basis for ethnographic analysis; see Blumer (1969) and Hammersley (1989a).

10 Several other researchers have used this technique, but without always showing full awareness of its distinctive features and/or providing details about the process of hypothesis testing and reconstruction involved. (See Becker 1963; Bloor 1978; Manning 1982; Katz 1983; and Strong 1988.)

11 See also the more recent work of Abraham (1989).

12 If the laws being searched for are probabilistic and/or vaguely formulated, then disconfirming evidence would be impossible to identify on

a case-by-case basis. Apparent exceptions could simply be oddities, and therefore not require the reformulation of the theory.

13 This is true even of those approaches like grounded theorising and analytic induction that appeal to the hypothetico-deductive method.

14 Atkinson argues that this mode of presentation is inconsistent with the interpretative character of symbolic interactionism. This is true, but I believe that the tension runs deeper: it pervades interactionism and ethnography in the form of a juxtapositioning of realism and constructivism (see Chapter 3). The constructivist element in symbolic interactionism, in terms of which ethnographic accounts may be seen as reflecting the perspective of the researcher (or the interaction between researcher and researched), has had little impact as yet upon ethnographic texts. There have been some experiments in textual strategy, but these have tended to be associated with the adoption of an anti-realist epistemology. For an extreme example of the 'post-modernist' rationale behind such textual experiments, see Tyler (1986). It is an assumption of my argument here that anti-realism is neither necessary nor desirable.

15 Rock (1973) has drawn particular attention to this feature of ethnographic work in the field of deviance. He argues that unless this commitment to faithfully reproducing the social world is amended, 'the sociology of deviancy may not be able to proceed in any useful fashion' (p.19). However, he does not reject the goal of reproducing social reality, but modifies it to include participants' conceptions of the macro-features of society. Even where the idea of representing a bounded social setting has been abandoned in favour of capturing the experience of participants and/or locating what is studied in a world-historical context, commitment to what I have called the reproduction model remains. In general, that model has only been abandoned by the 'post-modernists' who reject the very possibility of representation (Marcus and Fischer 1986: chs 3 and 4). My position is that representation should and can be our goal, but that it does not consist of *reproduction* of the social world, in whole or in part.

16 The argument that historical accounts are constructions was developed in its most systematic form by the neo-Kantians, particularly Rickert, Simmel and Weber. My arguments in this essay draw heavily on their work. See Rickert (1962 and 1986), Simmel (1977) and Weber (1949 and 1975). See also Burger (1976) and Oakes (1988).

17 I am assuming here that both factual and value claims may be justified by supporting argument. The idea that values are not open to rational justification has become widely accepted in the twentieth century. More recently, the idea that factual claims can be rationally defended has also been increasingly questioned. Both of these ideas are based on the assumption that unless we have some foundation of immediate and certain data from which to start, no knowledge is possible. From this point of view there is no defence against scepticism and relativism. However, if knowledge is possible without a foundation in the factual realm, and I think that there are good arguments for believing that it

is (Scheffler 1967; Newton-Smith 1981), then it may also be possible in the value realm. See Booth (1974) and MacIntyre (1981) for interesting discussions of this issue.

18 What I have in mind here is the application to the research process of the type of rational analysis of goals and means advocated by Weber (see Bruun 1972). This is possible whether or not one agrees with Weber that ultimate values are not rationally justifiable. Note that while truth should be the guiding principle of empirical descriptions and explanations, the implications of other values (such as protecting the interests of those studied) must also be taken into account.

19 Of course, the argument that social research cannot be 'value free', in the sense of being untouched by values, is hardly novel. But recognition of the role of values seems to have had little impact on the *practice* of social researchers. Furthermore, and ironically, the argument I am presenting here is substantially that of Weber (Weber 1949).

20 See Chapter 4 and Hammersley (1991a) for my attempt to answer this question. See also Haan *et al.* (1983) and Marcus and Fischer (1986).

2

SOME QUESTIONS ABOUT THEORY IN ETHNOGRAPHY AND HISTORY

Concern has sometimes been registered, even by ethnographers themselves, about the ahistorical character of much ethnographic research. Stephen Ball, for example, has pointed out how we often neglect the temporal patterns operating in the settings we study and that this seriously threatens the validity of our accounts (Ball 1983a). Others have pointed to the importance of biographical factors in sociological explanations (Pollard 1982). It has also been noted how, over the past forty years, ethnography has come to be identified with participant observation, life-history work suffering a serious decline; though there are now signs of a revival (Bertaux 1981; Plummer 1983). Lynch (1977) raises the issue in a particularly striking manner, criticising ethnographers for a lack of interest in the 'future history' of the groups they study. He cites the case of Lofland's work on a 'Doomsday Cult' (Lofland 1966), suggesting that we can now recognise the latter as having been one of the seed groups of the Moonies. He bemoans the fact that we have no study of how this small cult was transformed into the widespread movement of today.

While these criticisms contain much truth, the days have long gone when ethnographers laboured under theoretical perspectives, notably anthropological functionalism, which specifically denied the importance of history. And, indeed, recent anthropology seems to have become a major source of ideas for some historians (Walters 1980; Stone 1981). In this chapter I want to argue not only that history and ethnography are complementary but also that they share much in common. In particular, they both display a primary concern with describing social events and processes in detail, and a distaste for theories which, as they see it, ride roughshod over the complexity of the social world. Frequently too, they share a commitment to documenting 'in their own terms' the perspectives of the people involved in the events and settings they describe. Historians and ethnographers are often reluctant to move to general classifications of these perspectives, in which their uniqueness – and it seems much of their interest – is lost.

It is this attitude to theory which has sometimes led both ethnography and history to be criticised as empiricist.[1] They are accused of engaging in description for its own sake and of presenting their accounts of the world as if these represented theoretically neutral facts. Such criticisms have generally been rejected or ignored, and in many respects quite rightly. Sometimes they have come from critics practising theoretical dogmatism and speculative excess. The theory demanded has simply been the critics' *a priori* views about how the world 'must be'; the task of the ethnographer or historian being, at most, to fill in the details.[2]

In the face of dogmatic theoreticism, empiricism has definite virtues. In terms of method, systematic search for evidence and its careful handling must be applauded. Equally, the products of empiricism frequently have considerable value. The description of 'other cultures' (whether of the past or contemporaneous, of other societies or of segments of our own) can often serve to challenge our routine assumptions about the nature of social life or about particular groups of people or social situations. This explains the popular appeal of historical and anthropological work like *Montaillou* (Le Roy Ladurie 1978) and *The Mountain People* (Turnbull 1973). But such description performs important functions for social science too. For one thing, it can challenge the preconceptions we bring to our research and which so easily get built into the accounts we produce.

Nor is the value of description limited to what is, for us, the exotic. We often discover that there are features of even the most familiar settings of which we are unaware, recognition of which may subtly, perhaps even dramatically, change our understanding of those settings. Much recent ethnographic work in sociology has been concerned with 'making the familiar strange' in precisely this manner. Historical research can serve the same function, for instance by documenting the origins of contemporary phenomena whose existence we take for granted as 'natural' rather than as the product of history. A good example is the way in which we tend to take academic disciplines as basic forms of knowledge, forgetting the struggles which were involved in their establishment, the alternative versions which were promoted by different groups, and the changes in content they have undergone over time (Layton 1973; Shayer 1970; Ball 1982 and 1983b; Goodson 1981, 1983b and 1983c).

However, while empiricism has its virtues, it is ultimately indefensible. And there is a tendency within the thinking of both ethnographers and historians towards naïve realism, towards a neglect of the way in which theoretical assumptions inform their descriptions and explanations. Description is never 'pure', a direct and unchallengeable representation of the world. All 'facts' involve theoretical assumptions. Moreover, a description or explanation is only as good as the theory by which it was produced. We neglect theory at our peril.

While ethnographers often express a commitment to theory, there has been relatively little discussion of the nature of the theory used in ethnographic work. By contrast, there has been considerable discussion of this issue among philosophers concerned with the work of historians. In general, they have agreed about the central role that theory plays in historical explanations.[3] For example, while defending a conception of history as ideographic, Mandelbaum (1977: 6) points out that historians nevertheless often rely on generalisations (for which in this context we can read 'theory'):

> It is my claim that any work we take to be historical in nature purports to establish what actually occurred at a particular time and place, or is concerned with tracing and explaining some particular series of related occurrences. However, this does not entail that in fulfilling such a task the historian may not, at certain points, have to rely on generalizations in order to offer a coherent account of some of the occurrences with which he deals. For example, in attempting to give an account of a particular revolution, a historian often has to make use of certain general assumptions concerning how individuals generally behave in particular sorts of situations, such as those that arose in the course of that revolution.[4]

Hayek (1955: 72) makes the point even more strongly:

> If the dependence of the historical study of social phenomena on theory is not always recognized, this is mainly due to the very simple nature of the majority of theoretical

schemes which the historian will employ and which brings it about that there will be no dispute about the conclusions reached by their help, and little awareness that he has used theoretical reasoning at all. But this does not alter the fact that in their methodological character and validity the concepts of social phenomena which the historian has to employ are essentially of the same kind as the more elaborate models produced by the systematic social sciences.

Generalisations or theoretical claims are not difficult to find in ethnographic accounts either. For example, in her work on the attitudes of girls towards science in school, Measor (1983) argues that they have been socialised into a set of attitudes about what kinds of knowledge and activity are appropriate and inappropriate to their sexual identity. Thus, science, particularly physics and chemistry, is very definitely regarded as masculine. Moreover, she suggests that in school some girls actively use this feature of science to establish identity and status, and in the process put pressure on their peers to do likewise. This is an explanation for the behaviour that she observed in a particular school during her research: a tendency on the part of girls to find the activities unappealing if not abhorrent and to express fear about some of the equipment and materials. Implicit in this explanation is a theoretical idea: that if children are socialised into a perspective in which different types of knowledge are thought of as appropriate to contrasting identities, then they will not only tend to react more favourably to the knowledge which is 'appropriate' to the identity to which they aspire, but they will also tend to use displays of ignorance and incompetence in relation to 'inappropriate' skills and knowledge in order to underline that identity. Also, this tendency will be greater to the extent that the children are insecure about their own identities, or where there is strong competition for relationships between those having different identities, for example for boyfriends and girlfriends. Interestingly, as Hayek suggests is the case with history, it also seems to be true that the theories employed by ethnographers are often, if not simple, at least highly plausible. What is more usually at issue is whether the theory applies to the particular case.

However, despite substantial agreement that theory plays a role in historical analysis, there has been considerable disagreement about the nature of such theory and the character of its role.[5] An influential approach involves the application of ideas about the nature of explanation in natural science to the understanding of historical research. Here theory is treated as a statement which explains what will happen and why under given circumstances, and whose validity can be tested by checking whether or not its predictions are accurate. From this point of view, the claims which theories make are conditionally universal; in other words, they hold generally, given certain conditions, and the latter must not refer to particulars, to limits of time and space (Hempel 1959 and 1963). Such theories, it is suggested, form one of the crucial elements of historical explanations. Furthermore, on this view, theories should be selected for use in explanations solely on the grounds of their general validity and relevance to the phenomena to be explained. I shall call this the positivist model.

Many have rejected this model as inapplicable to historical explanations, on a variety of grounds. Some of the reaction against it has been founded upon misinterpretation of its implications. Often, for example, the conditional nature of this kind of theory has been ignored. Leff (1969: 3), for instance, denies the applicability of universal laws to history because of 'the absence of uniformity from human affairs'. But the positivist model of universal laws, in the form outlined above, does not presuppose uniformity in the sense of the repeated occurrence of identical situations undergoing identical processes of development. Nor is it 'historicist' in the sense popularised by Popper (1957): it does not presume a fixed sequence of stages of societal development leading to some in-built goal. It does not even involve the claim that all social events are causally determined:

> the covering law analysis of explanation presents a thesis about the logical structure of scientific explanation but not about the extent to which individual occurrences in the world can be explained: that depends on what laws hold in the world and clearly cannot be determined just by logical analysis. In particular, therefore, the covering law analysis of explanation does not presuppose or imply universal determinism.
>
> (Hempel 1963: 149–50)

Another basis for rejection of the positivist model has been the argument that historical explanation deals with unique events whose explanation requires appeal to a wide and uniquely relevant range of factors and their contribution over time, rather than to a set of general laws. And this is often taken to reflect a fundamental difference between the natural and social sciences. This is a mistake, however, as Hayek (1955: 66–7) points out:

> If I watch and record the process by which a plot in my garden that I leave untouched for months is gradually covered with weeds, I am describing a process which in all its detail is no less unique than any event in human history. If I want to explain any particular configuration of different plants which may appear at any state of that process, I can do so only by giving an account of all the relevant influences which have affected different parts of my plot at different times. I shall have to consider what I can find out about the differences of the soil in different parts of the plot, about differences in the radiation of the sun, of moisture, of the air-currents etc., etc.; and in order to explain the effects of all these factors I shall have to use, apart from the knowledge of all these particular facts, various parts of the theory of physics, of chemistry, biology, meteorology, and so on. The result of all this will be the explanation of a particular phenomenon, but not a theoretical science of how garden plots are covered with weeds.
>
> In an instance like this the particular sequence of events, their causes and consequences, will probably not be of sufficient general interest to make it worthwhile … or to develop their study into a distinct discipline. But there are large fields of natural knowledge, represented by recognized disciplines, which in their methodological character are no different from this. In geography … and at least in a large part of geology and astronomy, we are mainly concerned with particular situations, either of the earth or of the universe; we aim at explaining a unique situation by showing how it has been produced by the operation of many forces subject to the general laws studied by the theoretical sciences. In the specific sense of a body of general rules in which the term 'science' is often used these disciplines are not 'sciences', … but endeavours to apply the laws found by the theoretical sciences to the explanation of particular 'historical' situations.

The distinction between the search for generic principles

and the explanation of concrete phenomena has thus no necessary connection with the distinction between the study of nature and the study of society. In both fields we need generalizations in order to explain concrete and unique events. Whenever we attempt to explain or understand a particular phenomenon we can do so only by recognizing it or its parts as members of certain classes of phenomena, and the explanation of the particular phenomenon presupposes the existence of general rules.

In my view, what Hayek's argument here suggests is the need to draw a distinction between explaining (in the sense of trying to show why a particular event or feature occurred) on the one hand, and what I shall call 'theorising', on the other. In theorising the aim is not to explain a particular event but to develop and test a theory, an interrelated set of propositions making claims of a conditionally universal kind about general classes of events. Here propositions relating to particular factors are included or excluded according to whether or not they seem likely to form part of a coherent theory. Our primary interest is not in the events studied themselves. Indeed their only significance is the opportunities they provide for developing and testing the theory. Moreover, theorising demands investigation of a range of cases, where the theoretical variables take on different values and relevant extraneous variables are controlled. The comparative method is central to theorising, in the sense intended here.

The role of comparative analysis in historical research is usefully summarised in Sewell's (1967) commentary on the work of the historian Marc Bloch:

> If an historian attributes the appearance of phenomenon A in one society to the existence of condition B, he can check this hypothesis by trying to find other societies where A occurs without B or vice versa. If he finds no case which contradicts the hypothesis, his confidence in its validity will increase, the level of his confidence depending on the number and variety of the comparisons made. If he finds contradictory cases, he will either reject the hypothesis outright or reformulate it and refine it so as to take into account the contradictory evidence and then subject it again to comparative testing.
>
> (Sewell 1967: 208–9)

This process of testing, reformulating and retesting through comparative analysis is also to be found in the ethnographic tradition, in varying forms such as grounded theorising (Glaser and Strauss 1967; Glaser 1978) and analytic induction (Lindesmith 1968; Cressey 1950; Denzin 1978).

As Hayek makes clear, what I have called theorising and explaining, while distinct activities, are also complementary:

> Theoretical and historical work are ... logically distinct but complementary activities. If their task is rightly understood, there can be no conflict between them. And though they have distinct tasks, neither is of much use without the other.
>
> (Hayek 1955: 73)

And this is as true in the study of natural as of social phenomena.

While there is no shortage of promising theoretical ideas in ethnographic and historical work, there are few examples of explicit and sustained attempts at theorising in the manner defined above.[6] It is tempting to regard this with regret and to call for more studies of this kind. The logic of progress in ethnography and history would seem to involve development from descriptive and explanatory accounts, through theory development and testing, back to better descriptions and explanations, and so on. If this is correct, in many areas where ethnographic studies have been carried out we are at the point where theorising, of the kind I have recommended here, becomes an essential prerequisite for further progress. However, I think we must pause and consider the viability of such a programme. While in my view some of the criticism of the positivist model has been misguided, this is not true of all of it. There are two criticisms that seem to me to be sound and the problems they raise are as yet unresolved.

The first is the argument that explanation (like description) is a pragmatic matter. What should count as an adequate explanation of a phenomenon does not depend solely on the nature of that phenomenon and/or on the current state of relevant theory. It also depends on the particular purposes for which and context in which the explanation is being developed (Collingwood 1940; Hart and Honoré 1985; Scriven 1959; Garfinkel 1981). Collingwood provides an entertaining example:

> if my car fails to climb a steep hill, and I wonder why, I shall not consider my problem solved by a passer-by who tells me

that the top of a hill is farther away from the earth's centre than its bottom, and that consequently more power is needed to take a car uphill than to take her along the level. All this is quite true; what the passer-by has described is one of the conditions which together form the 'real cause' ... of my car's stopping .... But suppose an A.A. man comes along, opens the bonnet, holds up a loose high-tension lead, and says: 'Look here, sir, you're running on three cylinders'. My problem is now solved. I know the cause of the stoppage. It is *the* cause, just because it has not been 'arbitrarily selected'; it has been correctly identified as the thing that I can put right, after which the car will go properly. If I had been a person who could flatten out hills by stamping on them, the passer-by would have been right to call my attention to the hill as the cause of the stoppage; not because the hill was a hill but because I was able to flatten it out.

(Collingwood 1940: 302–3)

Put a different way, in explaining any phenomenon we are faced with an infinite range of factors to which we might appeal. There will be a variety of local causes and conditions, and each of those will be explainable in terms of a range of other factors and so on, *ad infinitum.* What we pick out from this corpus of potential 'causes' will depend on the purposes which our explanation is to serve. It will differ, for example, according to whether we are concerned with ascribing blame, identifying remedies, or something else. And, of course, even if we agree about the purpose of the explanation, there is room for disagreement about the cause. For example, in the case of a road accident: was its cause carelessness on the part of one or other of the drivers, the poor visibility, the dangerous junction, the failure of automobile manufacturers to give sufficient attention to safety, inadequacy in the training and testing of drivers etc.[7]

But if it is the case that explanation is always pragmatic, always directed towards particular purposes, this raises the question of what those purposes should be, and on what grounds they should be adopted. What sorts of purposes are relevant to ethnographic and historical research, and how do we decide about this? Where ethnographic research is very closely related to particular practical activities, these relevances may presumably derive from practitioner knowledge. But to the extent that research is designed to be of more general use, as is usually the case, on what basis should these relevances be determined? I do not know the answer to this question.

The second unresolved problem concerns the nature of the theoretical assumptions that are used in historical and ethnographic explanations. Hempel suggests that these may often be probabilistic rather than universal in character. Others have moved further away from conventional views about the nature of scientific laws. Thus, Scriven (1959) argues that historical explanation draws on quasi-laws which have neither the precision of scientific laws, nor do they provide the basis for prediction, and therefore are not open to systematic testing; though it is unlikely that we would wish to test them since they take the form of truisms. Dray (1957), following Collingwood, departs even further from the positivist model, arguing that historical explanations involve appeal not to sociological or even psychological laws but to intelligible and context-specific principles or rationales for courses of action that map the deliberations, or potential deliberations, of the actors involved. Such views have very important implications. If theories are probabilistic, or if they have the character of quasi-laws or intelligible principles, then we cannot test them by searching for negative cases and reconstructing them when we discover such cases. Exceptions would not count against such theories, indeed they are to be expected. This seems to undercut the very possibility of the sort of theorising that I outlined earlier and that I have argued elsewhere is a priority in the social sciences (Hammersley 1985a and 1987a). And, of course, few ethnographers today would claim that universal laws of human behaviour exist to be discovered. But if we accept this we are faced with questions about the validity of the general principles that ethnographers and historians employ in their explanations and how that validity is to be determined.

CONCLUSION

In this paper I have looked at one area where there are strong parallels between historians and ethnographers: in their attitudes towards the use of theory. I have drawn on the literature dealing with historical explanation in order to clarify some of the problems that surround the role of theory in ethnographic research. I argued that some of the criticisms of the positivist model of historical explanation are misdirected, but that there are at least two that raise difficult questions about the validity of historical and ethnographic studies and their assessment. These are the pragmatic character of explanation and the quasi-law-like character of social science theory. At present I see no obvious resolution to these problems. What is clear, though, is that what solutions we adopt to deal with them could have profound implications for the practice of ethnographic research.

NOTES

1 For a discussion of criticisms of ethnography for being empiricist, see Hammersley (1980). For the charge against history, see Hindess and Hirst (1975).
2 This has been a criticism sometimes directed at Marxist ethnography by non-Marxist ethnographers: see, for example, Hargreaves (1978) and West (1984).
3 There are exceptions, see Oakeshott (1933).
4 For more on Mandelbaum's rather complex position, see Dray (1979).
5 For a useful overview of the disagreements, see Dray (1967).
6 The only clear example with which I am familiar is the work of Hargreaves (1967), Lacey (1970) and Ball (1981). See Hammersley (1985a) and Chapter 12.
7 There are those who have sought an objectivist solution to this problem of explanatory indeterminacy on a different basis to the positivist model. An example is Max Weber, see Turner and Factor (1981). See also the references in Dray (1967).

3

ETHNOGRAPHY AND REALISM

In this chapter I want to discuss some of the philosophical under-pinnings of ethnographic research. For some ethnographers such a discussion may seem irrelevant at best. There is a strong anti-philosophical strand in ethnographic thinking that places value on the practice and products of research and has little patience with or interest in discussions *about* research.[1] I have some sympathy with this. Philosophical discussion and debate can easily become a distraction; a swapping of one set of problems for another, probably even less tractable, set. Certainly, I do not believe that philosophy is foundational, in the sense that the problems in that realm can or should be resolved before we engage in social research. Indeed, in my view empirical research, accompanied by reflection on its practice and products, has much to contribute to philosophy. But there is no escape from philosophical assumptions for researchers. Whether we like it or not, and whether we are aware of them or not, we cannot avoid such assumptions. And, sometimes, the assumptions that we make lead us into error. I believe that this is the case with some of the epistemological ideas current amongst ethnographers. These ideas are my concern in this chapter.

At the centre of these problems is the doctrine of realism, by which I mean the idea that there is a reality independent of the researcher whose nature can be known, and that the aim of research is to produce accounts that correspond to that reality. There can be little doubt about the widespread acceptance of this view. It is a philosophical doctrine on which much ethnography is founded. One of the most common rationales for the adoption of an ethnographic approach is that by entering into close and relatively long-term contact with people in their everyday lives we

43

can come to understand their beliefs and behaviour more accurately, in a way that would not be possible by means of any other approach. This was the reason for the shift within social and cultural anthropology in the late nineteenth and early twentieth centuries from relying on the reports of travellers and missionaries to first-hand fieldwork by anthropologists themselves. Similarly, within sociology, the same idea motivated Robert Park's advocacy of case-study research in Chicago in the 1920s. One of the most developed versions of the argument is to be found in the methodological writings of the Chicago sociologist Herbert Blumer. He criticises experimental and survey research for failing to grasp the distinctive nature of human social life, and the key feature of the naturalistic research strategy that he recommends is 'getting close' to naturally occurring social phenomena. The metaphors he uses to describe this approach – notably, 'lifting the veils' and 'digging deeper' – illustrate the realist assumptions that underly his views (Hammersley 1989a: 127–8). In much the same way, David Matza advocates 'naturalism', arguing that its core is a commitment to capture the nature of social phenomena in their own terms. And today this idea is found in explicit form in many introductions to ethnographic method (Lofland 1972; Schatzman and Strauss 1973; Hammersley and Atkinson 1983). From this point of view the goal of ethnographic research is to discover and represent faithfully the true nature of social phenomena. And the superiority of ethnography is based precisely on the grounds that it is able to get closer to social reality than other methods.

Despite this commitment to realism, however, there is an important strand in ethnography that pushes in a contrary direction. Central to the way in which ethnographers think about human social action is the idea that people *construct* the social world, both through their interpretations of it and through the actions based on those interpretations. Again, Blumer is an influential figure here; though the same idea can be found in many other sources.[2] Blumer argues at one point that even people in geographical proximity to one another may live in different 'social worlds' (Blumer 1969: 11). Furthermore, the implication seems to be that these worlds are incommensurable, so that one cannot be treated as superior to another (and certainly not in the sense of being a truer representation of reality because these worlds *constitute* reality for the people concerned). This same idea has long been central to social and cultural anthropology, with its attempts to understand alien belief systems 'from inside', rather than judging them from a Western, scientific point of view.[3]

This constructivism is quite compatible with realism so long as it is not applied to ethnographic research itself. It can be taken simply to require ethnographers to seek to understand (rather than judge) other people's beliefs, and to document the multiple perspectives to be found within and between societies. But we must ask: why should ethnographers be treated in a different way to others? To do so implies that they are outside of society, and this is surely unacceptable. Yet, once we treat ethnographic research as itself a social activity and seek to apply the constructivist approach to it, the question of the epistemological status of ethnographic findings is immediately raised. What may seem to follow is that in their work ethnographers create a social world (or worlds), rather than merely representing some independent reality (more or less accurately). And, it may be concluded, this world is no more nor less true than others; for instance than the perceptions and interpretations of the people studied. In this way, ethnographic constructivism seems to result in a relativism that is in conflict with ethnography's commitment to realism.

Faced with this apparent contradiction within ethnography, there are two obvious candidate solutions: to apply either realism or relativism consistently across the board, to both ethnographic method and to the social life that is studied. As I shall try to show, however, neither of these strategies is satisfactory.

If we apply ethnographic realism to our understanding of the people studied as well as to the research process, this implies an approach that is at odds with what is characteristic of ethnography. It means interpreting people's beliefs as the product *either* of contact with reality *or* of cultural bias. This abandons what is in my view one of the most valuable features of ethnography: its commitment to seeking to *understand* the perspectives of others, rather than simply judging them as true or false. It also involves the adoption of an asymmetrical approach to explaining beliefs, so that we appeal to different explanatory factors, depending on whether we take the beliefs to be valid or invalid. Those that are true are explained as products of the impact of reality, while those that are false are explained as the result of causal (probably cultural) factors producing error. There are good reasons to avoid this approach. One is that it is implausible, since it is clear that true conclusions can be reached on the basis of false premises; and even vice versa if there are implicit assumptions that are false. And, given that we can have no direct contact with reality, beliefs can never be a simple product of such contact. Cultural assumptions and social interests are always involved in perception and cognition, and they may mislead us or they may lead us towards the truth (or more likely they may do both at the same time, in different respects). Given this, in my view there should be no difference between the mode of explanation we employ to deal with what we take to be true beliefs (or rational actions) and those we believe to be false (or irrational). Another reason why the asymmetrical approach is counterproductive is that we can never know for sure whether beliefs are true or false. Hence, we can never be certain which of the two explanatory schemes ought to be applied in any particular case. As a result, what we treat as a sound explanation at one point in time may later need to be abandoned in favour of a different explanation, not because we have found out anything new about the production or functioning of the belief itself, but simply because our assessment of its validity has changed.[4]

The alternative strategy for solving the conflict between realism and relativism within ethnography is to apply relativism to the research process. This has been more popular among ethnographers than the first strategy, especially in recent times. And this reflects, in part, the influence of a variety of trends in philosophical ideas. In the 1960s and 1970s the impact of phenomenology often encouraged relativism.[5] What was taken from Husserl and other phenomenologists was primarily the idea that our understanding of the world is constructed on the basis of assumptions, those assumptions being interpreted not as universal givens (in the manner of Husserl), but as culturally relative. Particularly influ- ential here was Schutz's discussion of multiple realities; an idea derived from William James rather than from Husserl. While Schutz specified these as the worlds of everyday life, dreams, science and religion, his discussion has sometimes been interpreted as predicating multiple realities constituted by different cultures; and indeed this is compatible with some of what he says, and certainly with James's treatment of the idea (Schutz and Luckmann 1974: 22–3; Berger and Luckmann 1966).

Similar relativistic conclusions have been drawn from the later Wittgenstein's view that our language sets the limits of our world, and his discussions of forms of life and language games. Particularly influential here was Winch's application of these ideas to the understanding of other cultures. Winch argues that we can understand the beliefs and actions of people in a society very different from our own, for example those surrounding Zande magic, only by seeing them in the context of the cultural rules characteristic of that society. Furthermore, he claims that we cannot judge those beliefs without presupposing our own mode of thinking, the validity of whose assumptions and criteria can no more be established independently of our culture than can those of the Azande (Winch 1958 and 1964). In a rather similar manner to Schutz, Winch treats science and religion as different cultural worlds.

Both these philosophical traditions had an impact on ethnography during the 1960s and 1970s. Often, their influence was diffuse, blending with constructivist and relativist thinking generated within it. In the case of ethnographers influenced by ethnomethodology, though, their impact was more focused; and it led to distinctive forms of ethnographic work.[6]

Running alongside these developments, and having a similar effect, was the emergence of revisionist ideas in the philosophy of science. Up until the early 1950s there was a substantial consensus among Anglo-American philosophers of science that the distinguishing feature of science was that the knowledge it produced was based on observation and logic. However, at that time, this 'received view' came under increasing criticism, to the point where there was wide recognition that it could not be sustained (Suppe 1974). A variety of alternative views were developed, though none has formed a new consensus. Much the most influential product of this debate was Thomas Kuhn's book *The Structure of Scientific Revolutions* (Kuhn 1962). Kuhn argued that we cannot see the history of science as the cumulative development of more accurate and precise knowledge about the physical world. Rather, what we find in each field is a sequence of periods in which research is dominated by a particular paradigm, consisting of assumptions about the phenomena investigated and how they are to be studied and understood, these being embodied in investigations treated by scientists as exemplary. These periods of paradigmatic consensus are punctuated by what Kuhn calls 'scientific revolutions', in which one paradigm is gradually abandoned and a new one takes its place. Kuhn argues that the replacement of one paradigm by another is not, and cannot be, based entirely on a rational appraisal of each paradigm in terms of the evidence for and against it. This is because what counts as evidence, and its significance, are determined by the paradigms themselves; so that scientists operating in terms of different paradigms effectively see the world in different ways. There has been much debate about whether Kuhn's views are relativist, and Kuhn has sought to clarify this matter himself (Kuhn 1970, appendix). However, there is no doubt that his views have been interpreted in relativistic terms by many social scientists, including ethnographers.

These developments in the philosophy of science also stimulated changes within Anglo-American philosophy more generally, and in recent years there has been intense debate over realism. Here anti-realists have drawn both on resources present within the Anglo-American tradition, such as the early phenomenalism of the logical positivists and the later work of Quine, as well as on Dewey's pragmatism and continental European ideas (especially hermeneutics and post-structuralism). This anti-realist renaissance has also recently begun to have an impact on ethnography.[7]

The consequence of all these influences has been to encourage the application of a constructivist perspective to the research process itself; and thereby to undercut the realist rationale for ethnography, with its associated claim to objective description. Instead, it has been concluded by some ethnographers, often more informally than formally, that their accounts are simply one version of the world amongst others. This view is becoming increasingly popular, for example with ethnography being presented as a research paradigm that is incommensurable with others (Smith and Heshusius 1986; Smith 1989a), or ethnographic accounts being treated as *creating* cultural realities through the rhetorical devices they employ (Clifford and Marcus 1986; Tyler 1985). Here, any vestige of ethnography as representation of an independent reality is abandoned. Thus, Tyler (1986: 138) suggests that 'no object of any kind precedes and constrains the ethnography. It creates its own objects in its unfolding and the reader supplies the rest'. Without the ethnographer there is 'only a disconnected array of chance happenings'. This has led some to argue for ethnographic texts to be multi-vocal or dialogical, with the voice of the ethnographer playing only an equal, or perhaps even a subordinate, role to those of the people studied. Yet others have stressed the necessarily rhetorical character of ethnographic accounts and have advocated modernist and post-modernist textual experiments.[8]

In my view, however, applying relativism to ethnographic method is no less problematic than extending the realism assumed in much ethnographic methodology to our understanding of social life. The problems of relativism are well known. Central is the old question of what status we are to give to the claim that all knowledge is culturally relative. If it is true, then it applies to itself; and therefore it is only true relative to a particular culture or framework, and may be false from the perspective of other cultures or frameworks. Moreover, how are we to identify cultures or paradigms in a way that does not result in their proliferation, with people perhaps drawing cultural boundaries simply to protect the validity of their beliefs? In fact, any claims about the nature and boundaries of particular cultures would themselves presumably have to be treated as relative. This leaves us abandoned in circularity (Hammersley 1991e).

Over and above the self-refuting character of relativism it is also worth pointing out its practical implications for ethnography. If it is true that what ethnographers produce is simply one version of the world, true (at best) only in its own terms, what value can it have? And there is no reason to suppose that ethnographers produce just one version of the world. Given that they differ among themselves in cultural assumptions, we must surely conclude that their accounts are to be viewed as creating multiple, incommensurable worlds on the basis of the same or similar research experience. In the words of one of the advocates of anti-realism, we may have to conclude that 'there are as many realities as there are persons' (Smith 1984: 386). If this is so, what is the point in spawning yet more versions of 'reality', especially given the relative costs of ethnography compared with, say, armchair reflection? And why should some 'realities' be published and discussed at the expense of others? Of course, in place of the claim to provide true representations of the world we might appeal to the idea that our accounts, while not true, are useful in some way; for example, in providing instructive ideas or even entertainment. But do not etiquette books, books counselling how to make friends and influence people, political tracts, novels, plays, films, as well as newspaper articles and television programmes fulfil these functions? What need is there for ethnography given all this? The practical implications of relativism for ethnography are worth reflection.

It seems to me, then, that we can resolve the ambivalence

towards realism that is built into ethnography neither by extending ethnographic realism to our theorising about human social
life, nor by applying relativism to ethnographic method. In what
direction does a solution lie, then? The first step, I think, is to
recognise that the realism often built into ethnographic methodology is of a relatively naïve or crude kind. Effectively, it assumes not
only that the phenomena we study are independent of us, but that
we can have direct contact with them, contact which provides
knowledge whose validity is certain.[9] In practice, most ethnographers probably assume a weaker version than this: that the
closer we can get to reality the more likely it is that our conclusions
will be true. But the implication is the same: that if we could only
get rid of the barriers lying between us and reality, most obviously
our cultural preconceptions, we would be able to see reality itself.
Once these barriers have been overcome, once the veil has been
lifted, once we have dug below the surface impressions, reality
itself will be revealed. Such a view is clearly indefensible. It assumes
that there is some foundation of direct knowledge to which we can
get access. But what form could that foundation take? All perception and observation are assumption-laden. And even if there were
such a foundation, there is no means by which we could logically
induce knowledge from our observations in such a fashion that its
validity would be guaranteed.

The next step in the argument is to recognise that relativism is
not the only alternative to naïve realism. There is a great danger of
backing ourselves into a corner by deploying a dichotomy which
obscures the wide range of epistemological positions available. We
can maintain belief in the existence of phenomena independent
of our claims about them, and in their knowability, without
assuming that we can have unmediated contact with them and
therefore that we can know with certainty whether our knowledge
of them is valid or invalid. The most promising strategy for
resolving the problem, in my view, then, is to adopt a more subtle
form of realism. Let me summarise the key elements of such a view.

1 The definition of 'knowledge' as beliefs whose validity is known
   with certainty is misconceived. On this definition there can be
   no knowledge, since we can never be absolutely sure about the
   validity of any claims; we could always be wrong. In my view, we
   should instead define knowledge as beliefs about whose validity
   we are reasonably confident. While we can never be absolutely

certain about the validity of any knowledge claim, and while we may sometimes be faced with a choice between contradictory claims that are equally uncertain in validity, often we *can* be reasonably confident about the relative chances of validity of competing claims. Assessment of claims must be based on judgements about plausibility and credibility: on the compatibility of the claim, or the evidence for it, with the assumptions about the world that we currently take to be beyond reasonable doubt; and/or on the likelihood of error, given the conditions in which the claim was made (see Chapter 4).

2 There are phenomena independent of our claims about them which those claims may represent more or less accurately. And true knowledge is true by virtue of the fact that it corresponds to the phenomena it is intended to represent (though, as I indicated, we can never be *certain* that any knowledge claim is true). This assumption is clearly an essential element of any realism. However, we must consider the issue of what the term 'independence' means in this basic tenet of realism. This is complex. In one sense we are all part of reality and from that point of view cannot be independent of it. The same is true of any knowledge claims we make. However, what I mean by 'independence' here is simply that our making of a claim does not itself change relevant aspects of reality in such a way as to make the claim true (or false). And it seems to me that most social science accounts are neither self-fulfilling nor self-refuting. While some predictions may become self-fulfilling, even here the relationship is not entirely determinate. Whether a prediction is fulfilled as a result of its being made public always depends on other conditions: on whether it is believed and on whether other factors intervene, for example. And I suspect that most social research findings have (at best, or worst) only an extremely weak influence on what they predict or describe. Other powerful factors are always involved. In this sense, then, for the most part reality is independent of the claims that social researchers make about it.

3 The aim of social research is to represent reality, but this is not to say that its function is to *reproduce* it (that is, to represent it 'in its own terms'). Rather, representation must always be from some point of view which makes some features of the phenomena represented relevant and others irrelevant. Thus, there can be multiple, non-contradictory and valid descriptions and explanations of the same phenomenon.[10]

This subtle realism retains from naïve realism the idea that research investigates independent, knowable phenomena. But it breaks with it in denying that we have direct access to those phenomena, in accepting that we must always rely on cultural assumptions, and in denying that our aim is to reproduce social phenomena in some way that is uniquely appropriate to them. Obversely, subtle realism shares with scepticism and relativism a recognition that all knowledge is based on assumptions and purposes and is a human construction, but it rejects these positions' abandonment of the regulative idea of independent and knowable phenomena. Perhaps most important of all, subtle realism is distinct from both naïve realism and relativism in its rejection of the notion that knowledge must be defined as beliefs whose validity is known with certainty.[11]

What are the implications of subtle realism for the way we think about and practise ethnography? For one thing, subtle realism requires us to be rather more vigilant regarding the dangers of error than naïve realism would lead us to be. We must accept that we necessarily rely on cultural assumptions, and that these can lead us astray, just as easily as leading us in the right direction. Certainly, we cannot legitimately claim that simply because we were 'there' we 'know'. Yet this is the fundamental rhetorical strategy employed by ethnographers, as Geertz points out:

> The ability of anthropologists to get us to take what they say seriously has less to do with either a factual look or an air of conceptual elegance than it has with their capacity to convince us that what they say is a result of their having actually penetrated (or, if you prefer, been penetrated by) another form of life, of having, one way or another, truly 'been there'. And that, persuading us that this offstage miracle has occurred, is where the writing comes in.
>
> (Geertz 1988: 4–5)

Nor can we rely on the fact that because participants are 'there' that *they* 'know', as do those who define credibility in terms of respondent validation (Guba and Lincoln 1982). What we have here are rhetorical appeals to naïve realism, and they are not sustainable because of the weakness of that philosophical position. However, the fact that the observer was there and/or that partici-pants believe the account to be true are important sorts of *evidence* for the validity of an account. As researchers, we must develop the ways in which we monitor our assumptions and the inferences we make on the basis of them, and investigate those we judge not to be beyond reasonable doubt. This is not suggesting something that is new or novel. Ethnographers have become increasingly concerned with ways of checking their conclusions. Subtle realism simply encourages greater concern with this.[12] However, it runs counter to the implications of relativism, which undercut the rationale for such checks by denying that there is any reality to be known and implying that this rationale is based on arbitrary philosophical or political assumptions; assumptions which might, with equal warrant, be replaced by others, such as those generating fictional accounts.

What is implied by subtle realism is not, then, a complete transformation of ethnographic practice. We must still view people's beliefs and actions as constructions, and this includes their accounts of the world *and* those of researchers. At the same time, though, we should not assume that people's accounts are necessarily 'true' or 'rational' in their own terms. Whether we should be concerned with the truth or falsity of any account depends on how we plan to use it. There are two sorts of interest we can have in accounts, implying different requirements. First, we may treat them as social phenomena that we are seeking to understand and explain, or as indicators of cultural perspectives held by the people producing them. Here we must ignore our judgements about their validity or rationality, since this is not relevant to the task of understanding them. Indeed, the ethnographer should suspend any of her/his own beliefs that conflict with those being described and explained; otherwise there is a danger of misunderstanding. As I argued earlier, the question of the truth or falsity of an account carries no implications for how it should be explained. On the other hand, we may use accounts as a source of information about the phenomena to which they refer. They may, for example, provide us with information about events that we could not ourselves witness (for example that happened in the past or in settings to which we do not have access). Or they may allow us to check our own or others' observations through triangulation. Here we *must* be concerned with the truth or otherwise of the accounts, and we must judge this as best we can, both in terms of the likelihood of error of various kinds and according to how the information relates to our other knowledge. We can, of course, apply both these approaches to the same account; indeed, understanding an account may well help us in assessing its validity. However, it is very important to maintain the distinction between these two ways of analysing informants' accounts. Only if we do so can we retain the valuable ethnographic approach of seeking to understand and explain people's behaviour and beliefs independently of their supposed rationality or truth, while not lapsing into relativism.[13]

There is one area where subtle realism does imply something of a break with conventional ethnographic practice founded on naïve realism. This arises from its abandonment of the ideal of reproduction in favour of selective representation. Given that what is produced is, at best, only one of many possible valid accounts of the phenomena studied, it is a requirement that ethnographers make explicit the relevances on which their accounts are based. This is not always done.

CONCLUSION

In this chapter I have addressed what seems to me to be one of the central ambiguities in ethnography: between a commitment to a methodology based on naïve realism and a theoretical approach founded on constructivism that is often taken to imply relativism. I looked at each of the two most obvious solutions to this problem: the adoption of a consistent (naïve) realism or a consistent relativism. However, I concluded that neither of these offered an adequate solution. The first involves unacceptable assumptions about the asymmetry of explanations of true and false beliefs and of actions based upon them. The second leads to all those problems that usually follow from the adoption of a relativist epistemology, notably internal inconsistency. I argued that satisfactory resolution of this problem requires us to recognise that we are not faced with a stark choice between naïve realism and relativism, that there are more subtle forms of realism that avoid the problems of these two positions. I outlined what seem to me to be the main components of such a subtle realism, and sketched some of its implications for the principles and practice of ethnographic method.

NOTES

1 Something of this attitude is to be detected, for example, in Geertz's attack on 'anti-relativism' (Geertz 1984).

2 Blumer draws this idea from pragmatism; but it can also be found in one or another form in nineteenth-century historicism and in the eighteenth century in the writings of Vico and Herder (Berlin 1976).

3 For useful discussions of this idea in anthropology, see Jarvie (1964 and 1983), Winch (1964), Tennekes (1971) and Herskovits (1972). See also Geertz (1984).

4 For an application of this argument to social scientists' use of the concept of ideology, see Hammersley (1981a).

5 This is ironic since the origins of phenomenology lie in Husserl's attempt to ground knowledge in fundamental essences that are constitutive of human experience and therefore of the world, an enterprise resolutely opposed to scepticism and relativism: see Kolakowski (1975) and Bell (1990).

6 See, for example, Sudnow (1967) and Wieder (1974). For a useful general discussion of ethnomethodology in this respect, see Atkinson (1988).

7 Bernstein (1983) provides a useful overview of recent anti-realist trends. An example of the impact of these ideas on ethnography is the recent work of Denzin which seems to combine them in a relatively indiscriminate fashion (see, for example, Denzin 1989 and 1990). The differences and inconsistencies among the views I have outlined are at least as important as the similarities. And, as I have indicated, many of them are by no means unambiguously relativistic, even though that is often how they have been interpreted.

8 See the discussion of anthropological examples of 'experimental' ethnographic writing in Marcus and Fischer (1986). In sociology, Krieger (1983) provides an example of a text in which the voice of the researcher is suppressed in favour of those of the people studied.

9 It is also worth noting that to think of the phenomena studied as consisting of a reality independent of the ethnographer is misleading. We can treat them as independent of the researcher while recognising that both are part of the same reality.

10 Here I am adopting the neo-Kantian idea that reality is infinitely extensive and intensive (Rickert 1986). However, I do not believe that reality is structureless. In constructing our relevances we must take account of what we know and can discover about that structure if we are to get the information we need to serve our purposes (that is, in part at least, we must *discover* what is relevant). See Chapter 1.

11 Relativists' attitude to this definition is often ambivalent. On the one hand, they adopt it in arguing against realism, claiming that because there can be no knowledge of reality in this strong sense there is no sense in which we can reasonably claim to understand phenomena that are independent of us. In more constructive mode, however, relativists define knowledge in terms of what is taken to be certain within a particular culture or paradigm. While my conception of

knowledge shares something with this latter view, it differs from it in treating agreement as an indicator not as a definition of validity; and like all indicators it is subject to error.

12 For a more extended account of the assessment of ethnographic claims, see Hammersley (1991a).

13 Once again, this is not to recommend something that is entirely novel. Ethnographers have long employed both these forms of analysis, though they do not always distinguish between them sufficiently clearly. Something like this distinction is to be found in McCall and Simmons (1969: 4). The sort of subtle realism I have outlined clarifies the basis, and underlines the need, for this distinction.

4

BY WHAT CRITERIA SHOULD ETHNOGRAPHIC RESEARCH BE JUDGED?

There is considerable debate about what constitutes good ethnography; and, indeed, about what counts as ethnography.[1] These issues raise important questions both about the relationship between ethnography and other forms of social research, and about that between the methods of the social and natural sciences. And the point at which all these issues bite most deeply is the question of what criteria should be employed in the assessment of ethnographic studies.

There are three basic positions on this issue to be found among ethnographers, though they are not always as sharply distinguished as I shall make them here.

1   There are those who argue that we must apply the same criteria to ethnographic research as are employed by quantitative researchers, perhaps on the grounds that these are the criteria by which all scientific work should be judged. From this point of view, ethnography is one method among others and is not associated with a distinctive methodological philosophy.

2   Others, probably the majority, insist that ethnography represents an alternative paradigm to quantitative social research. Sometimes they claim that it represents true scientific method, being equivalent to that used by the natural sciences, thereby denying that quantitative social research matches this model (Blumer 1928; Znaniecki 1934). More common today, though, is the view that ethnography represents a different form of science to that characteristic of the physical sciences and the quantitative research modelled on them, one whose methodology is more appropriate to the nature of human social life (Blumer 1969; Lincoln and Guba 1985). Others see ethno-

graphy as closer in function and character to art and literature than it is to science, and the criteria by which it should be assessed are in their view aesthetic.[2] From these points of view the criteria to be applied in judging ethnography are rather different to those used by quantitative researchers, though there is disagreement about what the appropriate criteria are.

3 Finally, there are those who argue that the character of qualitative research implies that there can be no criteria for judging its products. In other words, it is suggested that the very notion of assessing research products in terms of a set of criteria is itself incompatible with the nature of the social world and how we understand it; or at least with the ethnographic approach.

I shall begin by examining each of these three positions, in reverse order. In the second half of the chapter, I want to outline what seems to me to be the most productive direction in which to search for a solution to the problem of criteria.

THE REJECTION OF CRITERIA

A distrust of theoretical and methodological abstraction is characteristic of the thinking of many ethnographers, and this sometimes extends to criteria for assessing research. However, few have argued explicitly against the very possibility of such criteria. An example is John K. Smith, who claims that in interpretive inquiry 'there can be no criteria to reconcile discourse (to sort out the trustworthy from the untrustworthy results)' (Smith 1984: 384; see also Smith 1989b). He argues that attempts to establish 'nonarbitrary' criteria for ethnographic research will inevitably be marked by confusion and inconsistency. This is because the quest for such criteria is incompatible with the basic philosophical assumptions of the qualitative tradition. He conceives of that tradition as representing one of two distinct perspectives on social inquiry that have been in competition since the nineteenth century. He views the quantitative tradition as realist, in the sense that it assumes that true accounts correspond to how things really are and judges competing accounts in terms of whether the procedures adopted ensure an accurate representation of reality. By contrast, according to Smith, the qualitative tradition is idealist. In terms of this tradition '"valid" is a label applied to an interpretation or description with which one agrees' and 'the ultimate basis for such agreement is that the interpreters share, or come to share after an open dialogue and justification, similar values and interests' (Smith and Heshusius 1986: 8–9). Smith argues that since we can have no direct and certain knowledge of an independent reality, the correspondence theory of truth is inappropriate. Along with this, the idea that by following particular methods we can ensure the validity of our findings also collapses. And so, too, does the notion that there are criteria by which we should judge research studies. Thus he claims that:

> To accept that social reality is mind-constructed and that there are multiple realities is to deny that there are any 'givens' upon which to found knowledge. If one accepts these assumptions, different claims about reality result not from incorrect procedures but may simply be a case of one investigator's interpretation of reality versus another's.
>
> (Smith 1984: 383)

It is important to separate out several elements of Smith's argument:

1 the claim that there can be no algorithmic criteria, in other words that the assessment of ethnographic claims necessarily involves judgement so that there is always a potential for disagreement about the application of any proposed criterion;
2 the argument that there are no criteria whose appropriateness or validity is fixed and certain, so that the considerations underlying the assessment of claims are themselves always open to disagreement and potential change; and
3 the suggestion that there are no criteria in the sense of judgements that assume the reality of the phenomena studied to be independent of the researcher. Rather, the considerations in terms of which assessment is and should be made refer solely to particular, historically located forms of social practice. The only legitimacy that they can have is that they belong to such a practice, that they are agreed upon by those who engage in that practice.

In my view, the first two points provide useful clarification of the concept of criterion. I, too, do not believe that there are algorithmic criteria whose validity is simply given. The application of criteria necessarily involves judgement, and the criteria themselves are always potentially open to challenge and reformulation. However, I do not accept the third element of Smith's argument. Here he adopts an anti-realist position in which he rejects the idea both that our knowledge can correspond to the phenomena it is intended to represent and that achieving such a correspondence is one of the aims of inquiry. In my view there are no good reasons for adopting this point of view.[3]

Let me begin by pointing out that the fact that we have no direct access to reality, and thereby to knowledge that can provide a foundation of certainty for our understanding of the world, does not necessarily imply rejection of truth as correspondence. Nor does it undermine the idea that some methods are more effective than others in producing knowledge of reality, or the idea that there are criteria by which we can judge empirical claims. These conclusions only follow if we assume that for claims to be called knowledge they must be known to be true with *absolute* certainty, that to be of any value methods must *ensure* true findings, and that criteria must produce assessments that are *beyond all possible doubt*. But there is no reason to make these very strong assumptions, and there are good reasons for not doing so. Effectively, Smith implies that we are faced with a choice between only two positions: realism (interpreted as *naïve* realism) and some form of idealism. But this is true neither historically nor philosophically. In the history of philosophy there is a much wider, and more complex, range of positions than this; and Smith's account of the history of two traditions within the methodology of the social sciences is not accurate for this reason (Hammersley 1990c). Furthermore, many of these positions are philosophically defensible, even though none can be established beyond all doubt.

More fundamentally, it is not clear on what basis Smith could reply to this criticism: after all, applying his own arguments to this issue, what grounds could he have for disagreement other than the sheer fact that he disagrees? This problem arises because he defines truth (within the interpretive tradition) simply as what is agreed upon: 'for interpretive inquiry, the basis of truth or trust-worthiness is social agreement; what is judged true or trustworthy is what we can agree, conditioned by time and place, is true and trustworthy' (Smith 1984: 386). This seems to undercut any basis for rational discussion.[4] Another problem with this approach is that it is logically impossible: how can we decide whether something is true on the basis of whether we have decided that it is true?

We have a circular definition here. Finally, we should note the curious way in which Smith discusses the validity of the quantitative tradition. Quite consistently, he treats the choice between paradigms as simply a matter of personal preference. If we were to adopt the quantitative paradigm, we could have criteria. 'However, if the interpretive assumptions are more satisfying, then we must put aside the desire to be foundational' (Smith 1984: 390). This points to the most decisive weakness of his position: its relativism. Smith urges us to embrace relativism, but can (of course) offer no grounds for us to do so unless we already share his position. This is the long-recognised internal inconsistency built into relativism: if true it applies to itself, thereby rendering its own truth relative, which means that there are conditions under which it is false (Scheffler 1967).

In my view, then, Smith's argument against the legitimacy of criteria for judging the validity of the findings of empirical research is not convincing. There do seem to me to be reasonable grounds for specifying such criteria. Indeed, I believe this is essential if qualitative research is to be of any value, since otherwise it allows no rational basis for distinctions between sound and unsound, and more and less valuable, accounts. At the same time, though, I think that we can conclude from Smith's discussion that it would be unreasonable to expect fixed and certain criteria whose application is algorithmic, telling us what is and is not true with absolute and precise certainty. Any criteria must be heuristic, relying on tacit and always questionable assumptions in their application, these applications therefore being subject to potential debate.

ETHNOGRAPHIC CRITERIA

A few ethnographers have presented criteria that they believe to be distinctive to ethnographic research.[5] For example, Lofland (1974) has sought to explicate the criteria of assessment employed by referees in reviewing articles for two sociological journals specialising in ethnographic research. While he presents his account of these criteria as a descriptive finding, it becomes clear that there is implicit prescription if we compare the discussion in this article with that in his text *Analyzing Social Settings*, where the same criteria underlie the recommendations (Lofland and Lofland 1984). Lofland presents what he calls the 'generic style' of ethnography. He recognises that there are other styles, but he concentrates on the evaluation of ethnographic research from this point of view. On this basis he suggests that we should look for several, perhaps even all, of the following features.

(a) A *generic* conceptual framework; that is one that identifies patterns that apply to a wide variety of social phenomena. One of the examples that Lofland cites is Bigus's analysis of the strategy of 'cultivation' employed by milk delivery workers in dealing with their customers. This research is *generically* focused because it is concerned with developing the concept of 'cultivating strategies', an idea that may be applied to other service relationships, and perhaps to relationships in general, rather than being concerned with the particularities of the milk round (Lofland 1976).

(b) A *novel* framework of concepts.

(c) An *elaborated* framework of concepts. This requires that the report 'goes beyond sketching out the frame ... [specifying] constituent elements of the frame, draws out implications, shows major variations ...' (Lofland 1974: 106).

(d) An *eventful* framework. 'Eventful' here means 'full of or rich in events', 'to what degree is the frame of [the] report grounded in, and illustrated by, concrete episodes and accounts of action' (Lofland 1974: 107).

(e) A framework *interpenetrated* with the empirical materials. In other words, the conceptual framework and the empirical account of particular events 'coexist as one whole, each depending on the other for the "interest" a reader has in the frame or in the qualitative material' (Lofland 1974: 108).

The generic style that Lofland advocates stands opposed to those forms of ethnographic research that are focused on topical issues alone, that are concerned simply with detailed description of a culture or behaviour pattern, that rely on generalised description rather than including detailed extracts from concrete data, or that separate analysis and data.

A somewhat similar set of criteria is provided by Athens (1984). For him, ethnographic work should be judged according to the extent to which it:

(a) *generates formal* theories. Work that merely refines existing theory or which produces only substantive theory is regarded as less valuable. (The concept of formal theory here seems similar to Lofland's 'generic' theory.)

(b) is *empirically grounded*: the concepts must be consistent with the empirical observations from which they were derived; and for the reader to make an assessment this requires at least some of those observations to be included in the research report.

(c) is *scientifically credible*, this being achieved by provision of an account of the research process.

Athens's first criterion seems to combine the first two of Lofland; while his second perhaps covers Lofland's last two, though it is less specific in its requirements. Only his last criterion seems distinctive.

The other attempt to specify criteria for judging ethnographic research that I shall examine is that of Guba and Lincoln (Guba 1981; Guba and Lincoln 1982; Lincoln and Guba 1985). They are more explicit than the previous two authors about the wider intellectual context in which their account is located. They set out from a position somewhat similar to Smith's: that there are two main paradigms of inquiry, namely the rationalistic and the naturalistic. They define these both in terms of contrasting axioms (that cannot be compromised) and postures (that may be compromised, though the axioms 'almost compel the adoption of particular postures') (Guba and Lincoln 1982: 249). They regard the rationalistic paradigm as the most appropriate for the study of physical phenomena, but argue that human social life has features that make this approach inappropriate for its study. Here the naturalistic approach is required. They argue that while naturalistic research should be committed to what they take to be the four major traditional criteria (truth value, applicability, consistency and neutrality), these must be formulated in a different way than in the rationalistic paradigm, as follows.

1 Commitment to truth value is represented by concern with credibility, with whether the people studied find the account produced to be true.

2 Applicability takes the form of transferability. The naturalist rejects 'generalisability' and 'the assumption of context-free laws'. But he or she 'nevertheless believes that some degree of transferability is possible under some circumstances' and 'those circumstances exist if enough "thick description" is available about both "sending" and "receiving" contexts to make a

reasoned judgement about the degree of transferability possible' (Guba and Lincoln 1982: 247).

3 Commitment to consistency is represented by concern with dependability. Since designs are emergent in naturalistic research, replication is not possible. Instead, the naturalist must seek to assess the effects of research strategies employed on the findings, and distinguish these from variations in the phenomena studied.

4 Neutrality takes the form of confirmability. The key question here is whether the data are 'qualitatively confirmable'; in other words, whether the analysis is 'grounded in the data' and whether inferences based on the data are logical and of high utility (Lincoln and Guba 1985: 323).

Lincoln and Guba's account only partially overlaps with those of Lofland and Athens, and therefore adds some additional criteria. Putting all the criteria together, we get the following list:

1 the degree to which generic/formal theory is produced;
2 the degree of development of the theory;
3 the novelty of the claims made;
4 the consistency of the claims with empirical observations, and the inclusion of representative examples of the latter in the report;
5 the credibility of the account to readers and/or to those studied;
6 the extent to which the findings are transferable to other settings;
7 the reflexivity of the account: the degree to which the effects on the findings of the researcher and of the research strategies employed are assessed and/or the amount of information about the research process that is provided to readers.[6]

There are several questions that need to be asked about these criteria. First, are they to be applied to *all* ethnographic research? For instance, should all ethnographic research be concerned with the development of formal theory? By no means all ethnographers adopt this goal, and in my view there is no reason why they should. We need to modify the application of any criteria according to the intended product of the research. I shall develop this point later.

Second, while the criterion of credibility is important, it requires a subtler interpretation than those provided in existing accounts. It should not be *defined* in terms of whether readers or the people studied judge the account to be true. There are several reasons why the responses to the researcher's account even of the people studied will not necessarily give a sound indication of its truth. They may feel that it is in their interests not to accept or admit certain truths or to accept falsehoods. Equally, they may not themselves be aware of key features of what has happened to them, for example of the impact of remote causal factors on their lives. To assume that respondents can validate or even falsify accounts in some definitive way is to forget the social character of the relationship between researcher and participants and to assume that they have privileged access to the truth. Neither of these assumptions is sustainable. Furthermore, to treat respondent validation as a criterion is to ignore the distinction between criteria (on the one hand) and the strategies we use to gather information about the adequacy of the research (on the other). The responses of participants to ethnographic accounts are a useful source of data, but their agreement with those accounts should not be a *criterion* for assessing such research. If we were to adopt this as a criterion, the obvious recommendation to follow would be that we should produce bland and/or flattering accounts, since these are probably more likely to be accepted as true by participants than those which portray them in a less flattering light.[7]

Finally, we must ask whether there is any reason to believe that, in so far as they are appropriate, these criteria should be applicable *only* to ethnographic research. It seems to me that, suitably modified, they apply to all social research.

APPLYING QUANTITATIVE CRITERIA

The most common evaluative frameworks discussed in the methodological literature dealing with quantitative method centre on one or both of two sets of concepts: 'internal and external validity' and 'reliability and validity'. These two frameworks are compatible; indeed the first can be taken to subsume the second. Several writers have applied these sets of concepts to ethnographic research, though often reinterpreting the concepts in the process (Berk 1974; Denzin 1978; Dobbert 1982, ch.7; Evans 1983; LeCompte and Goetz 1982; Goetz and LeCompte 1984; Kirk and Miller 1986).

The most serious problem with this strategy in my view is not that such criteria are not applicable to ethnographic research, but that even in their application to quantitative research they are not adequate. Their conceptualisation is unsound in some respects, and they are not always necessary and are never sufficient as a basis for assessing research.

Campbell's development of the concepts of internal and external validity takes the experiment (or rather the quasi-experiment) as its model of research; but the framework is held to apply to other forms of research as well (Campbell 1957; Campbell and Stanley 1963; Cook and Campbell 1979). The focus is on hypothesis-testing and how research can be designed so as to rule out various types of threat to validity. There is some ambiguity about the meanings of the terms 'internal' and 'external' validity (Hammersley 1991c). However, broadly speaking, 'internal valid-ity' refers to the issue of whether, *in the experiment concerned*, mani-pulation of the treatment produced variation in the outcome. 'External' validity concerns whether a relationship discovered in an experiment can be generalised to other situations. From this point of view, the findings of an experiment may be internally valid in the sense that it seems highly likely that the treatment produced the outcome, but may not be generalisable because the outcome is an artifact of laboratory conditions.

There are some serious problems with this framework for thinking about validity. Most important of all is that the distinction between internal and external validity is not cogent. In claiming that the treatment produced the outcome in a particular experi-ment we are making a causal claim and therefore necessarily implying that in other situations that are similar in relevant respects the same relationship would be found. And if we investi-gate such situations and find that the relationship is not present there, and we are confident that this result is not a methodological artefact, we must revise our views about the validity of the findings of the *original* experiment. For this reason, to talk of different types of validity is misleading. The findings of a study are either valid or they are not (or they approximate being valid to some degree); we cannot have findings that are valid in one sense but not in another. While Campbell's discussions of validity issues are useful, in particular his itemisation of threats to validity, the distinction between internal and external validity is fundamentally misleading (Hammersley 1991c).[8]

The other framework drawn from quantitative methodology that is often applied to ethnographic research is the distinction between reliability and validity. Even more than in the case of internal and external validity we find ambiguities of definition in the use of these terms (Hammersley 1987c). However, there is a conceptually sound distinction implicit here. Validity in this context refers to the accuracy with which a description of particular events (or a set of such descriptions) represents the theoretical category that it is intended to represent and captures the relevant features of these events. For example, if we are concerned with documenting the 'survival strategies' (Woods 1979) that secondary-school teachers employ in the classroom, we must ensure that the examples of teacher action which we treat as instances of survival strategies *are* instances of that concept; and that our descriptions of the teachers' actions do not misrepresent them. Reliability refers to the degree of consistency with which instances are assigned to the same category by different observers or by the same observer on different occasions. It provides evidence about validity and also tells us about the usefulness of the particular research strategy used.

While the concepts of validity and reliability, suitably defined, are appropriate criteria for judging the methods and products of research, they are not sufficient. The internal/external validity framework covers additional issues that must sometimes be addressed, even though that framework is itself not soundly constructed. And, over and above these, there are other issues that require attention, notably what I shall refer to below as the question of relevance.

A REFORMULATION OF THE CRITERIA

As I noted, a drawback of some discussions of the criteria by which ethnographic (and other social) research should be judged is that they do not make a clear distinction between these criteria and the means or evidence by which judgements may be made about whether or not the criteria have been met. Within the quantitative tradition this can be seen in the common treatment of reliability (defined in terms of mere consistency of result) as a criterion of assessment standing side by side, if not a little above, validity. Yet, defined in these terms, it cannot be more than a means of assessing the likelihood of invalidity.[9] This confusion of ends and means in the quantitative tradition probably arises from the influence of operationalism. However, we sometimes find it in discussions of qualitative methodology too. Thus, some of what Lincoln and Guba identify as criteria are means by which the validity of qualitative research may be assessed, rather than criteria themselves. As we have seen, this is certainly true of 'credibility', and it also applies to 'consistency' and 'neutrality', and perhaps even to 'transferability'.

In this discussion I shall be concerned only with criteria of assessment in the sense of standards by which research results should be assessed, not with the means used to apply these criteria. In order to decide what are appropriate criteria for judging the products of ethnographic research, and indeed of social research in general, we must consider a fundamental question: what is the purpose of such research, what goal is it intended to serve? And, of course, this is a matter of some debate. Answers to it involve assumptions and disagreements, both about what is desirable and about what is possible. My own view is that the function of research is to provide information that is both true and relevant to some legitimate public concern.[10] On the basis of that definition there are two obvious criteria in terms of which research findings should be judged: truth (or validity) and relevance. And these criteria apply to both qualitative and quantitative research.

I take the importance of validity to be obvious, and directly or indirectly it has been the primary concern of most discussions of assessment criteria; though as we shall see it is by no means unproblematic. However, research must not only produce findings that seem likely to be true, these findings must also be of some human relevance. It is not uncommon for criticisms to be made of the triviality of research findings. Often these criticisms reflect ignorance about the significance of the findings within the field concerned. None the less, the issue of the relevance of the findings of social research to people outside the research community is a crucial one. In my view social science would have no value if its findings were not relevant in this sense. Again, though, we shall see that there is room for considerable dispute about what does and does not count as relevant.

It seems to me that seeking in a rational way to meet the criteria of validity and relevance, to some satisfactory degree, is a necessary and sufficient condition of sound research practice; though I recognise that false claims can sometimes be fruitful, and that we cannot always anticipate the future relevance of true but apparently trivial claims. I shall now discuss each of these two criteria in more detail.[11]

Validity

In conceptualising validity, I adopt a position of what might be called subtle (as opposed to naïve) realism (see Chapter 3). I use 'validity' as a synonym for what seems to have become a taboo word for many social scientists: 'truth'. An account is valid or true if it represents accurately those features of the phenomena that it is intended to describe, explain or theorise. Assumed here, then, is a correspondence theory of truth, but the correspondence involves selective representation rather than reproduction of reality. Furthermore, I recognise that we can never know with certainty whether (or the extent to which) an account is true; for the obvious reason that we have no independent, immediate and utterly reliable access to reality. Given that this is the situation, we must judge the validity of claims on the basis of the adequacy of the evidence offered in support of them.

Of course, this concept of adequacy is itself not simple. One of the implications of rejecting naïve realism is that we must recognise that all judgements about the truth of knowledge claims rest on assumptions, many of which we are not consciously aware of, and most of which have not been subjected to rigorous testing (Hammersley 1991a). This gives a pragmatic dimension to the assessment of knowledge claims. Given that there is no bedrock of truths beyond all doubt which we can use as a basis for our assessments, the process of assessment is always potentially subject to infinite regression. Whatever evidence is offered for a claim, the validity of that evidence may always be challenged; and any further evidence provided may in turn also be challenged; and so on, *ad infinitum.* Clearly, we have to stop somewhere. The question is, though, at what point and on what grounds?

We face this problem in everyday life, and we seem to resolve it there in terms of a variety of considerations: judgements about what is beyond reasonable doubt; the likely costs of error; the scope available for acquiring further evidence before a decision has to be made; the likely value of that evidence and the costs of getting it etc. It seems to me that the situation of the researcher is distinctive in degree but not in kind. I take it that, first and foremost, there is a requirement placed on researchers routinely to subject the validity of claims and assumptions to more scrutiny than is normal in other circumstances. This is part of the function of research. However, since no point of absolute certainty can be reached, even among researchers some notion of reasonable doubt must be operative beyond which it is judged not necessary to go.[12] And over and above this principled restriction on the possibility of doubt, there are also practical limitations. There are pressures of time and limits to resources facing researchers; and these are, if anything, becoming more restrictive.[13]

On what basis, then, should social researchers, and readers of research reports, decide about sufficiency of evidence? It seems to me that there are three important considerations here.

1 The first concerns the issues of plausibility and credibility (see Hammersley 1991a). First, we must consider whether the claims made are sufficiently plausible, given our existing knowledge. If they are themselves beyond reasonable doubt we can simply accept them. If they are not, we must ask whether the claim is credible, by which I mean whether it is of a kind that we could reasonably expect to be accurate, given what we know about the circumstances in which the research was carried out. For example, in Pollard's study of the impact of differences in teaching style on pupils' friendship groups I think we can reasonably accept his claim that one of the teachers employed a star system to motivate the pupils (Pollard 1984b: 36). It is common knowledge that teachers sometimes do this, and it is a matter about which an observer in the teacher's classroom, like Pollard, could come to a judgement with relatively little danger of error. On the other hand, when the same author claims that the children in this teacher's class tended to have friends of the same level of academic achievement, I think it would be unreasonable for us to accept this as plausible or credible at face value. Indeed, Pollard does not expect us to, he provides further evidence for this claim. And in such cases we must then, of course, assess the evidence itself, but once again we can do so only in terms of *its* plausibility and credibility.

In their work researchers must seek to establish their findings as sufficiently plausible and credible to be accepted not only from their own point of view, but also by anticipating the likely judgements of fellow researchers. In writing their research reports they should provide sufficient evidence to convince that audience; and, in the face of expressions of doubt, they should be prepared to supply further evidence.[14]

Where the intended audience is not other researchers in the relevant field, for example where it is practitioners concerned with the substantive matters researched, the author must consider how that audience deviates from the researcher audience, reducing or eliminating evidence where it is judged likely to be found unnecessary and introducing additional evidence where this audience is likely to need more persuasion.

2 The second consideration that should determine the amount and kind of evidence provided is the centrality of the claim to the argument presented by the researcher. Where a claim is central, more convincing evidence will be required than where it is marginal. This is analogous to the common-sense tendency to require more evidence where a costly decision is involved.

3 The third consideration is the type of claim made. We can distinguish between a variety of types of claim that may be found in ethnographic (and other) research, though these are not always clearly differentiated. It seems to me that we need to distinguish, at a minimum, between definitions, descriptions, explanations and theories.[15] What is involved in assessing the validity of a claim varies according to which of these types it belongs. Let me illustrate this by contrasting descriptions and theories. Descriptions are claims about what occurred in a particular place at a particular time (or a finite set of spatio-temporal locations). Evidence must therefore relate to that location (or set of locations), and of course to the particular event(s) to which the description is claimed to refer. We must show that the phenomena described fit the categories built into the description, and that the information about the phenomena on which their categorisation is based is accurate. (This corresponds to the concern with the consistency of claims with empirical evidence that was included in the summary of ethnographic criteria above, and to quantitative researchers' concern with construct validity.) By contrast, theories are concerned with relationships between types of phenomena, wherever instances of those types occur; for example the claim that, other things being equal, labelling someone deviant will increase their deviance. The validity of such claims is more complex than that of descriptions. In trying to support a theoretical claim we

71

will have to provide descriptive evidence about some case (or, more likely, cases) relevant to the theory, which documents the correlation of instances of the type of phenomena produced with those of the type claimed to produce them. In addition, though, we will have to try to show that, *in this case and others*, the occurrence of the first type of phenomenon is not a product of factors other than the one claimed. This requires information about such other factors as are judged potential alternative causes. And inference from what happened in the case(s) studied to a conclusion about the validity of the theory is notoriously problematic. In short, then, different sorts of evidence are required depending on the type of claim involved. And this implies the use of a variety of sources of information, even though the criterion – validity – is the same whichever type of claim is involved.

From my point of view, then, the assessment of validity involves identifying the main claims made by a study, noting the types of claim these represent, and then comparing the evidence provided for each claim with what is judged to be necessary, given the claim's plausibility and credibility. Some claims may be beyond reasonable doubt in themselves, in which case they will be judged not to need evidence. In other cases evidence will be required, evidence whose nature will depend in part on the type of claim involved. This evidence will, in turn, need to be assessed in terms of its plausibility and credibility. What should be clear from this is that while the criterion of validity applies across qualitative and quantitative research, and across research aimed at various products and audiences, its requirements in particular cases may vary considerably.

Relevance

Sometimes research seems to be presented as if the discovery of truth were sufficient justification in itself. In practice, though, most researchers recognise that their work must also be judged in terms of its relevance. But, of course, the question should be addressed: relevance to what and for whom? It may be tempting to think that research reports can be addressed to humanity at large, but this is not a defensible position. Much of the output of social research, and especially of ethnographers, is concerned with particular events in particular places which are of interest to only limited audiences.[16]

It is essential, then, in assessing the relevance of a study, as with judging its validity, that we consider the question of audience. There is a variety of types of audience that ethnography may address. One is fellow researchers. But, of course, not even all social researchers will find every piece of social research relevant to their work. Who will and will not (or should and should not) is complicated by the fact that the social research community is differentiated not only by specialisation in terms of substantive field and specific research problems, but also by commitment to different methodological and theoretical approaches. Thus, a piece of research may be judged relevant or irrelevant not only in terms of its relation to some topic of interest but also on the basis of its exemplification of some methodological or theoretical paradigm. In my view, while there is a role for judging research in terms of method exemplification, the primary emphasis should be on substantive relevance.

The functions that research studies can serve for the community of researchers are diverse and depend somewhat on the nature of the product. But we can identify a couple of aspects of relevance here.

(a) *Importance of topic.* This concerns the centrality of the topic studied to a substantive field. Some issues within a field are more important than others. Within the sociology of deviance, for example, the question of the causes of delinquency would be judged by most researchers to be more central than investigation of the practices of naturists, though there is research on both topics.[17] These ideas about importance reflect, and should reflect, wider societal values and circumstances. However, in my view it is important that social scientists retain some autonomy in making judgements on the basis of these values (Hammersley 1991a).

(b) *Contribution to the literature.* Research that confirms what is already well known is of little value. Rather, it must make a significant contribution to what is taken by researchers to be established knowledge. It is here that Lofland's (1974) and Athens's (1984) concern with novelty and theoretical development are appropriate.

These, in my view, are the two aspects of relevance, as they relate to the assessment of studies by the research community.

There are other audiences for social research besides fellow researchers, of course. Very often there are groups of practitioners who work in areas related to the substantive foci of research; and of course they may well also be among the subjects of the research. The attitudes of practitioners to the work of researchers is variable and complex. It is not uncommon for practitioners to claim that research is irrelevant to their work or that it misrepresents it or the problems they face.

Debates about the relevance of research to the work of practitioners often founder on the problem of what relevance entails. It is sometimes understood on the basis that effective practice involves the mere application of the findings of research, those findings being formulated in prescriptive terms as rules to be followed. It is not surprising that social research in general, and ethnography in particular, is rarely (if ever) relevant in this sense. In my opinion this view involves misconceptions about both practice and research. We have noted the variety of possible products of research, and prescriptions are by no means the most common research product. Nor can prescriptions usually be formulated as rules that apply algorithmically. In general, what is appropriate action in any situation depends on one's goals, local circumstances, and judgements about the likely consequences of various possible courses of action and their value implications. It can never be reduced to the application of rules. This is no more than to reiterate a conception of the nature of practice that goes back at least to Aristotle (Lobkowicz 1967). He drew a sharp distinction between theoretical science, involving the contemplation of eternal truths, on the one hand; and the more uncertain knowledge on which practical activities like politics are based, and which derives from experience. He seems to have seen little role for theoretical knowledge in informing practice; even in the field of medicine, where few today would doubt it. Later writers recognised the role of theory in informing practice and this included the idea that lessons could be learned from history in order to improve political practice. Machiavelli was not the first to advocate such a role for history, but he has come to symbolise one view of the practical relevance of social research. His emphasis on providing the means of effective action and his downplaying of the issue of the value justification of the goals pursued and the means adopted fitted well with an influential conception of science as concerned only with fact and theory, not with values other than truth; a view that became quite influential among social scientists in the nineteenth and twentieth centuries.

What we have here, then, is a gradual shift from Aristotle's view that practice could learn little or nothing from theoretical science, to the view (in its most extreme form) that practice is nothing more than the application of the findings of theoretical science. That view has rarely been explicitly advocated and defended, and has often been attacked. However, something like it has been the effective basis on which much social science in the twentieth century has operated.[18] Much more effort and resources have been put into the clarification of factual compared to value issues, the latter being treated either as outside the scope of rationality or as following from the facts.[19] In practice, of course, value judgements are made in social science research, but they are often effectively disguised as factual judgements, and justification for them is often not presented. This is as true of ethnography as of other kinds of social research (see Hammersley 1991c).

In my view, while we should not return to Aristotle's complete separation of theory and practice, his conception of the nature of practice as involving judgement and knowledge derived from experience is sound.[20] This implies a much more limited role for research in influencing practice than is often claimed for, or expected of, it. It can never provide an alternative to experience and judgement. This is not to say that it cannot play a useful role in informing practice. But the question remains: in what sense might social research be relevant to practitioners? The same two aspects of relevance seem likely to apply here as within the research community, albeit with slightly different implications.

(a) *Importance of topic.* What is important to practitioners will often be different to what is important to researchers. Importance here seems likely to relate to problems that practitioners face that are pressing and/or have major consequences for achieving the goals they are pursuing. Practitioners are likely to judge research in terms of whether it helps them with their current problems. Their judgement is therefore likely to be more short term and specific than that of researchers. This is as it should be; though their judgements should not be treated as a valid general assessment of the value of the research.[21]

(b) *Contribution of findings.* Here again, mere confirmation of what is already known is of limited value. Obviously, though, what is taken to be already known will rightly differ between researcher and practitioner communities. At the very least, the former will question some of what the latter take for granted.

An obvious question that arises from this discussion is: which is the most important audience for ethnographic research, fellow researchers or practitioners? There is no simple answer to this apparently straightforward question. While, in my view, the ultimate justification for social research is its contribution of relevant knowledge useful to other forms of practice, that contribution is a collective one. It often is, and should be, the result of a combination of studies rather than of a single one. Furthermore, this fact (plus the specific and necessarily changeable character of practitioners' judgements) means that assessments of the practical relevance of research are subject to a considerable degree of uncertainty. This does not mean that reasonable judgements cannot be made, simply that we must recognise the danger of error and consider what sorts of error we most and least prefer to avoid. Furthermore, it seems to me that while practitioners' judgements of the relevance of research are important, since they may provide a different perspective to that of researchers, their position involves no epistemological, moral or political privilege about this matter. Indeed, I still believe that it is researchers who must make decisions about what lines of research are and are not to be pursued, albeit in the light of the views of others, both practitioners and funders. A crucial consideration in any decision about the selection of research topics is the question of feasibility, and researchers are in the best position to judge this. Also, for research to be successful it is necessary for researchers to be fully committed to the project. If they doubt its feasibility, or any other aspect of it, the necessary commitment of time, energy and intelligence is unlikely to be forthcoming. Research is not like filling shelves in a supermarket, which can be done effectively with little commitment to any larger organisational goal.

Whatever the audience, it is clear that judgements of the relevance of studies, particularly their importance, depends upon prior value judgements. Given this, the question might be raised: how are we to justify such judgements? In the realm of values, scepticism and relativism are even more widely accepted than they are in the realm of facts. However, it seems to me that they are not convincing in either sphere. Few would deny the dangerous implications of value scepticism or relativism, for example in possibly rendering us unable to condemn, or to justify action against, the perpetrators of genocide. But there remains the problem of how the arguments for knowledge in the sphere of values can be justified. Ironically, though, I believe that the inroads that scepticism and relativism have made into the philosophy of science may stimulate not just the defence of realism in the factual domain (which has indeed happened), but also arguments supporting the rational justification of value judgements.[22] After all, if it is possible to make rational decisions about the validity of factual claims despite the absence of a foundation of certain knowledge, why is it not possible to make rational judgements about value issues even though there are no ultimate values that we can establish beyond all possible doubt? In the case of value judgements, as in that of providing evidence for factual claims, we must argue from assumptions that we believe, and which we may justifiably expect our audience to assume, are beyond reasonable doubt. And in the face of disagreement over value judgements (motivated by good faith), we must search for assumptions on which we can agree and try to show how our conclusions can be justified on the basis of them.[23]

I would not want to suggest that producing research that meets the criterion of relevance is a straightforward task. Indeed I believe that there are important questions about the capacity of ethnography to produce relevant results. These stem from the fact that the situations studied by ethnographers rarely have intrinsic relevance. Rather, the findings have to be made relevant by appeal to empirical generalisation or theoretical inference, neither of which are unproblematic (see Chapter 5). Nevertheless, relevance is a criterion that must be taken into account in any assessment of the value of ethnographic work.

CONCLUSION

In this chapter I have sought to identify the criteria by which ethnography, and in fact all social research, should be assessed. I began by addressing the argument that no such criteria are appropriate, suggesting that while algorithmic and absolutely conclusive methods of assessment are not likely to be available, we can specify reasonable criteria that ought to be taken into account in making assessments. I then examined some attempts to put forward criteria distinctive to the ethnographic or qualitative tradition. I argued that some of these were not criteria at all but means of providing data relevant to assessment. Furthermore, those that were criteria were not always distinctive to ethnography or relevant to all research goals. Some ethnographers have, of course, sought to apply the criteria developed by quantitative researchers to their work. I looked at the potential of this strategy, suggesting that while these criteria certainly identify important issues, they involve some misconceptions and are not sufficient in themselves as the basis for assessment. In the final section of the chapter I identified what seem to me to be the two overarching criteria that must govern assessment of the value of social research: validity and relevance. By 'validity' I mean the truth of the claim made. Validity is interpreted in terms of selective representation of reality, with the amount and nature of the evidence that is necessary depending on the type of claim involved, and on judgements about its plausibility, credibility and centrality (judgements whose own validity can never be certain). Relevance, on the other hand, concerns the importance of the research topic and the contribution to our knowledge made by the findings of the study. As with validity, it has varying implications depending on the audience addressed.

My focus in this chapter has been on the criteria that are appropriate for assessing ethnographic (and other kinds of social) research; rather than on the means that can be employed in making such assessments. Clarification of these criteria is an essential first step before we can develop more effective strategies to meet them.

NOTES

1 For example, Lutz (1981), Rist (1980), McDermott (1982) and Wolcott (1980 and 1982). I am using the term 'ethnography' here in a broad sense to cover what is also generally referred to as 'qualitative method', 'the case study approach' etc.
2 See, for example, Clifford's (1986b) analysis of the allegorical character of ethnography. Also, Nisbet (1962) and Brown (1977), though these authors argue that aesthetic criteria apply to science in general, not just to ethnography or even to social science.
3 I am not arguing that the criteria adopted for assessing ethnographic findings should themselves correspond to reality; but I do want to

argue that the establishment of criteria should be based on assumptions that have such a correspondence, and that one of the assessment criteria should be correspondence to reality. See the discussion of validity later in this chapter, and also Chapter 3.

4 Those who disagree with one another could each provide reasons and go on doing so until they found beliefs they shared, but it is not clear why (on Smith's argument) the discovery of such common ground should lead either side to change their original views. The only possible bases for the revision of views within Smith's scheme seem to be inconsistency and the desire for solidarity. Consistency is the one criterion that Smith does accept, but he recognises that there are multiple coherent perspectives about anything. The idea that the aim of inquiry should be solidarity rather than truth comes from Rorty (1984). The problem with this, even putting aside general doubts about anti-realism, is that on this view whether we agree or not, that is whether some claim is treated as true or trustworthy, is determined by our judgement as to the balance of our interests, whether the desire for solidarity with those we currently disagree with outweighs our desire for solidarity with others and our other preferences. This may be a reasonable description of some people's behaviour, but it is not a convincing epistemology. And, contrary to Rorty, there is no escape from epistemology. We necessarily make assumptions about what is knowable and under what conditions, whether or not we wish to or are conscious of doing so.

5 For other attempts to identify criteria for assessing ethnographic research besides those discussed here, see Wolcott (1975), Owens (1982), Miles and Huberman (1984), Mishler (1990) and Wolcott (1990).

6 For an account of this concept of reflexivity, see Hammersley and Atkinson (1983).

7 I am drawing a distinction here between the standard(s) in terms of which claims should be assessed and the means or indicators by which that assessment should be carried out. The term 'criterion' has sometimes been used to refer to both, and this leads to confusion. Here, I shall use the term to refer only to standards of assessment.

8 This criticism has less force in relation to the way in which the concepts of internal and external validity are sometimes applied to ethnographic research, where internal validity refers to the accuracy of description of the particular case (situation, person, organisation etc.), and external validity to the extent to which that case is representative of some wider population. Here the two issues *are* distinct, so long as the claims which are being generalised are descriptive and not explanatory or theoretical ones. Thus, if we were assessing a study of a prison that documented some key features of the relationships among inmates and between inmates and staff, it would be quite reasonable to ask first how accurate was the description of the relationships in that particular prison at that particular time; and second, whether those relationships would also be found in substantially the same form in some population of prisons over some time period.

However, this separation of internal and external validity would not apply if we were concerned with an explanatory claim, for example that some feature of the prison's organisation produced some feature of the documented social relationships. While we could assess separately the issue of how typical the prison studied was in the relevant features of its organisation and how typical it was in its social relationships, the question of whether the causal relationship occurred in the particular case is inseparable from the question of whether a similar relationship would be found in other cases. In claiming that it occurred in the particular case, we are necessarily claiming that under other relevantly similar conditions the same relationships would be found. To the extent, then, that ethnographic accounts are concerned with explanation as well as description, the distinction between internal and external validity is just as misleading as it is for quantitative research with the same goal.

9 Defined in terms of consistency *and* accuracy of result, it may be a criterion, but it is a criterion for the assessment of methods or instruments, not of research results. Vagueness about the object being assessed (whether it is research design, results or instrument) is a feature of many discussions of validity and reliability in the quantitative literature. See Hammersley (1987c).

10 For discussion of some competing definitions of the function of research, see Chapters 6 and 8.

11 Some have sought to collapse these two criteria, treating them as identical or regarding relevance/usefulness as an indicator of validity. The most influential advocate of this view among philosophers was William James. While his writings are by no means unequivocal on this issue, in many places he does suggest an equivalence between truth and usefulness, as in his famous remarks about religion: that the truth of religious belief lies in its consequences for the believer (James 1902 and 1909). It is important to recognise that James does not mean that whatever pleases us is true. His concept of satisfaction or utility is a wide-ranging and long-term one: it applies to what it generally serves our purposes to believe to be true. This is a substantial reinterpretation of Peirce's pragmatic maxim, but Dewey also adopts an instrumentalist conception of truth. On James, Peirce and Dewey, see Scheffler (1974). A somewhat similar view is advocated by Habermas (1987 and 1988). He argues that the validity of critical theory can only be judged on the basis of its practical success in enlightening the audience to which it is directed, liberating them from the effects of ideology.

Sometimes these views are put forward on the anti-realist grounds that we cannot know validity, whereas we can judge whether the effects of something are useful. Alternatively, it may simply be argued that usefulness is far more important than validity. The first argument is not effective, as we can see if we ask how we are to know that our judgements about the usefulness of a belief are valid. In other words, claims about usefulness presuppose validity claims, and therefore cannot replace them. The second argument is a value judgement and one that I think it would be unwise to adopt as a general rule. There are occasions when the fact that something apparently worked may be enough for us. But on many occasions it is *useful* to know whether it was indeed the supposed remedy that had the desired effect and why.

12 Interestingly, the level of what is taken to be reasonable doubt about basic assumptions varies among intellectual enterprises, so that philosophers typically exercise much more fundamental doubts than do most scientists.

13 On the increasing importance of the limitations of resource for natural science, see Rescher (1984). Over and above this, the extension of administration and teaching within higher education institutions in recent years has reduced the time available for research, and financial resources for social science research have also declined in many Western countries. This cannot but have an effect.

14 However, this holds only where such expressions are judged to be based on good faith, rather than on a refusal to be convinced about the issue whatever the evidence. Audiences with the latter characteristic simply cannot and should not be taken into account. There is, of course, room for disagreement about whether a critic is acting in bad faith, and in general it seems to me that researchers must err on the side of treating bad faith as genuine rather than vice versa.

15 For a fuller account of these types, see Hammersley (1991a).

16 There may be some knowledge that everyone should be concerned with, but much knowledge is not of this kind. How directly relevant are many of the findings of the natural sciences to most of us? How could we keep up to date with advances in all of their branches? The problem of relevance arises in an acute form in the case of ethnography because of its idiographic approach (see Chapter 5).

17 Of course, naturism may be a topic that is used for developing formal theory, in which case it may gain importance from that source. There is a massive literature on the causes of delinquency: for an interesting review of some of the main alternative explanations, see Kornhauser (1978). There is a much smaller literature on naturism, see Weinberg (1973) and Parry (1987).

18 For criticisms of research in political science along these lines, see Storing (1962).

19 These two positions seem to have had much the same consequences for social science.

20 Several writers have recently emphasised the independence of practice from theory. See, for example, Schwab (1969), Schon (1986) and Carr (1987).

21 There is a further complication surrounding the question of the audience for ethnographic research. This is that researchers are usually also teachers in higher educational institutions who prescribe the reading of research reports for their students. Some of those students will be proto-practitioners in relevant fields, some may already be practitioners taking part in in-service courses, while others may be destined to become researchers. Students, along with their teachers, constitute an especially salient audience for ethnographic

researchers. And this audience may have its own distinctive requirements, for example for research reports that facilitate teaching and
learning as these are defined in higher educational institutions today.

22 For examples of defences of realism in the philosophy of science, see
Bhaskar (1978), Trigg (1980), Smith (1981), Newton-Smith (1981),
Aronson (1984), Devitt (1984), Churchland and Hooker (1986),
Miller (1987), Papineau (1987) and Vision (1988). There are also
signs of a renewed challenge to scepticism and relativism in relation
to the sphere of values, see for example MacIntyre (1981 and 1988).

23 For attempts to apply such an approach in assessing ethnographic
research, see Hammersley (1990b, 1991a and 1991c). How value
issues are resolved may differ somewhat between researcher and
practitioner communities, however, because of the different priorities
of those communities, given their different goals.

Part II

ETHNOGRAPHY, RELEVANCE AND PRACTICE

5

THE GENERALISABILITY
OF ETHNOGRAPHY

In this chapter I want to look at an issue in the methodology of ethnographic research that has not been given the attention it deserves: the question of the generalisability of its findings.[1] I argued in the previous chapter, that the goal of any research is to provide information that is not only true, but which is also of relevance to issues of human concern (see Chapter 4). I could provide a true description of the items that are currently on the table at which I am writing and an explanation for their presence; but there are few, if any, circumstances under which this would or should be of interest to anyone, even me. Such an account, true though it might be, would be of little relevance. In planning, as well as in assessing, ethnographic research, we must consider its relevance as well as its validity. Of considerable importance here is the question of how, as researchers and readers, we are able to generalise from findings about particular situations studied to conclusions that have such general relevance.

Ethnographers usually study one or a few small-scale cases (settings, groups or people) over periods that range from a few days to several years. A primary concern in this research is the description and explanation of what is observed in the particular case(s) studied. It should be noted that only in rare circumstances will non-local audiences have intrinsic interest in these cases. There may be such interest in Fielding's account of the leadership of the National Front (Fielding 1981). Similarly, if it is true that the religious group that Lofland studied was one of the seed groups of the Moonies (Lynch 1977), then we might be interested in it for itself in a way that we would not be if it were just another 'doomsday cult' (Lofland 1966). In the case of most ethnographic studies, however, there is no widespread intrinsic interest in the particular case(s) studied. Yet ethnographers publish their work in national and international journals, or in commercially published books, and teach it to their students. In doing so, they are claiming that their work has general relevance beyond the local circumstances in which it was produced.[2] The question is, though, on what basis can this claim to general relevance be justified? How can we find within, or make out of, the detailed description of a particular case an account that is of value to those who have no intrinsic interest in that case?

I shall examine here the two forms that claims about the general relevance of ethnographic work can take: empirical generalisation and theoretical inference. Ethnographic studies often trade on both of these without distinguishing clearly between them.[3] Neither is straightforward and the requirements that must be met in each case for the claim to be valid are quite different.

EMPIRICAL GENERALISATION

It may be claimed that the particular setting investigated is typical of some larger whole or aggregate. Here, for example, an ethnographer might claim that a comprehensive secondary school he or she has studied is typical in relevant respects of all or most comprehensive schools during some time period (see, for example, Ball 1981: 20). If this claim is sound, the implication follows that what is said of the particular setting is true of all or most of the settings in the aggregate; and the account should be of interest to anyone who is interested in the aggregate or any of its members.

It is worth noting that for empirical generalisation to provide relevance, the setting studied does not have to be typical: indeed, its relevance may derive from its atypicality. For example, Cicourel and Kitsuse (1963) studied Lakeside High, a school that they pointed out was atypical of US high schools, not just in serving an exclusively high income neighbourhood, but also in its large size, bureaucratic structure and professionalised counselling service. However, they argued that this school was in the vanguard of changes that were taking place among US high schools so that more and more schools would become similar to Lakeside High in respects relevant to their research findings. Here, of course, the validity of the empirical generalisation depends on the accuracy of Cicourel and Kitsuse's claims about trends in US high schools. The same sort of rationale (but in reverse) was used by Goldthorpe *et al.* to establish the general relevance of their survey of Luton car workers. It had been claimed that increased affluence among manual workers was leading them to abandon traditional working class solidarity in favour of a more middle-class orientation. The authors argued that if even the comparatively affluent workers that they studied had not adopted such an orientation, then there was no reason to conclude that the bulk of manual workers were coming to adopt middle-class values or would do so in the future. (Goldthorpe *et al.* 1969).

Sometimes, ethnographic studies involve a multiple form of empirical generalisation. Parts of a setting may be studied and the results generalised to the whole; and then, in order to provide for the general relevance of the study, the setting may itself be treated as typical of a larger population of settings. For example, Jerome Skolnick studied some of the lawyers and police officers at work in a US city. He generalises his findings to the justice administration system of that city as a whole, and then treats his findings as a basis for discussion of the administration of justice in the US (though he notes the distinctive features of the city he studied, and carries out a brief investigation in another city) (Skolnick 1966).

It is important to remember that besides inferring from findings about one phenomenon to an aggregate of phenomena, empirical generalisation also involves inference from facts about events at the time at which the setting was studied to events in that setting and others *at other times*. Indeed, it is necessary to be very clear about what is involved in empirical generalisation. Ethnographers sometimes write as if they are generalising to a category of phenomena occurring in unspecified times and places, rather than to an identified aggregate of settings during a specific time period (or set of time periods). For example, the study of one police department, or a number of police departments, may be used as a basis for making claims about police work in general. The temptation to do this is revealed in the subtitle of Skolnick's book which is 'law enforcement in democratic society'. Gone here is the reference to a particular democratic society, the implication is that the findings apply to *all* democratic societies. This is illegitimate. Empirical generalisations can only be to finite populations (though these do not necessarily have to be specified very precisely). Claims about categories of phenomena (that are open-ended and therefore refer to an infinite number of instances past, present, future and possible) are theoretical claims (on which, see below).

Ethnographers do, then, often make claims about the typicality of the settings that they study: though these are sometimes hedged, the institution studied being described, for instance, as 'not atypical' (for example, Rist 1970: 417). Making such claims is quite legitimate in principle in the case of both descriptive claims (claims about what occurred or was present at some time and place) and explanatory claims (claims about why something happened at some time and place). We must give some thought, though, to the question of to what aggregate and time period generalisation is being made. In part this will depend on the purpose of the research and the audience for it. What aggregate and period would or should our audience be interested in? But audience interest is not the only important consideration. We must also, of course, think about the likely degree of homogeneity of the features we are studying across units within the various populations to which we might try to generalise. There is little point in selecting a population that would be of great interest to our audience if it is likely that the features we are studying are so heterogeneous within it that generalisation from our investigation is likely to be ill-founded.

Having decided what is an appropriate population to which generalisation might be made, we must then actually assess and present evidence about the validity of that generalisation. Of course, this is a task to which statistical sampling techniques can be applied. But these techniques are rarely appropriate in the case of ethnographic studies because the ratio of settings studied to the number of settings in the aggregate is usually too low.[4] However, this does not in itself rule out the possibility of empirical generalisation. We must not confuse probability methods with the goal of making claims about representativeness or typicality. After all, in practice such methods are rarely used in pure form even by survey researchers: stratified random sampling, for example, involves reliance on background knowledge about the most significant forms of heterogeneity to be found within the relevant population. Conversely, being unable to use probability methods does not rule out the possibility of making reasonable judgements about the representativeness of findings drawn from a particular setting in relation to some wider population. There are a number of sources of information that may provide a basis for such judgements.

(a) Information about relevant aspects of the aggregate in the appropriate time period may be available in published statistics, whether produced by the state, by non-state organisations or by independent researchers.[5] Wolcott (1973) provides an example of the use of this strategy in an ethnographic study, seeking to establish the representativeness of the school principal he studied by drawing on a nation-wide survey of US elementary school principals. Of course, there is a limit to the relevant information that is available. We may not always be able to obtain information about the particular aggregate in the particular period to which we wish to generalise. In this situation we may be able to make reasonable judgements about the population we are interested in from information about a population for which we do have information (for example, where the former represents a substantial proportion of the latter). Another problem is that the particular information relevant to our concerns may not be available for the population to which we wish to generalise. For instance, in studying longshoremen in Portland, Oregon, in the US (the equivalent of dockers in the British context), Pilcher wanted to document their income. Unfortunately, this information was not available. However, he was able to obtain official statistics about the average earnings from waterfront work of longshoremen in Oregon as a whole. This information obscured variations in earnings between workers in different ports in Oregon, and between longshoremen of different ages. Even more important, it omitted income from other forms of work (the uncertain nature of waterfront work makes other sources of income a necessity for many) and fringe benefits (official and unofficial) (Pilcher 1972: 15–17). Nevertheless, in this case, as in others, information available in official statistics may be better than nothing.[6]

(b) Another possibility is increased collaboration between ethnographers and survey researchers, or the combination of case study and survey methods in the same investigation.[7] The advantage of this strategy over reliance on already available statistics is of course that information that is not provided in those statistics can be collected. However, because of the practical constraints involved in survey research, reliance would probably often have to be placed upon indirect indicators for some of the information required.

(c) Another strategy is the coordination of ethnographic studies so as to provide accounts of the range of variation in an aggregate or larger system. This coordination might be based upon stratified sampling. At present there is little coordination among ethnographic studies, even where these are studies of the same type of phenomenon.[8]

There is no doubt that ethnographic studies can, and probably already do, provide descriptive information about settings that are typical in relevant respects of larger aggregates that are of interest to us. However, in general, ethnographers are not very effective in establishing the typicality of what they report. Greater use of the strategies outlined above would improve this, and it is worth noting that these strategies are complementary, not mutually exclusive.

Of course, ethnographers not only offer *descriptions* of phenomena but also often present *explanations*. We must be especially careful to distinguish the process of generalising explanations from theoretical inference. The crucial difference is between generalising to a finite population on the one hand, and to a category that subsumes an infinite number of actual and potential instances on the other. As with generalising descriptions, in generalising explanations we must begin by deciding what the most appropriate aggregate and time period is. Much the same considerations apply as before, but the range of possible populations is more limited. The most obvious candidates are populations of cases displaying the same explanatory factor or similar ones to that identified in the setting studied. For example, if we explain the attitude of a doctor towards a patient in terms of the system of patient typifications she employs, then the appropriate aggregates would be finite populations of doctors sharing the same type of typification system. If the doctor's use of these typifications were itself explained in terms of, say, the type of training she received, her career pattern, and/or her gender, then generalisation might be attempted to populations sharing these features. Once again, of course, having decided upon an appropriate aggregate and time period to which generalisation might be made, we must seek evidence about the validity of the generalisation and assess it. The same strategies are appropriate here as in the case of description.[9]

Summarising then, generalisation from a study of a single case (or a small number of cases) to a larger population is a legitimate means of making ethnographic findings generally relevant. Such generalisation does not necessarily require the use of statistical sampling techniques; though these should, of course, be used where appropriate. It *does* require reflection and clarity about the population and time period to which generalisation is to be attempted, use of aggregate data, extant and generated by survey research, and/or systematic coordination of ethnographic studies to sample across populations and over time.

THEORETICAL INFERENCE

The second and quite different way that ethnographers may seek to give their work general relevance is by drawing conclusions about one or more social scientific theories from the features of the local events they observe and describe. What I mean by 'theory' here is statements about necessary relationships among categories of phenomena. An example of a theory that has been developed largely through the medium of ethnographic work is labelling theory: the claim that the frequency and intensity of deviance on the part of an individual are increased by the labelling and treatment of that person as deviant. This formulation of the theory, though, captures only one of several, mutually incompatible, strands to be found in the literature, the conflation of which renders the theory unclear (Fine 1977). These strands parallel the range of alternative justifications for theoretical inference that can be detected in the methodological writings of ethnographers (see Chapter 1). In brief these consist of:

(a) the claim that ethnographic work produces theoretical insights whose validity and value are to be judged by the reader;
(b) the idea that theories are universal claims that can be derived from the study of a single case which exemplifies a type;
(c) the argument that by studying critical cases we can, on the basis of the hypothetico-deductive method, draw inferences about the truth or falsity of universal laws.

None of these arguments is entirely convincing. The insight model leaves open the question of how we are to decide what there is about the situation studied that is generally relevant. We must anticipate what readers will find insightful, and on what basis are we to do this? Furthermore, are all such bases, including for example political prejudice and aesthetic fancy, reasonable grounds for providing 'insights'? If not, how should readers decide the value and validity of ethnographic accounts? And is ethnography necessary for generating insights; cannot this be done as effectively by reflection on experience? The type model also involves problems. It assumes that in some, rather mysterious, sense there are ideal types of phenomena that provide the basis for understanding any of their instances, however much these may deviate from type. But on what grounds can we assume that there are such types? And how do we discover them? The third argument is found in its most explicit form in analytic induction (Znaniecki 1934; Lindesmith 1968; Cressey 1953).[10] The advocates of analytic induction argue that true scientific method involves in-depth analysis of individual cases, leading to the discovery of universal laws. They contrast this with the statistical method which can produce only probability statements. It should be noted, though, that few ethnographers today believe that universal laws of human behaviour exist. It is argued that such laws cannot exist because human actions are not causally determined, or at least not fully determined, and do not conform to lawlike patterns (Blumer 1939 and 1969; Matza 1964 and 1969). If this is true, analytic induction is not an appropriate model for theoretical inference.[11]

Given these problems, it is not clear what basis there can be for making claims about the general relevance of ethnographic studies in terms of their contribution to the development of theory. I would not want to dismiss the possibility of universal laws of social phenomena, at least of a generative rather than a regularity kind. However, we must recognise the force of the arguments against the existence of such laws, and also what is required if they are to be identified by means of ethnographic research. It may also be that my criticisms of the other rationales for theoretical inference are ill-founded. I hope I have shown, however, that ethnographers need to give some thought to these questions.

CONCLUSION

In summary, there are serious problems with arguments for the general relevance of ethnographic studies. These studies are often structured by appeals to empirical generalisation and/or to theoretical inference. But the nature of these appeals, and the requirements they place on the researcher, are not often given attention. In this chapter I have tried to clarify the bases on which claims to general relevance can be made, and to assess their potential as justifications for ethnographic research.

Empirical generalisation does provide a sound basis for claims to the general relevance of ethnographic studies in the case of both descriptions and explanations. Its use does not necessarily require the study of a large proportion of instances in an aggregate, or a sample selected on the basis of statistical sampling theory. It does, however, require ethnographers to make rational decisions about the population to which generalisation is to be made, and to collect and present evidence about the likely typicality of the case(s) they study. It also suggests that there should be more collaboration with survey researchers and increased coordination among ethnographic studies so as to cover the main lines of assumed variation within a domain.

The second kind of appeal to general relevance, on the basis of theoretical inference, raises more serious problems. There are several kinds of theoretical inference to which appeal may be made, but all of these involve problems. The strongest, analytic induction, is premised on the existence of universal, deterministic, sociological laws. Yet, most contemporary ethnographers reject the claim that there are such laws, arguing that human behaviour is creative and formative, at least within limits. They also reject the search for probabilistic laws. But if neither deterministic nor probabilistic laws are available, then attempts to justify ethnographic work as a basis for theoretical inference do not seem to be legitimate.

If ethnography is to have a clear and convincing rationale we must clarify the issues surrounding the bases on which claims to the general relevance of its findings are made. And we must develop ethnographic practice in such a way as to sustain those claims.

NOTES

1 This chapter addresses one aspect of validity, but it is one that has great significance for the issue of relevance. For some other discussions of this issue, see Stake (1978), Kennedy (1979), Tripp (1985), Donmoyer (1990), Schofield (1990) and Becker (1990). In

my view, useful as they are, all of these treatments of the problem are weakened by a failure to make two important distinctions: between empirical generalisation and theory (on which see the discussion later in this chapter); and between establishing the validity of a generalisation or theory and deciding on its usefulness in making sense of a particular case. One aspect of the latter relates to the distinction I drew between theorising and explanation in Chapter 2.

2 Advocates of action or collaborative research make participants one of their prime audiences (as well as drawing them into the practice of the research). But even in these kinds of research this local audience is rarely the only one intended.

3 Even when they are distinguished, their relationship is not always understood correctly, in my view. Thus, Mitchell (1983) draws the distinction between what he calls 'statistical' and 'logical' inference, but treats them both as means of what I have referred to as 'theoretical inference' (see Chapter 10). And while Yin (1984) does recognise the distinction, he denies (quite wrongly in my view) that case studies can be a basis for what he calls 'statistical generalisation', which is equivalent to what I refer to here as 'empirical generalisation'.

4 Probability sampling may be applicable in ethnographic research where the aim is to generalise *within* the setting studied, for example across participants in that setting.

5 A model for the combined use of aggregate statistics and case studies was provided by Ernest Burgess and Clifford Shaw in the 1930s (Burgess 1927 and 1930; Shaw 1931). For them these two sources of data were complementary: the case studies provided in-depth knowledge of people's perspectives and of processes of social interaction; the quantitative data offered information about how typical the cases studied in depth were (see Bulmer 1980 and 1984; and Harvey 1987).

6 Bulmer (1980) notes a general reluctance to use official statistical data on the part of British sociologists, including ethnographers, compared with those in the US, and argues that this reluctance is ill-founded.

7 Survey researchers have sometimes complemented their work with more detailed case studies; and ethnographers sometimes use questionnaires to provide information from a broader sample (though often this is generalisation within, rather than across, cases). See, for example, Olesen and Whittaker's (1968) study of the socialisation of nurses in which they used a questionnaire to collect background information about the nurses they studied, and those in preceding and succeeding years. Similarly, Rock employs a small social survey of public knowledge and opinion to complement his ethnographic study of the process of debt collection in London in the 1960s (Rock 1973). There are also some investigations that represent a more even balance between case study and survey, including the work of the Institute of Community Studies (see Platt 1971) and, more recently for example, Millham *et al.*'s (1986) study of children in care and their families (though in key respects these are still closer to the survey than the ethnographic tradition). There have long been calls

for more systematic combination of these data sources, but there has been only limited progress: see Zelditch (1962), Sieber (1973) and Bryman (1988).

8 One reason for this is probably the great emphasis placed upon theoretical originality by the ethnographic community, and the resulting variability in focus of such studies. This is not to deny that there is some loose coordination of investigations. For example, Punch justifies his study of policing in Amsterdam's Warmeosstraat on the grounds that previous studies of the police have neglected the distinctive characteristics of cosmopolitan, inner-city areas (Punch 1979). However, something more formal and systematic than this is surely required, along with more clarity about the larger domain to which generalisation is being made. There have been some moves in this direction in the evaluation field, with the development of multi-site studies. However, these have often involved relatively superficial investigation of the cases studied: see the discussion in Schofield (1990: 212–14).

9 In Chapter 4, note 6 I suggested that the generalisation of explanations is not possible. The contrast between this and what I have written here reflects my continuing uncertainty about this issue.

10 Znaniecki's position seems to straddle the type model and the hypothetico-deductive method.

11 The other major strategy for theory development within the ethnographic tradition, grounded theorising (Glaser and Strauss 1967), is less clear in character than analytic induction. But to the extent that, as Strauss (1987) claims, it is a version of the hypothetico-deductive method, it too must presuppose the existence of scientific laws of human behaviour. Given this, it too must be regarded as being at odds with other elements of the current perspective of most ethnographers (Hammersley 1989a).

6

CRITICAL THEORY AS A MODEL FOR ETHNOGRAPHY

In recent years there have been an increasing number of calls for a 'critical ethnography'. This term is used in a variety of ways, but the most common implies an 'appropriation' and 'reconstruction' of conventional ethnography so as to transform it into a project concerned with bringing about human emancipation; this usually being interpreted in socialist and/or feminist terms.[1] Conventional ethnography is criticised by advocates of critical ethnography both for adopting an inappropriate theoretical perspective that neglects oppression and its causes, and (even more importantly) for not being closely enough related to political practices that are designed to bring about emancipation. Thus, in a review of Peshkin's study of a fundamentalist Christian school (Peshkin 1986), McClaren advances the following criticisms:

> Peshkin's interpretive research paradigm sorely lacks a critical praxis-oriented dimension. ... The researcher [should] take seriously the establishment of a theoretical context which enhances the possibility of critical analysis capable of transforming the asymmetrical relations of power and privilege that constrict human life and limit human possibility. ... Peshkin seems to believe that ethnography can and should confine itself to a cultural analysis, to analysis of symbols, statements and values. ... This is ethnographic insularity with a vengeance, field work devoid of necessary theoretical and activist dimensions.
>
> (McClaren 1987: 136, 138)

As I shall use it, then, the term 'critical ethnography' refers to a form of qualitative research that contrasts with more traditional approaches in being closely, perhaps one should say organically, linked to socialist and/or feminist politics. In this chapter I want to assess the rationale for this approach.

THE CRITICAL MODEL

The sense of the term 'critical' used by critical ethnographers derives from Hegelian and Marxian philosophical ideas and their development by twentieth-century Marxists.[2] As Lobkowicz (1967) shows, Marx adopted a view of the relationship between theory and practice, based on the writings of Hegel and Kant, that is quite different from what is found in earlier thinking about this issue. Thus, for Aristotle, practice was distinct from theory, and neither had much relevance for the other.[3] They were concerned with different domains, the universal and the contingent. He believed that there is practical knowledge, but that this is necessarily only probabilistic and of uncertain validity; and it is directed towards the achievement of the good, not towards truth *per se.* Theory, on the other hand, is concerned with the contemplation of eternal verities and is of value in itself. There is an implied contrast here between the human and the divine (Lobkowicz 1977). Kant, however, identified the practical with the ethical, and thereby with a higher metaphysical realm which is quite separate from the reality dealt with by theory (in the form of natural science), and is necessarily unknowable in scientific terms (Kroner 1914). What we have here is in many respects an inversion of the Aristotelian view: the practical partakes of the divine, while theory deals with human experience. Hegel's contribution was to 'overcome' these distinctions by reintroducing Kant's metaphysical reality back into the world, and knowledge of it back into theory. He argued that the point in history had been reached (its end-point in fact) at which theory (that is, the ideal) and reality were reconciled. He believed that his own philosophy represented the world become conscious of itself. While, like other left Hegelians, Marx did not accept that this reconciliation had already occurred, he did adopt the view that history had arrived at the point where all the contradictions that had previously characterised human society could be overcome (that is, humanity could be emancipated and realise its true being). And he believed that the potential for that reconciliation was embodied in his own theoretical work. All that remained was for reality to come into line with theory, and this would be achieved through the development of the proletariat and its adoption of his 'scientific socialism' (and the social transformation that would ensue from this).[4]

What we have here is a teleological view of history as at least potentially leading towards the self-realisation of humanity, the actualisation of all that human beings have striven for in the past but have previously been unable to achieve. This view is central to the ideas of influential twentieth-century Marxists such as Lukács, Korsch and the Frankfurt School (though some of the latter, notably Adorno and Horkheimer, later became pessimistic about the prospects for emancipation).[5] A crucial feature of this perspective is what is sometimes called negative critique: the criticism of existing social relations in terms of the ideal immanent in history; in such a manner as to stimulate the process by which ideal will become reality. This plays a particularly important role in the thinking of the Frankfurt School, for whom a key feature of advanced capitalism was an ideology that denies (on technical grounds) that social arrangements could be different. From this point of view, negative critique is, at the very least, an essential preliminary to bringing about emancipation. Indeed, it has been argued in relation to Horkheimer and Adorno that: 'critical theory had no active theory of politics and was left only with the notion of "immanent critique"' (Dickens 1983: 134). More sympathetically, we can see the Frankfurt theorists as seeking to keep critical consciousness alive at a time when, they believed, even the very possibility of an alternative socio-cultural order had almost been expunged (Buck-Morss 1979).

Critical theory became influential among a substantial minority of Western social scientists in the 1960s, 1970s and 1980s. A key figure here has been Jürgen Habermas.[6] It has become commonplace for critical theorists to adopt the typology of approaches to inquiry that he presents (Habermas 1987; Fay 1975; Bernstein 1983; Popkewitz 1984; Angus 1986a; but see also Overend 1978). He identifies three models of scientific inquiry.

1 The *empirical-analytic sciences*, comprising natural science, but also including attempts to apply natural science methods to the study of human behaviour (notably in the form of quantitative social research). Habermas argues that this approach is constituted by a technical interest in the instrumental control of phenomena.

2 The *historical-hermeneutical sciences*, consisting of the discipline of

history and those parts of social science that are guided by an interpretative orientation, such as Weberian sociology (though also including phenomenological, interactionist and ethnomethodological approaches). According to Habermas these sciences are constituted by the practical interest that is characteristic of human communication, a concern with achieving the mutual understanding that is essential for the survival of human society. Conventional ethnography is generally treated as conforming to this model.

3 *Critical theory,* or critical social science, is exemplified to varying degrees in the work of Marx, Freud and the Frankfurt School. It is grounded in an emancipatory interest in the overcoming of social oppression, notably that which is characteristic of advanced capitalism. Clearly, this is the category into which critical ethnography is intended to fall.

Habermas challenges attempts to model social science on the natural sciences; he regards the empirical-analytic approach as inappropriate in that field.[7] There are several grounds for this view. One is that, by seeking to exclude values from the realm of science and treating science as the only source of reliable knowledge, whole areas of life (including politics and ethics) are left as matters about which only arbitrary decisions can be made, based on taste or other irrational factors. Second, that despite the claim to be value-neutral, positivist social science incorporates and reinforces values that support the status quo.

Habermas also criticises interpretative social science, and these criticisms have been elaborated by critical ethnographers. As we saw above, conventional ethnography is challenged both for the inaccuracy of its theoretical assumptions and for its (often implicit) political commitments and effects, these being regarded as closely related. Thus, it is claimed that such research neglects the constraints operating on the people studied, who are portrayed as simply exercising their freedom. This criticism has two aspects. One is that people's understandings of the world are taken at face value rather than their distortion by ideology being recognised. Another is that there is a failure to identify the macrosocial structural determinants of people's behaviour. Associated with this, it is claimed, is a neglect of social conflict and contradictions, and of power differences. In short, it is argued that simply to describe people's behaviour as if it were the product of a freely expressed culture is systematically to misrepresent that behaviour. Furthermore, doing so reflects a misguided political commitment to the idea that socio-political problems are simply the product of inter-cultural misunderstandings, and this has unacceptable conservative political consequences, reinforcing the ideological misunderstandings of participants and thereby protecting the exploitative macro-social structures that produce them.[8] As Moon comments:

> Thus, a purely interpretive or *verstehende* social science is necessarily conservative, for it gives rise to a form of political practice that is closely bound to the existing traditions of society, and that divests itself of any standpoint from which these traditions might themselves be called into question.
>
> (Moon 1983: 147)

On this basis, the critical model is advocated as the most appropriate approach to social research, at least at the present time. Habermas portrays this model as combining features from both the other types of science, but also as having some important distinctive characteristics. Critical theories are aimed at producing the emancipation of oppressed groups through enlightenment, that is by enabling members of such groups to recognise their interests. It is claimed that ideology prevents oppressed groups from seeing their true situation and interests, and is therefore a major factor in sustaining their oppression. A central feature of the work of critical theorists is therefore ideology-critique. This begins with the attempt to understand and document the culture of the oppressed. But it subsequently operates in a manner analogous to empirical analytic science in documenting the quasi-causal production of ideological consciousness. However, critical theory differs from the sort of theory characteristic of natural science in at least two respects. First, whereas natural-science theories are applied in an instrumental way through the manipulation of variables to bring about the desired result, critical theory operates by freeing people from the coercion of ideology through enabling them to recognise the reality of their situation and thereby giving them more control over their own lives. Second, the success or otherwise of a critical theory in bringing about enlightenment and emancipation is a crucial, perhaps *the* crucial, aspect of any assessment of its validity. Here Habermas uses the analogy of psychoanalysis, the validity of psychoanalytic interpretations being partly judged by whether they are recognised as true by the patient and whether that recognition eliminates the symptoms; in other words they are judged by the success or otherwise of the therapeutic process, viewed as a self-reflective movement towards personal autonomy. Thus, critical theories set out to explain the nature of a social order in such a way that they serve as catalysts for the transformation of that order:

> Critical theory seeks to provide an interpretation of social conditions which begins with the self-understandings of the social actors, but ... subjects them to sustained criticism with the objective of uncovering their basic contradictions, incoherences and ideological distortions. Further, critical theory seeks to explain the power and persistence of such ideological distortions by showing how systematically distorted ideas and belief systems arise, and the role they play in maintaining a system of social interaction. Moreoever, it also provides an analysis of the workings of the social system, showing the ways in which a system crisis could arise, thereby providing for the possibility of critical theory's becoming itself a material force leading to system change.
>
> (Moon 1983: 175)

Up to now I have presented the critical theory tradition as if it were consensual. But, as with most traditions, there are considerable internal differences. To illustrate these I want to identify three broadly defined versions of the critical model. First, there is the orthodox Marxist position which assumes the teleological view of history outlined above, and envisages critical theory as both the product of intellectuals committed to a revolutionary socialist party and as addressed to the working class so as to enable it (through understanding the nature of capitalist society and its role in the transformation of that society) to bring about the revolution that will emancipate all humanity.

A second version of the critical model is to be found among members of the Frankfurt School. In general, the latter did not regard the working class as an emancipatory force, nor did they see the Communist Party as playing a positive role in emancipation. And in some cases, including Habermas, they also seem to have abandoned the teleological conception of history. However, the rest of the Marxist position is retained, including the key role of intellectuals and of the critical theory that they produce.

Finally, there are positions, influenced by feminism as well as by Marxism, that often seem to have abandoned most elements of the orthodox position apart from the idea that some form of critical theory or research can play a consciousness-raising role and bring about a social transformation (of one kind or another). Here, the abolition of patriarchy may be as central as the overthrow of capitalism; indeed the latter may not figure at all. Thus, multiple sources of oppression may be identified. A consequence of this is variation in the assumed audience for critical theory. Whereas for Marx it was the working class, for Habermas it seems to be all humanity (Dickens 1983), and for many feminists it is women (see Lather 1984). Such diverse target audiences may be thought of as primarily emancipating *themselves*, though in some versions (as in the case of the working class for Marx) they are believed to have the capacity to emancipate everyone. Many recent versions of critical ethnography also depart from orthodox Marxism in presenting critical theory as the outcome of collaboration between researchers and oppressed, rather than the former bringing to the latter a theory that will dispel their ideologically generated ignorance and/or confusion. Indeed, the distinction between intellectuals and others is often regarded as one of the alienating features of modern society that is to be overcome. A final area of disagreement I shall mention is that, whereas for Marx and Habermas critical theory is true in the sense of capturing tendencies inherent in existing society (indeed this is what is held to be distinctive about Marxism compared with utopianism), critical ethnography sometimes seems to be regarded not as an approach whose validity in relation to other theoretical perspectives can be established but as one ideological view, or one incommensurable paradigm, among others (Simon and Dippo 1986; Lather 1986a and 1986b; Burawoy 1987).

Clearly, which of these positions is adopted has considerable significance for the assessment of what is being recommended, though critical ethnographers are not always explicit about their views on these issues. In assessing critical ethnography I shall look first at the criticisms its proponents make of conventional ethnography, and then at some aspects of the approach to social research they advocate.

CRITICISMS OF CONVENTIONAL ETHNOGRAPHY

As we saw, Habermas and others criticise interpretative research for simply reproducing ideological common sense, and for thereby neglecting the effects of macro-social factors on people's behaviour under capitalism. Two responses need to be made to this criticism, I think. The first is that it is based on an overly narrow view of the nature of interpretative research. In practice most ethnography is concerned not just with describing people's perspectives and behaviour, but also with explaining them.[9] Second, often the explanations presented by ethnographers *do* appeal to relatively macro factors; though it is true that their accounts do not always refer to capitalism or patriarchy as explanations for the events they describe. To criticise them for this, however, is simply to point out that conventional ethnographers are not critical ethnographers. The superiority of critical ethnography has been assumed in such criticisms rather than established.[10] Furthermore, as we shall see later, there are good reasons for conventional ethnographers' reluctance to use some Marxist concepts, including 'oppression', 'emancipation' and 'ideology'.

Another aspect of conventional ethnography that critical ethnographers challenge concerns the role of values. It is argued that such research, like quantitative research modelled on the natural sciences, is wedded to the concept of value neutrality. It is directed towards describing behaviour from some objective, albeit culturally sensitive, point of view. It thereby neglects the value commitments it adopts and the political effects it has. And the suggestion is that in both respects it is conservative. In relation to this criticism, it should be noted that to the extent that ethnographers have not been concerned simply with describing, it also loses some of its force, since it hinges on the idea that their work simply reproduces common-sense knowledge, and thereby ideology. Nevertheless, it is true that in general non-Marxist and non-feminist ethnographers have not adopted an explicit political position and that often they have been unclear about the role of values in their work. Of course, there has been recognition of the fact that values often affect research, so that few ethnographers would claim that their own or others' work is completely unbiased. But this is seen as a contingent matter that, in principle, could be eliminated by strengthening commitment to objectivity and by scrutinising research more intensively. What is often neglected is the way in which practical/political values necessarily inform decisions about what should be studied, and what is relevant and not relevant in the description and explanation of phenomena. Also, there is a tendency for evaluation to creep into ethnographic descriptions without being explicitly presented as such or being supported by the necessary justificatory arguments (see Hammersley 1991c). The values underlying decisions about relevance and evaluation that are central to conventional ethnography are rarely made explicit or provided with justifications, then. And the rationale for conventional ethnography, the question of what it is for and how it relates to practice, has not been given sufficient attention either (see Chapter 1).[11]

Critical ethnographers raise important issues here, then. However, their treatment leaves much to be desired. In its crudest form it implies that researchers must *either* be for emancipation *or* serve to perpetuate oppression. As I have noted elsewhere, this is a naïve view of politics in which the only roles are the good, the bad and the naïve (Hammersley 1985b). It also assumes a much more straightforward relationship between political commitment and effect than is plausible. More fundamentally still, it represents a misinterpretation of Weber's principle of value neutrality.

The rejection of value neutrality plays a key role in the argument for critical ethnography since it serves both as a critique of more conventional work and opens the way for the legitimacy of an ethnography committed to particular political values (though it should be noted that it does not of itself indicate what those values ought to be). The implication is that ethnography is always necessarily political in the sense of serving someone's interests, wittingly or unwittingly; and that only by consciously linking it to the right sort of politics can we ensure that it will serve the right interests.

However, while in my view critical theorists are quite correct to recognise that values do and must play an important role in social research, they are wrong to believe that this is denied by Weber's principle of value neutrality. And as a result of this they neglect an important distinction that is central to this issue and fail to recognise the significance of value conflict. For Weber, the phenomena investigated by the social scientist are *defined* in terms of practical values. There is no question of those phenomena being value free in some absolute sense. At the same time, he argues that once defined these phenomena should be investigated in a way that (as

104

far as possible) suspends practical value judgements in the attempt to discover the truth about them. It is not clear whether critical theorists would accept or reject this position. And this reflects a deep-seated ambiguity within the Marxist tradition about the concept of truth. As Prokopczyk (1980) demonstrates, Marx took over the Hegelian concept of truth whereby what is involved in its pursuit is not modifying our beliefs to correspond with reality but rather modifying reality to correspond to our understanding of the ideal immanent in history. As we shall see, this teleological view involves enormous problems. It is rare for critical ethnographers to make an explicit commitment to this position. But if they are not committed to this view they are left with the option either of seeking some other basis for the justification of values (Habermas's position) or of treating value judgements simply as irrational commitments (Weber's position). While critical ethnographers are rarely clear about which of these positions they adopt, some at least seem closer to Weber than to Habermas or Marx in this respect, in the sense that they treat critical theory as an ideology or as a paradigm based on value commitments, without any indication of how those commitments might be justified (see, for example, Popkewitz 1984; Simon and Dippo 1986; Burawoy 1987).[12]

However, whether one follows Habermas or Weber in this regard, there are difficulties. Seeking some rational basis for value judgements opens up the prospect of an infinite regress, since any evidence offered in support of a value judgement may be challenged and further evidence demanded, and so on *ad infinitum*. Habermas seeks to avoid this problem by appeal to what would be decided in the ideal speech situation, viewed as a context in which decisions would be rational because free from constraint. I shall look at the problems involved in this idea later. Weber's position, on the other hand, is that there are ultimate value commitments from which particular value judgements can be deduced, but that by their very nature these commitments cannot be rationally justified (otherwise they would not be ultimate). The problem with this position is that all of our value choices are rendered irrational because they are based on a fundamental and necessarily irrational commitment to some set of ultimate values. This is, of course, precisely the sort of 'decisionism' that Habermas seeks to avoid.[13]

There is some truth, then, in the criticisms that advocates of the critical model make of conventional ethnography. They point to problematic features of it, such as ethnographers' neglect of the necessary role that values play in their work, and above all their failure to deal with the question of the purposes that ethnographic research should serve. However, the criticisms are rather over-drawn; and often rely on the assumption that a Marxist theory of society has been established as valid beyond all reasonable doubt, when it has not. They also frequently rest on a misinterpretation of the principle of value neutrality and a failure to resolve the problem of the role of values in social research.

THE CRITICAL MODEL ASSESSED

I want to look next at some problematic aspects of the assumptions on which the critical model is based. I shall examine four issues: the teleological view of history built into orthodox Marxism; the relationship between research and practice that is assumed by critical theorists; the question of the criteria by which critical accounts should be evaluated; and the problems that critical ethnography inherits from conventional social research.

The teleological model of history

As I noted earlier, the orthodox version of the critical model is based on a very distinctive philosophical view that can, in large part, be ascribed to the influence of Hegel and Marx. It involves a conception of history as moving (in dialectical not linear fashion) towards the realisation of human ideals. This does not need to be seen as an inevitable historical trend: there is room for delays and perhaps even for derailments. However, what is crucial is the idea that what is involved in Marxist politics is not simply the pursuit of some ideal that is to be imposed on reality (as in the case of utopian thinking), but rather of an ideal that is built into history. Associated with this is a conception of truth in which normative and factual elements have been fused, and where the pursuit of truth requires not just discovering what corresponds in past and present reality to the true (that is, to the ideal), but also changing future reality in order to bring it more completely into line with that truth (Prokopczyk 1980).

This point of view has considerable appeal. It combines both radical and realistic emphases, thereby providing the optimism required to motivate research and political action that are committed to actually bringing about radical social change. And it has particular appeal to intellectuals because it portrays the process of history as analogous to an idealised form of intellectual debate, and as involving the ultimate realisation of ideas in pure form, in contrast to the messy and intellectually unsatisfying compromises of all hitherto existing politics. Also, in some versions of critical theory, emancipation is conceived in highly intellectualist terms as involving the adoption by the masses of 'high culture'.[14] And, finally, intellectual work (in the form of negative or ideology critique) is assigned an important, indeed a revolutionary, role so that the potential contribution of intellectuals to politics is believed to be considerable. What we have here is the unity of theory and practice very much on the terms of intellectuals.

The orthodox model also apparently solves a number of problems that face other sorts of research and political practice: it may seem to obviate the need to justify the ideals to which political practice is directed, since it is claimed that they can be shown to be immanent in the history of humanity. In this way, they have an objectivity that other ideals lack. Nor, for the same reason, does there seem to be any need to show that they are feasible goals, even though they involve a radical transformation of society and of human nature. Furthermore, the teleological model provides a ready way of dealing with doubts about its validity. It incorporates an explanation for the disbelief of others that, effectively, explains it away: disbelief is the product of false consciousness, a failure to recognise the truth because of a false understanding of one's interests which is the product of ruling class ideology (or in the case of members of the ruling class themselves, perhaps, of a neglect of long in favour of short-term interests). Here, then, we have what claims to be a scientific solution to the problem of values, yet one which promises heaven on earth.

Despite its coherence, comprehensiveness and appeal, however, the teleological model of history is far from convincing. What reasons are there to believe that the history of the world represents a progressive development towards perfection, even potentially? What sense can we give to the idea that some single set of beliefs and values represents humanity's true self-consciousness? How could these conclusions ever be established? As Lowith (1949) has shown, this is a secular version of influential Jewish and Christian theologies, and they demand a kind of faith that is hard to reconcile with modern philosophical assumptions. Furthermore, the idea that how things ought to be can be divined by discovering the tendencies present in the current organisation of society suffers from a variety of defects: one cannot legitimately derive 'ought' from 'is'; it is difficult to see why we should believe that there is only one coherent set of tendencies within a society at any one time; and the strategy places an enormous methodological burden on the factual analysis of society, one that it cannot sustain if we accept post-positivist ideas about the nature of scientific inquiry.

As I noted earlier, many critical theorists have abandoned the orthodox model, along with its teleological version of history; and with good reason. Yet it seems to me that once this is done, the rationale for critical theory becomes difficult to sustain. Marx provides a coherent, if rather implausible, explanation for why his scientific socialism is true, why the realisation of socialist ideals in pure form is possible despite what seems to be implied by political 'reality'. And he shows how this can come about (in principle at least), and the role of the working class as an emancipatory force in bringing it about. But once the teleological model has been abandoned, there is no longer any guaranteed potential for change of the kind to which critical theorists are committed, and therefore it is no longer clear why one set of ideals should be regarded as 'true human consciousness', rather than another. Indeed, we may even be plunged into value relativism. Nor is it clear why we should believe that these ideals are realisable, especially when they seem to lack political feasibility. As a result, we are forced to ask why it should be assumed that one particular political struggle should have priority over others, and why it is in the interests of groups engaged in different struggles to support one another (apart from for merely tactical considerations). Similarly, the purpose of and audience for social research no longer seems to be so well defined. It becomes possible that there will be multiple, contradictory critical theories advanced by researchers who are linked with different oppressed groups. And the linchpin of critical theory, that it is concerned with the emancipation of all, even of the oppressors, has been lost. The useful simplification, whereby politics is a matter of identifying and supporting 'progressive' and opposing 'regressive' forces, cannot now be sustained. A more complex, and less intellectually satisfying, political reality emerges in which intellectuals can play a much less grand and more uncertain role, a reality with which (as we shall see) the theoretical ideas associated with critical ethnography are not well designed to deal.

It seems that critical ethnographers are caught on the horns of a dilemma here. They may either cling to an orthodox Marxism that has answers to the problems surrounding research and politics and the relationship between the two, albeit implausible ones; or they can abandon the teleological model of history as unconvincing, but only at the cost of undermining the rationale for critical theory.

Research and practice

As should be clear from the discussion so far, the conception of practice on which the critical model is based concerns *political* practice. Furthermore, that practice is conceptualised in terms of the overcoming of oppression. However, it seems to me that the oppressor/oppressed model does not capture the complexities of the roles and interests involved in social life, even in the narrowly political sphere. Some of the problems with this model arise from the point that I noted earlier: that it is not obvious that there is only one source of oppression. This threatens the coherence of the critical model, unless there are reasonable grounds for believing that a single form of theory-guided practice can lead to the simultaneous abolition of all sources of oppression. Without that assumption it seems likely that from the point of view of different critical theorists, or even that of a single one, many people may be simultaneously both oppressor and oppressed.[15]

Over and above this problem, there are difficulties involved in the very concept of oppression. As Geuss points out:

> It seems unrealistic under present conditions of human life to assume that any and every preference human agents might have can be satisfied, or to assume that all conflict between the preferences of different agents will be peacefully and rationally resolved. *Some* frustration – even some imposed frustration – of *some* human preferences must be legitimate and unexceptionable.
>
> (Geuss 1981: 16)

On these grounds 'domination', as used by Habermas, cannot simply mean repression, that is frustration of at least some human preferences. Geuss also questions whether unequal distribution of the power to exercise normative repression is always illegitimate; after all, Marxists recognise that 'at certain levels of development of the material forces of production an unequal distribution of repressive normative power is historically necessary' (Geuss 1981: 17). To take account of these problems it seems that we must define 'domination' or 'oppression' as 'unnecessarily unequal surplus repression'. Yet the methodological problems involved in judgements about what is unnecessary inequality and surplus repression should be obvious.

Furthermore, even this subtle definition of oppression involves the assumption that we can identify what are real or genuine needs. And as Geuss again points out, these are not a matter of simple description:

> the set of desires and preferences we attribute to the [oppressed] group is a theoretical construct which fills out the fragmentary evidence, removes some of the contradic- tions between avowals and behavior, and may end up ascribing to the group on the basis of its actual behavior, wants and desires of which no individual member is aware.

> (Geuss 1981: 45)

How do we smooth out the contradictions in what people say and do about their needs? How do we decide what are genuine desires, and what desires are against a person's own interests (or against those of others)? Geuss comments that: 'To speak of an agent's "interests" is to speak of the way that agent's particular desires could be rationally integrated into a coherent "good life"' (Geuss 1981: 47–8). This opens up the possibility of a critical theory defining the 'real needs' of an oppressed group falsely. Worse still, the question arises: are there not likely to be several alternative rational reconstructions, especially since such judgements depend on value and factual assumptions? If so, there is room for genuine disagreement about needs and interests (Moon 1983; Fay 1987).[16]

These problems with 'oppression', and with the associated concepts of 'needs' and 'interests', necessarily create difficulties for the other central concept underlying the critical model: emancipation. If oppression is multi-dimensional, and needs and interests are not easily and determinately identifiable, then the idea of emancipation as the freeing from oppression and the meeting of genuine needs becomes highly problematic. This is not to say that people's conditions of living cannot or should not be improved, simply that what is an improvement (and for whom) is always potentially subject to reasonable disagreement, that it is a matter of degree, and that improvements will be limited to particular respects, and may involve costs for others. What seems unlikely is the transport of all from the realm of necessity into that of freedom.

In its orthodox Marxist version, the critical model is founded on the idea that practice consists of bringing reality into line with theory. Of course, Marx was not unaware of the strategic and tactical problems involved in political practice; but he seems to have treated these as subordinate considerations that have no implications for the ultimate goal of that practice. Much the same applies to other versions of critical theory. Ironically, given Habermas's opposition to positivism's 'scientisation' of politics, his approach itself involves an exaggeration of the power of theory in relation to practice that, for all its differences, parallels the technical rationality of positivism, and does not capture the reality of even narrowly political practice in an adequate way. It seems to me that development of Aristotle's conception of practice is a more promising basis for considering the contribution that theory can make than is the work of Marx.[17] In these terms practice involves making decisions in light of multiple values that have to be interpreted in relation to concrete and changing situations about which we have limited information, and whose validity is uncertain. What is involved is *not* the pursuit of some fixed end state, but the seeking of improvements in some aspect of a situation (or the prevention of some worsening) in the light of values whose validity one accepts, while recognising that our understanding of them may need to be revised subsequently. Furthermore, while seeking to improve a situation in some respect, we must take account of the likely consequences of any strategies and tactics employed for other values and interests (our own and those of others). We must also note the social dimension of this. In specifying something that requires improvement, we are identifying the sufferer (whether ourselves or another) in terms of a particular identity to which other people belong and which captures only a small selection of the features that make up that person and her/his circumstances. Furthermore, these other features will be variable across members within the identity category. What I am emphasising here is the inevitably contextual character of practice; not just of judgement about what would be effective means, but also assessments of appropriate and reasonable goals.

An especially important consideration that makes practice much more complex than the critical model assumes is the heterogeneity of values. It is an essential assumption of the critical model that there is a single set of values that everyone would agree on if it were not for the effects of ideology on our thinking. This is, of course, one of the areas of sharpest disagreement between Marx and Weber. While, as I have explained, I do not regard Weber's position as entirely satisfactory, it seems clear to me that in practical terms there is no doubt that we do often face value conflict, both when we ourselves are attracted to competing possible courses of action, and when we come into contact with others committed to values discrepant with ours. It is certainly appealing to assume that there could be a situation in which these conflicts would be overcome forever, but I can see no good reasons for believing that this is the case.

Methodological basis

Another aspect of the critical model that requires attention is its methodological recommendations. In part, the epistemological base on which it relies is the Marxist view of history as the self-development of humanity, which I outlined and criticised earlier. In these terms the truth of critical theory is held to be itself a product of the process of historical development. Thus, in the work of Lukács and Korsch, truth (like ideology) is defined (in principle) in genetic terms, in terms of whose view it is. As I have already suggested, this philosophy of history is not convincing. And, of course, few Marxists have wished to define true working-class consciousness in terms of what members of that class actually believe at any given point in time. However, Habermas makes some important additional methodological recommendations. Using the model of psychoanalysis, he incorporates checks on the validity of a critical theory in terms of recognition of its truth by the oppressed group themselves, and in terms of its practical efficacy in bringing about emancipation. Other advocates of the critical model also frequently appeal to these criteria of validity (Burawoy 1987; Lather 1986a and 1986b).

At times, the idea of recognition by the oppressed as a criterion of validity is presented in simplistic terms relying on a naïve empiricism whereby the truth is there to be seen once the mists of ideology have been dispelled. But there are more sophisticated discussions of this issue within the literature. Thus, Geuss identifies two conceptions of the process of ideology critique to be found among advocates of the critical model. The difference between them concerns whether critical theories operate on the basis of historically specific epistemological principles embedded in the culture of the oppressed or on the basis of principles that are taken to be universal.

The first approach portrays ideology critique as internal or immanent criticism, as showing members of the oppressed group the implications of applying their own epistemic principles to their other beliefs and values in a consistent way. As Geuss comments:

> For Adorno we must start from where we happen to be historically and culturally, from a particular kind of frustration and suffering experienced by human agents in their attempt to realize some historically specific project of 'the good life'. The critical theories we propound in the course of this undertaking are extraordinarily fragile historical entities, which, even if effective and 'true', can never lay claim to any absolute standing – they are effective and 'true' only relative to this particular historical situation and are bound to be superseded.
>
> (Geuss 1981: 63)

What we must ask here, though, is: why should we assume that the oppressed group's epistemic principles are more immune to ideological distortion than the rest of their beliefs? And on what grounds is it believed that there is a single, consensual set of epistemic principles employed by the group? Furthermore, how do we identify any such set of principles in a way that avoids ideological error?

It was in response to these problems that Habermas came to propose the second, alternative, basis for ideology critique. Here, critique operates on the basis of those epistemic principles on which everyone would agree in the course of unlimited discussion in the 'ideal speech situation', that is in a situation free from ideological and other sorts of constraint. Habermas argues that such a form of dialogue is *implied* in all human communication. Thus, he claims that in speech aimed at reaching mutual understanding (which he takes to be the most fundamental kind), speakers make four types of validity claim:

1 that what they say is comprehensible;
2 that what they state is true;
3 that their expressed intentions are their true ones;
4 that the utterance is appropriate relative to some relevant normative context.

And he argues that only if these claims are accepted by other participants as what would be recognised as true in the ideal speech situation can understanding take place.

There are a number of reasons why this argument is not persuasive. One is that the claim that communication necessitates agreement about the truth of what is stated and that this truth is judged in terms of what would be agreed in the ideal speech situation seems to be false. We can understand what people say without agreeing with them, and the attribution to all human beings of Habermas's own consensus theory of truth is implausible. As Geuss comments:

> I find it quite hard to burden pre-dynastic Egyptians, ninth-century French serfs and early-twentieth-century Yanomamo tribesmen with the view that they are acting correctly if their action is based on a norm on which there would be universal consensus in an ideal speech situation. The notion that social situations should be based on the free consent of those affected is a rather recent Western invention. ... The notion that an action is morally acceptable or a belief 'true' if they would be the object of universal consensus under ideal conditions is an even more recent invention held perhaps by a couple of professional philosophers in Germany and the United States [the reference is presumably to Habermas himself and to John Rawls]. ... The point is not that pre-dynastic Egyptians couldn't formulate the 'consensus theory of truth', but that we have no reason to think that they had any inclination to accept as legitimate only those social

institutions on which they thought there would be universal consensus in ideal conditions.

(Geuss 1981: 66–7)

Also, it seems to me that Habermas's conception of the ideal speech situation is circular, since it is *defined* in terms of freedom from the effects of ideology, that is of forces generating false beliefs. Yet, presumably, we need to be free from ideology to recognise that situation? Furthermore, what seems to be involved in the notion of an ideal speech situation is that speakers subject all their assumptions to scrutiny and retain only those that are accepted by all participants in that situation. But this is to assume that each belief can be taken separately and its validity judged against some other belief whose validity is assured. And since such assurance can only be the product of the ideal speech situation itself, it is difficult to see how the process of assessment could ever get started. Finally, there is the question of how we are to know what would be decided in the ideal speech situation when none of us has access to it. We are in a double bind here: to know what is required for enlightenment and emancipation we must already be enlightened and emancipated (Geuss 1981: 54).

In my judgement, these arguments leave recognition by the oppressed as a very weak basis for the validation of critical theories. Let me look now at the other check on the validity of such theories that Habermas presents, the idea that they are tested by their success or otherwise in bringing about emancipation. This is an idea that is widely adopted by advocates of critical ethnography, including many feminists (see Hammersley 1990b). I have already argued that the concept of emancipation is deeply problematic. But even putting this aside, there is the fact that the emancipation test seems to presuppose that a critical theory is the only or main contributor to emancipation. I have suggested that this involves an exaggerated estimate of the role of theory in practice. Theories are not simply applied but *used* in association with practical knowledge. And, if this is the case, the achievement of emancipation depends on much more than the truth of the theory, and so failure to achieve emancipation does not tell us that the theory is false. This is one aspect of the problems that arise from any instrumental criterion of truth. Such a criterion presupposes that successful practice must be based on correct theoretical assumptions, and that incorrect assumptions must always lead to failure. There is

115

little justification for these presuppositions, it seems to me. Indeed, if they were true it would be difficult to understand how humanity has survived, given that we began and continue in relative ignorance.

In my view, then, the methodological assumptions of the critical model are not cogent. Neither the idea that critical theories can be validated on the basis of their genesis, nor the claims that they can be tested by recognition of their truth on the part of the oppressed, and that they are proven by their success in bringing about emancipation, can stand up to close scrutiny.

Problems inherited from conventional social research

As Habermas makes clear, critical theory represents a synthesis of features to be found in the empirical-analytic and hermeneutic approaches. Critical ethnographers are less explicit about this, but their orientation does seem to involve both interpretative understanding and causal explanation of people's attitudes and behaviour. The upshot of this is that many of the methodological problems that have long faced all social researchers face critical ethnographers too; over and above the more specific ones I have discussed in the previous sections. Indeed, if anything these inherited problems are heightened in the case of critical ethnography. There are several reasons for this.

One is that the critical ethnographer seeks to go beyond what conventional ethnographers attempt. For example, the sort of theory that must be developed is much more comprehensive than that typical of other sorts of social research. Fay lists the components of a critical theory as follows:

I. *A theory of false consciousness* which
1. demonstrates the ways in which the self-understandings of a group of people are false (in the sense of failing to account for the life experiences of the members of the group), or incoherent (because internally contradictory), or both ...;
2. explains how the members of this group came to have these self-misunderstandings, and how they are maintained;
3. contrasts them with an alternative self-understanding, showing how this alternative is superior.

II. *A theory of crisis* which
4. spells out what a social crisis is;

116

5. indicates how a particular society is in such a crisis. This would require examining the felt dissatisfactions of a group of people and showing both that they threaten social cohesion and that they can not be alleviated given the basic organization of the society and the self-understandings of its members;

6. provides an historical account of the development of this crisis partly in terms of the false consciousness of the members of the group and partly in terms of the structural bases of the society.

III. *A theory of education* which
7. offers an account of the conditions necessary and sufficient for the sort of enlightenment envisioned by the theory;
8. shows that given the current social situation these conditions are satisfied.

IV. *A theory of transformative action* which
9. isolates those aspects of a society which must be altered if the social crisis is to be resolved and the dissatisfactions of its members lessened;
10. details a plan of action indicating the people who are to be the 'carriers' of the anticipated social transformation and at least some general idea of how they might do this.

(Fay 1987: 31–2)

This is a daunting list of components, in comparison with more conventional versions of social theory; and meeting its requirements would raise most of the methodological problems that face conventional social research simultaneously.

A second reason why the methodological problems that face social research are heightened by critical ethnography is that it is expected to issue in results that are directly relevant to political practice. A common problem here is the different time scales characteristic of research and practice. A tendency towards condensed, or what Rist calls *'blitzkrieg'* (Rist 1980), ethnography seems likely to be necessary to overcome this problem.[18] And yet this clearly renders the problem of achieving and establishing validity even more serious than it is in conventional social research operating under a less pressing schedule. On the other hand, it seems obvious that we need to be even more confident of the validity of our findings if they are to be fed directly into political practice than in the case of conventional ethnography, where errors can be discussed and corrected by subsequent studies.

Third, there are difficulties arising from the fact that (unlike most ethnography but like some other forms of social research) critical theory incorporates an asymmetrical model of explanation whereby beliefs are accounted for in quite different ways according to whether they are assumed to be true or false. If the beliefs are held to be true, they are explained as penetrations through to reality (or as effectively being caused by reality), whereas if they are false they are the product of ideological distortion produced by macro-societal factors.[19] There are two problems with this. First, it assumes a naïve realist epistemology whereby belief in the truth is a result of contact with reality. Once we abandon this position, as surely we must, there is no good reason to believe that truth and falsity are produced by different sorts of mechanism. And, therefore, there is no justification for the asymmetrical approach to explaining beliefs. The second problem arising from use of this concept of ideology is that any error in assessments of the validity of beliefs automatically leads to error in their explanation. Yet, it seems prudent, wherever possible, to minimise rather than to compound errors. For both these reasons, in setting out to explain people's beliefs, ethnographers try to suspend their judgements about the truth of those beliefs so as to avoid misunderstanding them and the reasons why they are held. It is for this reason that they generally avoid the concept of 'ideology', except as a synonym for 'world-view' or 'perspective'. Here, as elsewhere, critical theory seems to add unnecessary problems to those already facing ethnographers, while also leading to potential misunderstanding of the causal production of beliefs.

Finally, it is worth noting that critical theory, and therefore presumably critical ethnography, assumes the existence and the identifiability of at least quasi-causal laws of the development of societies. Knowledge of such laws is essential for critical theorists if they are to be able to identify those points of system crisis at which political action is likely to be progressive and fruitful.[20] Yet, the problem of whether such laws exist, and if they do of how they are to be discovered, is a severe one that is given no attention in the discussions of their approach by critical ethnographers. While conventional ethnographers may be wrong to deny the possibility of such laws, this needs to be argued rather than merely assumed. Here, too, the adoption of a 'critical' perspective inherits and perhaps exacerbates the methodological problems faced by more conventional social research.

CONCLUSION

In this chapter I have sought to assess the rationale for critical ethnography. I outlined the basis for this type of research, drawing particularly on the work of Habermas. I argued that while the criticisms of conventional ethnography made by critical theorists include some sound points, it is not a viable approach to research. In orthodox Marxist form it provides a coherent and comprehensive view, but one that is highly implausible. In my view, belief in the teleological conception of history demands a leap of faith. Yet when this and other implausible features of the orthodox position are abandoned, critical theory loses coherence. It becomes simply research directed towards serving the interests of some particular group, whose interests may conflict with those of others, including those of other oppressed groups. Critical ethnography's claim to priority on the grounds of its emancipatory potential collapses.

There are some other problematic aspects of the critical model too. One is its conception of practice and of the relation of the latter to theory. There are good reasons for supposing that the oppressor–oppressed framework is not a sufficiently subtle social theory on which to base a conception of practice; and serious problems also arise with the concepts of need and emancipation. In addition, the critical model relies on a view of the relationship between theory and practice derived from Marx and Hegel, whereby the goal of practice is to bring reality into line with theory. In my judgement this is a utopian (and politically dangerous) orientation, since it neglects the complex character of practice and its irreducibility to ideals and theories. Another aspect of the critical model that is questionable is its strategy for assessing the validity of critical theories. In part their validity is assumed to be founded on the Marxist philosophy of history. But Habermas and others also suggest two checks on validity: recognition by the oppressed group and success in bringing about emancipation. However, I argued that neither of these provides a sound basis for assessing the validity of theories. Finally, I pointed out that in addition to these distinctive problems critical ethnography inherits most of the methodological problems that have long pre-

119

occupied social scientists; indeed, if anything it faces these in more severe forms. For all these reasons, it seems to me that the proposal for a critical ethnography is not a viable or desirable alternative to more conventional ethnographic work.

NOTES

1 Discussions outlining and promoting critical ethnography include Masemann (1982), Thomas (1983), Simon and Dippo (1986), Angus (1986a) (Angus (1986b) is a slightly different version of this article), Brodkey (1987), Quantz and O'Connor (1988), Anderson (1989), Gitlin *et al.* (1989), Gitlin (1990), Roman and Apple (1990) and Harvey (1990). A rather different version of critical ethnography is represented by Herzfeld (1987), reflecting what seems to me to be the much more ambiguous orientation of post-structuralism. I have specifically excluded post-structuralism from my discussion in this chapter because, while it is sometimes drawn on by critical ethnographers, it provides no basis for critique, only for indiscriminate affirmation of negation: see Dews (1987). In addition, there is work that, while not explicitly labelled as critical ethnography, conforms quite closely to that model. Thus, Anderson traces the origin of critical ethnography to the research of Sharp and Green (1975) and Willis (1977). Similarly, much writing about feminist methodology corresponds broadly to the genre; see Hammersley (1990b) for a discussion of the latter and for references.

2 This is, of course, by no means the only sense of the term 'critical' that is in current use. Indeed, the well-known 'positivist debate' between Adorno and Popper (and others) involved an explicit confrontation between critical theory and critical rationalism (see Adorno *et al.* 1976 and Albert 1985). For the purposes of this article, however, I shall restrict the reference of 'critical' to the meaning employed by critical theorists.

3 MacIntyre (1988) provides a rather different interpretation of Aristotle to the one I am presenting here. However, I think this stems in large part from his use of the term 'theory' to cover both philosophical and practical knowledge. See also Ball (1977).

4 There has, of course, been considerable debate about Marx's position and about changes in it over the course of his life. I take the view that there is no sharp break in his work and that he inherited much from Hegel despite their differences.

5 This teleological view of history was shared both by those, such as Kautsky, who believed that the transformation of capitalism into socialism was an inevitable result of the development of bourgeois society, and by those who placed greater emphasis on the role of revolutionary consciousness, political will and organisation, such as those mentioned in the text.

6 Arguments for the critical model draw on other sources, besides those

mentioned here, including Gramsci, Sartre and Bakhtin. However, Habermas's work represents the most developed version of this approach, and I shall draw heavily on it in what follows. For general introductions to the Frankfurt School, see Jay (1973), Kellner (1975) and Kolakowski (1978). See also Kortian (1980) and Connerton (1980). On Habermas, see McCarthy (1978), Dickens (1983), White (1983) and Ingram (1987). For excellent critical discussions, see Geuss (1981), Keat (1981) and Fay (1987).

7 It is worth noting that Marcuse treats the positivist account of science, on which Habermas's discussion of the empirical-analytic science is based, as incorrect even as an account of natural science (Geuss 1981: 28). It is a common criticism of Habermas that he takes over the positivist conception of science and assigns too important a role to instrumental reason. For an excellent discussion of this issue, see Stockman (1978).

8 In some versions this criticism of hermeneutic approaches is temporally restricted: once oppression has been overcome, hermeneutic-historical science will be sufficient for understanding human social life, since then ideology and the social structural determination of human action will have disappeared. This seems to follow from Marx's and Habermas's views, but it is not given much emphasis by critical ethnographers.

9 This point is sometimes obscured by the self-understandings of ethnographers, for example where these imply that the goal of ethnography is simply the description of cultures.

10 This seems to me to be the character of the criticism directed by McClaren against Peshkin (McClaren 1987), see above. For a discussion of similar criticisms in the field of education, see Hargreaves's (1978) assessment of the work of Sharp and Green (1975).

11 The issue of what the political effects of ethnographic work have been is more difficult to deal with. We have little or no information about this.

12 Similarly, in a discussion of feminist methodology, Reinharz declares that 'since interest-free knowledge is logically impossible, we should feel free to substitute explicit interests for implicit ones' (Reinharz 1985: 17). Lather (1986a and 1986b) adopts a similar position, quoting Reinharz. Here the implication seems to be that one must simply be open about one's commitments. There is no indication of the basis on which they should be selected or justified. Interestingly, Overend (1978) argues that this is effectively the position that Habermas resorts to as a result of his reliance on a consensus theory of truth.

13 I have sketched my own view of a possible solution to this problem in Hammersley (1991a), ch.3.

14 This is a feature that is especially characteristic of the Frankfurt School.

15 This point has been made by black feminists in criticising white feminists for ignoring the distinctive features of the lives of black women, notably the complex effects of racism (see, for example,

Carby 1982). But, of course, the argument could quite reasonably be pursued via more discriminating concepts than 'black', taking account not just of ethnic but also, say, of generational and regional differences. See Merton (1972) for a similar argument.

16 This problem could be superficially resolved by claiming that the oppressed themselves know what their needs are. However, this overlooks the likelihood of disagreement among this group about their needs, and it neglects the critical theoretical insight that people's understandings may be affected by ideology. For these reasons, in my view, this argument fails.

17 A variety of authors have built on the Aristotelian concept, see, for example, Schon (1986) and Carr (1987).

18 Though it should be noted that the examples of critical ethnography usually cited are much more conventional in character (Sharp and Green 1975; Willis 1977; McClaren 1986).

19 For an example of the use of this explanatory scheme, see Willis (1977). For a critique of this use of ideology see Hammersley (1981a).

20 This is one of the components that Fay (1987) identifies in the extract quoted earlier.

7

PARTS THAT EVEN ETHNOGRAPHY CANNOT REACH

Some reflections on the relationship between research and policy

Over the past twenty years methodological fashion in many of the social sciences has swung from quantitative to qualitative methods. The value of the latter is now widely accepted, and in some fields there may even be a danger that qualitative work will largely supplant quantitative research. One aspect of the popularity of ethnography, which has been given increasing emphasis in the current cold economic climate, is the belief that this method offers a better source of information for social and educational policy-making than does quantitative research. It is claimed that it provides a more relevant understanding of social events than quantitative research, and that it offers evidence in a form which is much more accessible and useful to policy-makers than are statistical analyses. In this way, ethnographers seek to capitalise on the failure of quantitative research to meet the expectations once held for it (Rist 1984; Pollard 1984a; Finch 1986).

In this chapter I want to assess these arguments for the policy payoff of ethnography. Since I shall be critical of some aspects of them, I must make clear at the start that I do not deny that ethnographic research can make a useful contribution to policy-making, or that such a contribution is important. In my view it is a necessary justification for social research that it should contribute to the thinking and activities of people outside the social research community (see Chapter 4). This means that, to be legitimate, ethnographic research must contribute to policy-making, in the broadest sense of that term.[1]

However, in my view, some of the arguments promoting the potential contribution of ethnography to policy-making are misleading. There is a tendency:

1 to over-estimate the validity of ethnographic findings compared to that of other sorts of social research;
2 to exaggerate the role that research can fulfil, even in principle, for policy-makers; and
3 to believe that ethnographic studies should make a *direct* contribution to policy-making, and can do this simultaneously with developing sociological theory.

THE VALIDITY OF ETHNOGRAPHY

Advocacy of the potential of ethnographic or qualitative research for policy often involves what is in my judgement an exaggeration of the likely validity of such work, both in general and in comparison with other kinds of social research. For example, in an article promoting the contribution of ethnography to the work of schoolteachers, Pollard declares at one point that 'in my view there is every reason to be more confident than of most methodologies that the validity of ethnographic data can be high' (Pollard 1984a: 183). And he leaves this conclusion standing, despite subsequent recognition of serious problems with the validity of such data. To illustrate his point Pollard argues that the emergence of what Woods (1985) has called 'phase two' ethnographic work (which involves coordinated theoretical development) promises higher levels of reliability and generalisability. Yet, there is little ground for such a belief. The developments that Woods identifies do not focus on single theories but relate to a range of theoretical ideas, nor do they involve systematic theory-testing (Hammersley 1987a; see also Woods 1987 and Hammersley 1987b).

I am certainly not suggesting that we should assume that the findings of ethnographic research have no validity, but I think that we need evidence for the claim that it can routinely produce findings that are more valid than quantitative research, and that are sufficiently valid to provide a sound basis for policy-making. What advocates of ethnography have succeeded in doing is to raise significant doubts about the validity of the findings of quantitative research. They have shown that these results are a good deal less reliable (in the common-sense meaning of that term) than some quantitative researchers and many users of social research findings have supposed. However, the more positive side of the argument, that ethnography can provide more valid results, has been much less cogent in my view. In general, it has relied on a naïve realism that is just as philosophically questionable as the positivist underpinnings of quantitative method, with its appeals to contact with (or closeness to) reality, and/or to the privileged insight of participants into the mainsprings of their behaviour (see Chapter 3).

Ethnography certainly has some strengths compared to quantitative research. Thus, Rist (1984) identifies a number of useful sorts of evidence which ethnography can provide. He argues that it is more able to take account of the diversity of perspective among people who are involved in and affected by policies, as well as of change over time in these perspectives. It also facilitates documentation of the actual beliefs and behaviour that occur behind official or public fronts, and the examination of these in context. In addition, it is able to use multiple sources of evidence, overcoming the danger of relying on a single, possibly biased, source. Finally, it allows the discovery of unanticipated aspects of the policy process and investigation of how policies are actually implemented, detecting deviations from how they were intended to be implemented that could be significant for policy outcomes. In a similar vein, Finch argues that ethnography can be more flexible than quantitative research, adjusting to changes in the situation studied and to changes in the policy-making context, that it studies social phenomena in their natural contexts, that it examines process as well as outcome, and that it provides explanations that are adequate at the level of meaning as well as at the level of cause (Finch 1986: 161).

However, while ethnography has these strengths, they do not add up to any general superiority over other methods. There are several reasons for this. First, in not all cases are these features exclusive to qualitative research. Thus, survey research is able to document diversity in perspective, and can also take account of change over time, for example by means of the panel method. More importantly, the gains offered by ethnographic research are bought at the expense of certain weaknesses, notably in its ability to generalise to larger populations and to identify causal relationships (see Chapter 11). These may not always be significant, and even where they are, qualitative research (alone or in combination with other methods) may still be appropriate. But it is important to recognise such weaknesses, not to ignore them or to pretend that they are of minor importance. Doing so may lead us to overestimate the likely validity of ethnographic findings.

Furthermore, there are some claims made about the advantages of ethnography that would be difficult to sustain. For instance, like many of its advocates, Rist appeals to the idea that it gives access to a different kind of knowledge to quantitative research. He argues that:

> Rather than presuming that human environments and interactions can be held constant, manipulated, treated, scheduled, modified or extinguished, qualitative research posits that the most powerful and parsimonious way to understand human beings and the social environments they have created is to watch, talk, listen and participate with them in these environments .... This is quite the opposite of claiming 'to know' about human behaviour by fracturing it into small, atomistic components that are then subjected to intensive scrutiny .... Qualitative research focusses on a different way of knowing – one based on experience, empathy, and involvement.
>
> (Rist 1984: 160)

This claim is open to serious challenge. On what grounds can we assume that experience, empathy and involvement are reliable bases for knowledge in particular cases? And why should the researcher's experience, empathy and involvement be a better basis than that of the practitioners? In my view, claims that ethnography represents a distinctive form of science are not convincing (see Chapter 9, and also Hammersley 1989a). Reliance on 'understanding' does not allow us to escape the methodological problems that face other sorts of social research.

Moreover, if we look at the areas where ethnographers have criticised quantitative researchers, we will find that their work often fares little better in dealing with those problems. For example, ethnographers often criticise quantitative research for the operationalisation of subtle theoretical concepts in terms of crude indicators. And sometimes they question the very logic of operationalisation itself. Thus, Herbert Blumer expresses doubts that it is possible to construct valid, definitive concepts in social research; concepts that are defined in terms of necessary and sufficient conditions. However, his solution to the problem of the relationship between concepts and data (the development and application of sensitising concepts) is not compelling. It fails to grapple with the problem of how such concepts can be related to data in an effective way and how they can be used to test theoretical hypotheses (Hammersley 1989b).[2] Similarly, ethnographers often criticise the use of statistical control of variables on the grounds that it reduces complex processes to the operation of discrete variables. Yet they have not shown how ethnographic analysis is capable of establishing the validity of causal claims. They put forward a range of different strategies for dealing with this problem, but none seems very likely to be successful (Hammersley 1989a).

In my view the relationship between ethnography and other sorts of research is not one of general superiority on one side or the other, but rather of relative advantages and disadvantages that have differential significance depending on the purposes and circumstances of particular pieces of research. Furthermore, I think ethnographic methodology has some way to go before it can make strong claims about the validity of its findings. There is a danger of complacency here, of taking the current products of ethnographic research as providing a solid basis on which policy-makers can rely. They may provide nothing of the kind, being better than the products of quantitative research in only limited respects at most. In my judgement ethnographic findings are often of uncertain validity. Indeed, there is even some dissensus among ethnographers about the standards by which the validity of their work should be assessed (see Chapter 4). This is not to suggest that ethnography is inferior to other sorts of social research, simply to deny that it has overcome the serious methodological problems that face all such research. I am not suggesting that ethnographic research tells us nothing, or adopting some sort of extreme scepticism. But I do believe that some ethnographers have made inflationary claims about the relative validity of the findings of ethnographic work compared with those of other sorts of research.

WHAT RESEARCH CAN PROVIDE

The second area of doubt I have about many of the arguments for the contribution of ethnography to practice concerns the issue of what it is possible in principle for research to contribute to policy-making. It seems to me that arguments for the policy relevance of ethnography often over-estimate this contribution. For example, Pollard talks of ethnography being a 'source of informed policy'. Yet, in my view, research cannot be a *source* of policy, informed or otherwise. It can aid policy formation, but no more than that.

A frequently used contrast in discussions about research and policy is that between the engineering and enlightenment models. In its most extreme form the first tends to see research as providing sets of policy prescriptions that policy-makers simply have to follow in order to achieve their goals. The enlightenment view, on the other hand, implies a less direct relationship between the knowledge produced and the policies adopted; and perhaps also an extension of the area of legitimate interest of researchers to include the goals of policies as well as the means of achieving them.[3] This is a rather more realistic and appropriate conception of the role of research than the engineering model, and it is the one that most ethnographers are likely to adopt. However, it still over-estimates the contribution that research can usually make to policy. The very term 'enlightenment' implies that practitioners are in the dark and need the light of research before they can see where they are and in which direction they should be going. This idea finds its most developed form in critical theory, where the audience (oppressed groups) is viewed as unable to understand their situation and their true interests because of the effects of ideology (see Chapter 6). However, the same assumption, in milder and/or less explicit form, is built into all versions of the enlightenment model. What is involved here, often, is a deficit view of policy-makers and practitioners.[4]

In my judgement, research is not the only or even the most important source of knowledge available to practitioners. Practice necessarily relies on experience and on a capacity for sound judgement acquired by practitioners over the course of their work. These are essential and cannot be replaced by research, since the two sorts of knowledge have different characteristics. Thus, experience is based on a synthesis of information and judgement from diverse situations that is sedimented over time in the form of skills, habits and knowledge-at-hand. Furthermore, this processing involves different levels of plausibility and credibility to those appropriate to research. This is not a matter of practical judgements requiring lower levels of evidence; sometimes practitioners will require more than researchers, as when an idea runs against what they believe on the basis of their previous experience. Rather, it is that plausibility is judged on the basis of practitioners' experience, not on the basis of what is taken to be beyond reasonable doubt by most researchers. In addition, in making judgements, practitioners often have to take into account a wider range of issues than do researchers, and more rapidly. Given different purposes, experience and circumstances of work, different constraints operate on knowledge. Research is more focused and operates over a longer time scale than the reflections and inquiries of practitioners; and research has to have this character if it is to make a distinctive contribution. (I shall take up this point later.)

As we saw earlier, Finch (1986) argues that one of the advantages of ethnographic research is its flexibility; it can adjust to changes in the situation facing policy-makers. However, while it is more flexible than much quantitative research, ethnography is not flexible enough to adjust immediately to all changes in the policy-making situation. Thus, Rist (1984) is quite realistic about the likely influence of ethnographic research on policy-makers; no doubt based on bitter experience. The same sorts of limitations on influence are likely to be found as with quantitative research. And, as I have argued, there are some good reasons for this, though there may well be bad ones too.

What I am suggesting here is that the conceptions of practice and of the relationship between research and practice that often underlie ideas about the contribution ethnography can make to policy-making are sometimes misconceived. They neglect the differences between the sorts of knowledge that research can produce and those required for practice, and especially the contextually (including temporally) specific character of much of the latter. This is not to say that research (in the sense of products of specialised inquiry) can make no contribution to practice, simply that it is only one source of information and ideas, one whose significance will never be overwhelming and may sometimes be negligible. In this respect, too, ethnographic research is no different from other types of social research.

THE MULTI-FUNCTIONALITY OF ETHNOGRAPHIC RESEARCH

Pollard argues that 'given a careful choice of topic and an acute awareness concerning research design', it may be possible to conduct studies which are relevant both to policy and to theory development (Pollard 1984a: 183). Indeed, he goes on to suggest that the requirements placed on ethnographic research are the same, whichever of these is the goal: what is required is good quality work. Finch endorses this point of view:

developments in ethnography which make it more policy
relevant would also be conducive to theoretical developments .... In other words, rather than being alternatives,
good ethnography which is theoretically grounded would
have an *enhanced* capacity to make an impact on policy.

(Finch 1986: 171)

This sounds like having it both ways; and, indeed, I think the
arguments of Pollard and Finch are mistaken in important
respects. I agree with both their insistence that theory is an
important product of ethnographic research and their argument
that all research should be policy-relevant, in a broad sense of that
term. However, there are some important qualifications.

First, I want to question the implication that there is a single,
standard product of ethnographic research, one that is simultaneously theoretical and policy-relevant.[5] It is necessary to recognise that such research can produce a variety of types of product
(see Chapter 4). It may present theories, but equally it may be
primarily concerned with description, explanation or evaluation
of some particular phenomenon.

Second, I think we need to reflect carefully about what we mean
by 'policy-relevance'.[6] In the previous section I argued that the
contribution that research can make to practice is more limited
than is sometimes believed. Here I want to suggest that its
intended contribution can vary in significant ways. For instance, it
may be designed to meet highly specific and explicit needs of
policy-makers, such as the requirement for some information that
is an essential prerequisite for the formulation or implementation
of a policy. What is provided in this case is a contribution to one
part of the work of one set of policy-makers at a particular point in
time; the information probably taking the form of description,
explanation or evaluation. At the other extreme, the information
provided by research may be of much more general relevance. For
example, it may throw doubt on the validity of assumptions that
are frequently made about some area of social life by policy-makers
and others. Here the product of research relates not to a particular
decision at a particular time and to a particular group of practitioners, but to an orientation that many people take towards some
aspect of the social world much of the time. Furthermore, it may
well not be information that policy-makers asked for or wanted, or
even information that they subsequently regard as of value. What

is and is not relevant is, of course, contestable.[7] Research products having such general relevance may be theories, but they could equally be descriptions, explanations or evaluations of macro-scale phenomena or of recurrent micro-scale phenomena; both types of phenomena can have implications for policy-makers across a variety of forms of practice.

In my judgement research is best able to produce findings of general rather than specific relevance. In order to make clear why this is the case, I need to be more explicit about what I mean by 'research'. For me, research is a process of inquiry which is collective not individual; and it is geared towards the production of valid and relevant knowledge, rather than to the solution of practical problems. I am not rejecting the value of more practically oriented forms of inquiry here (for example, what is sometimes referred to as action research), simply denying that they fulfil the same function as research, as I interpret that term (see Chapter 8). The great value of research on this model is that it produces knowledge that, on the average, is likely to contain fewer errors than knowledge from any other source. This arises from the role of the research community in checking the results of particular studies, and the fact that it deploys, or should deploy, a more sceptical form of assessment than is typical elsewhere. The orienta-tion to routinely sceptical colleagues is the main distinguishing characteristic of research, as compared with other sorts of inquiry, including the sorts of everyday inquiry that we all occasionally engage in as practitioners of one sort or another.[8] An important implication of this view of research is that any particular investi-gation should be geared towards the research community, even though it is judged by that community partly in terms of the relevance of its findings to issues that are of concern outside.

A second aspect of the collective character of research is that researchers operate (or should operate) a division of labour. It is often not possible for a manageable research project to tackle all aspects of a publicly relevant issue. A number of pieces of research are required, focusing on different parts of the problem.[9] Simi-larly, and in the case of ethnographic research in particular, there may be a need for multiple studies to allow for generalisation to a larger population that is of interest (see Chapter 5).

It is not difficult to see that research, on the model I have outlined here, is a slow and uncertain business. And for this reason researchers will rarely be able to meet the time-scale requirements of policy-makers for specific information. Indeed, attempts to do this are likely to undermine the functioning of the research community. On this basis, then, research is better suited to providing information of general rather than specific relevance. Equally, it seems likely that studies need to have findings of general relevance if it is to be worth while for the research community to make any sustained assessment of them.

There is a further implication of this view of research that is worth mentioning here. This relates to the question of the appropriate audience for ethnographic accounts. In my view, the immediate audience for research must be the research community, even though the ultimate aim is to produce knowledge that is of value to others. Therefore, communications to policy-makers from researchers should draw on multiple studies and on the necessarily always provisional conclusions of the research community about their validity, rather than reporting the outcome of a particular piece of research. Otherwise, the distinctive benefits of the research process as a collective enterprise will not be obtained.[10]

I agree with Pollard and Finch, then, that research should be policy-relevant. But I do not believe that this implies that there is a standard product of ethnographic research that is both theoretical and addressed to a policy-making audience. In my view, ethnography can provide a variety of types of product, all of which should be policy-relevant, but their relevance to practice should be general rather than specific, and indirect rather than direct.

CONCLUSION

In this chapter I have urged caution about some of the arguments used to suggest that ethnographic research can make a greater contribution to policy making than quantitative research. I have suggested that the claims sometimes made about the policy payoff of ethnography are excessive in three respects. First, the capacity of ethnographic research to produce valid findings is often over-estimated in comparison with that of other approaches. Ethnography offers no magic solution to the methodological problems that face all social research. There is a serious danger that, like the advocates of quantitative research before them, qualitative researchers will over-sell the validity of their findings. And the result of this will be yet more frustration and cynicism about research on the part of practitioners. This is not to imply that ethnography has no validity, simply that I do not believe that there are reasonable grounds for concluding that its findings are more likely to be true in some general and invariant fashion than those of quantitative research. While ethnographers have identified serious validity problems in quantitative research, they have not succeeded in resolving those problems themselves.

Second, there is the neglect of the limits to the contribution that any research can make to practice. Research cannot produce knowledge that can simply be applied to resolve practical problems. Practice is context-sensitive and involves judgement in which factual and value assumptions must be relied on, many of which must come from experience rather than research. Research cannot substitute for experience here, though it can inform it. Indeed, research findings must be assessed by practitioners in the light of their experience, and used in relation to their contextual knowledge and practical judgement. While there are reasons for believing that in general the products of research are less likely to be invalid than the practical knowledge of practitioners, in particular cases and for particular purposes this may not be so. Furthermore, usually, practitioners are not solely interested in the validity of specific factual and/or value claims, but rather in the effectiveness or likely effectiveness of a whole policy, to which the validity of those claims may be of only very minor relevance. This is not to deny that research can make a useful contribution, but rather simply to protest at the extravagance of the claims that are sometimes made about the scale of that contribution. Even the enlightenment model of the relationship between research and policy assumes an exaggerated role for research in this respect.

Finally, I considered the idea, present in some proposals for policy-relevant ethnography, that studies may be multi-purpose, simultaneously producing both policy-relevant information and theory, and thereby serving both practitioners and fellow researchers at the same time. I argued that ethnographic research may generate a variety of sorts of product, rather than just one. And while all of them should be policy relevant, this relevance will often be general rather than specific. Furthermore, the contribution of research to practice, as opposed to that of other forms of inquiry, depends on a division of labour among researchers and on the role of the research community in subjecting the results of particular studies to a higher level of routine scepticism than is common outside that community. A further implication of this is that research reports ought to be addressed to fellow researchers; communications to practitioner audiences being based on the research community's assessment of the whole range of relevant studies.

In summary, then, ethnography can and should be policy-relevant. However, we must beware of claims that it has a superior potential for making a contribution to policy-making compared with other methods. Like them, it has its strengths and weaknesses. Like them, its potential contribution to practice is limited by the nature of practice and the sorts of knowledge that practice demands. And like them it must take different forms depending on its intended product, and is usually most usefully directed towards producing valid knowledge that is of general relevance.

NOTES

1 With Pollard (1984a), I shall use the term 'policy-making' as a synonym for practical decision-making in general. It is worth noting that there has been some debate about whether ethnography can or should be used to serve policy needs (see Wolcott 1982).

2 See Hammersley (1986) for an attempt to spell out the issues surrounding the relationship between concepts and data in ethnographic research.

3 See Finch (1986) for a useful review of these models and for references.

4 In some versions of the argument policy-makers are regarded as morally deficient, as being simply concerned to defend their own interests or those of the powerful groups that they serve. While I would not deny that they, like others, are influenced by ulterior motives, it is not obvious to me that this is any more true of them than of researchers.

5 The term 'ethnography' is itself sometimes used to refer to the product of ethnographic research, and this is one source of the misconception that there is a single type of product. Another is the idea that such research is aimed at producing 'theoretical descriptions', see Chapter 1.

6 The argument of the next few paragraphs is spelt out in a little more detail in Chapter 8.

7 Both Pollard and Finch recognise the difference between meeting practitioners' needs and giving them what they desire.

8 See Hammersley (1991a) for a slightly fuller outline of this conception of the research community.

9 I have spelt out this argument in Hammersley (1980).

10 It should be obvious that I am presenting an idealised view of the social research community. But the aim is to present an ideal, not to defend the status quo.

8

ON PRACTITIONER
ETHNOGRAPHY

The predominant model of ethnography, inherited from social and cultural anthropology and from Chicago sociology, treats it as a form of pure rather than applied research.[1] From this perspective, it is not tied to any immediate practical purpose but is concerned rather with contributing to our knowledge of human society; whether in terms of identifying the latter's general principles of operation or the description and explanation of diverse forms of social and cultural organisation. Despite this, a minority of ethnographers have long advocated and practised more applied forms of research. In the US there is a well-established and influential tradition of applied anthropology (Eddy and Partridge 1978; van Willigen 1986). And since the late 1960s, on both sides of the Atlantic, ethnography has been used in other applied fields, for instance in educational evaluation (Walker 1978, see also Atkinson and Delamont 1985; Fetterman 1984; Fetterman and Pitman 1986). Indeed, there have recently been increasing calls for ethnographic research to be more directly related to policy issues, and strong claims made about its potential in this respect (see Chapter 7).[2] An influential, if extreme, version of this argument proposes what we can call 'practitioner ethnography'. Here, not only is research to be closely tailored to the needs of practitioners (of one kind or another), but it is argued that this can only be achieved if the practitioners participate in the research process, effectively taking it over themselves.[3]

One of the most influential versions of this argument arose in the field of education, in the form of the teacher-as-researcher movement. Thus, Stenhouse (1975) argues that when teachers become researchers investigating their own practice, this results in educational research that is more relevant and also transforms teaching. Moreover, the sort of research he advocated, often referred to as case study, can be seen as a version of ethnography.[4] Others have drawn on the critical theory of the Frankfurt School to put forward the view that the development of active groups of teacher-researchers could revolutionise the education system and perhaps also the wider society (Carr and Kemmis 1986). Similar developments have occurred elsewhere. Thus, within social psychology, 'new paradigm' research involves a strong emphasis on collaborative approaches (Reason and Rowan 1981), as do some versions of applied anthropology (van Willigen 1986), and of feminist method (see, for example, Mies 1983). In the field of adult education and development studies in the Third World there is a growing movement for 'participatory research', influenced by the work of Freire (1972). Freire advocates 'conscientisation', a process in which politically and economically oppressed groups are encouraged to investigate their needs and circumstances, to pursue political action to secure improvements in their conditions, and to reflect on the outcomes of these activities with a view to reformulating their political views and improving their strategies for bringing about change. Once again, there is a strong emphasis within this tradition on the use of qualitative methods.

It is not always clear whether practitioner ethnography is advocated to serve the same function as, and to replace, conventional ethnography; but many of the arguments used to support it carry one or other or both of these implications.[6] In this chapter I want to examine these arguments. There seem to be three major ones:

1 that conventional research is irrelevant to practice;
2 that it is invalid because it lacks an insider perspective; and
3 that it is exploitative.

I shall examine each of these claims in turn.

IRRELEVANCE

The criticism that conventional ethnographic research is irrelevant to practice involves two sub-claims.

1 That research is of value only in so far as it serves the needs of some group of practitioners.
2 That those needs cannot be served effectively by external,

specialist researchers; only by practitioners doing research themselves. To the extent that specialist researchers participate at all, their task should be to facilitate practitioner research.

1 Research must serve practitioners' needs

Subject to some important qualifications, this first argument is sound in my view. I find it difficult to see what justification there could be for research, especially for publicly funded research, that does not make some contribution to the needs of non-researchers. Research must be judged not just in terms of its validity but also on the basis of its relevance to practical concerns (see Chapter 4).[7]

However, we must clarify what 'serving practitioners' needs', means. I do not believe, to take the extreme case, that research only has relevance if it is directed towards a practitioner audience and provides information that is of immediate and acknowledged use to that audience. For one thing, research products can be relevant *indirectly* as well as *directly*; that is, they can have relevance through their influence on other research products that do have direct relevance. Needless to say, indirect relevance is more difficult to judge with confidence than direct relevance. But it is a legitimate form of relevance none the less; and the inevitable element of uncertainty surrounding it is independent of *degree* of relevance. Equally important, research may be directly relevant to practice in at least two ways: it may serve a *specific and acknowledged* need for items of information; or it may be of more *general value*, relating not to a particular policy decision but to some aspect of the approach that practitioners take to a whole range of decisions and problems. It may, for example, involve the investigation of assumptions that are routinely made, but about which there is some reason for doubt. Furthermore, the need for such generally relevant research may not always be acknowledged by practitioners. It is important that we do not assume that practitioners have privileged insight into what is and is not a useful contribution to practice at any particular time. They may have a distinctive, and will certainly have a valuable, perspective; but there is no guarantee that their judgements will be correct. One reason why this is the case is that the most pressing problems for practitioners are not always those that are the most important, yet practitioners will almost inevitably give greater weight to the problems that are most pressing. In short, practitioners' judgements will be shaped by the circumstances of their work and the perspectives generated to deal with these.[8] Another reason is that practitioners' judgements of the value of research will be relative to their expectations of it. If they expect it to provide solutions to their problems, an expectation reinforced by the claims of some researchers, then they are almost certain to be disappointed because of the limitations to the contribution that it can make (see Chapter 7).

I accept, then, that ethnographic research must be directed towards producing information that has relevance beyond the research community. However, I have suggested that relevance can be indirect as well as direct, and general as well as specific. And in my view all these forms of relevance are legitimate.

2 Only practitioner research produces relevant findings

Criticisms of conventional ethnography by advocates of practitioner research often involve the claim that the products of the former are irrelevant to practitioners, and (by implication at least) necessarily so.[9] I do not believe that this is true. But, what *is* true is that the findings of conventional research are usually of indirect and general, rather than direct and specific, relevance. And there are good reasons for this, arising from the fact that such research is a specialised activity involving a division of labour.

There are two aspects of the division of labour on which conventional research is based. First, the research community plays (or should play) a crucial role in checking the validity of the findings of particular studies. This process is at the heart of the justification for research as a source of knowledge. This justification rests on the claim that research-based knowledge is less likely to be in error than information from other sources because it is subjected to scrutiny in terms of a higher level of routine scepticism than is common outside the research community. In my view, it is this, rather than any appeal to a concept of brute data that constitutes immediate knowledge of reality and whose validity is guaranteed (or some other version of foundationalism), that is the major rationale for the intellectual authority of research.[10]

A second reason for the division of labour among researchers is that it is often not possible to answer questions that are directly relevant to practical problems adequately (that is, in a way that is persuasive to the research community) through a single piece of research. It will often require a research programme, a set of coordinated studies dealing with various elements of the problem.

The fact that research involves a division of labour carries some important implications. One is that most research reports will (and should) be directed towards fellow researchers, even though the research they report can (and should) be relevant to practice. In the terms I am using here, their relevance will usually be indirect. Indeed, I think there is a strong argument that reports of particular research projects should always be addressed to other researchers, and that communications directed to practitioners should draw on a wide range of studies, not just on one. Only then can the benefits of the collective assessment of findings by the research community be obtained. Second, because of its time-consuming and labour-intensive character, research will frequently not be able to meet the (often rigidly timetabled) demands of practitioners for specific information. For this reason, research is more usually directed towards issues of general relevance, where time constraints may be less pressing. There is also a positive reason for this: research having general relevance is more likely to be read and subjected to detailed assessment by the research community than research having only very specific relevance. This stems from the cosmopolitan, rather than local, orientation of that community.

What I have sketched here is in many respects a fairly conventional model of the specialist researcher doing research whose adequacy is judged, in the first place, by fellow researchers. But I am arguing for this not on the grounds that knowledge is of value for its own sake, or on the basis of a naïve and discredited positivism.[11] Rather, my argument is that this form of research can produce knowledge of general relevance that would not otherwise be accessible (because its attainment requires a division of labour) and that is, on average, more reliable (in the sense of being less likely to be false) than information from other sources. Of course, this model necessarily requires specialist researchers, in the sense of people who have the time, knowledge and skills needed to participate in the research community as well as to do research. However, this does not rule out practitioners. Indeed, many social researchers *are* practitioners, in that they also teach in higher education institutions. And there is no restriction in principle on other sorts of practitioners engaging in research.[12] However, the question of who can and should do research is not really what is at issue in the debate over practitioner ethnography. What *is* crucial is the nature of the research, and in particular its relationship to practice. I have argued the case for research of a relatively conventional kind whose relationship to practice is indirect and general rather than direct and specific, and it is precisely the value of such research that advocates of practitioner ethnography challenge. I have tried to show that their claim that the knowledge which this kind of research produces is irrelevant is based on too narrow a concept of relevance. To establish their case they would have to show that inquiries having direct and specific relevance are of more value than those whose relevance is indirect and general; or, more radically, that the latter are not of any value at all. This has not been achieved. Usually they have simply dismissed conventional research as irrelevant on the evidence that practitioners (or some of them anyway) profess to find it of little value. I have argued, however, that we cannot treat practitioners as having privileged insight into the contribution that research makes to practice.

It is important to stress that I do not regard the model of research I have outlined as the only legitimate form of inquiry. Indeed, it seems to me that the very origins of research lie in more everyday sorts of investigation. One of these arises where we are seeking to carry through a line of action and we run into an obstacle. A reasonable response to such a problem may well be to carry out an investigation of the situation with a view to finding a solution. This inquiry will be tailored to the particular context in which the problem arises, to the purposes that the practitioner is pursuing, as well as to the resources available and to other constraints. As such, this is quite clearly a very different kind of inquiry to the model of specialist research that I outlined above. In particular, such problem-solving investigation is directed primarily towards the production of information of direct and specific relevance, and its success is judged in these terms.

It is a terminological question whether one calls such problem-solving inquiry 'research', and what is most important is the distinction not the terminology. However, I think there are some good reasons for not applying this label.[13] One is that even though the advocates of practitioner ethnography often present themselves as defending practitioners against the imperialistic designs of researchers, the effect of their proselytising may well be to encourage the imposition of the methodological canons of research on to problem-solving inquiry, and this will often be inappropriate.[14] While both forms of inquiry should be concerned with validity and relevance, the character of the judgements about these matters in each case are likely to be different; and rightly so, because each form of inquiry requires a different orientation to these criteria for its success. I have already indicated their different orientation to relevance. In the case of validity, practitioners should accept what seems beyond reasonable doubt on the basis of their experience, and judge the results of any inquiry on that basis. Often that experience will be personal, and even where it is collective the collectivity will usually be relatively local in character. Furthermore, other considerations will play a key role in practitioners' deliberations, such as how important the decision is in practical terms, the chances of things going wrong, the legal situation etc. Researchers, on the other hand, must orient towards what would be accepted as beyond reasonable doubt by members of the research community, who are likely to have rather more diverse backgrounds, experience and assumptions than any local practitioner community. Indeed, it is in the very nature of this community that it is open-ended and cosmopolitan. As a result of these differences, researchers and practitioners may well come to different but equally justifiable judgements about what assumptions are and are not beyond reasonable doubt.[15]

The objection may be made that I have defined practical inquiry in a very narrow way, as responding to what Schutz calls imposed rather than intrinsic relevances (Schutz 1970). This omits a major aspect of some of the arguments for practitioner ethnography: that concerned with how it might change practice rather than with how it might change research. The argument here is that engagement in ethnography will encourage practitioners to be more reflective, to think more widely and deeply about their activity (about its goals and the means employed to achieve them, about the conditions in which they work etc), and will perhaps as a result lead to a reorientation of their activity. What is implied by this is a much more open-ended sort of practical inquiry, in some ways more analogous to that of specialist ethnographers than what I have called 'problem-solving inquiry'.

However, while such reflective inquiry may be oriented towards general rather than specific relevance, it still differs in significant ways from specialist research. It is important to recognise that ethnography is not isomorphic with reflexivity. Reflection does not necessarily require the systematic collection and recording of first-hand data. It may simply draw on experience, background knowledge and perhaps the reading of relevant literature; including, but not exclusively, the research literature. Furthermore, the process of analysis involved in reflection is likely to be less explicit and focused. To treat ethnography as identical with reflection may therefore, as in the case of problem-solving inquiry, lead to the imposition of inappropriate methodological guidelines. It might also encourage a neglect of explicit reflection on value issues, since research is often held (wrongly in my view) to deal only with facts and not values.

There is also a danger arising from the somewhat loaded character of reflexivity as it is advanced by some advocates of practitioner ethnography. For instance, Stenhouse's writings are strongly informed by assumptions about what is and is not good teaching. In part, at least, these seem to be built into the very concept of the teacher-as-researcher, with teaching being regarded as a form of discovery learning modelled on renaissance humanism and Popperian philosophy of science. Similarly, critical theory has been a very influential model of reflective thinking, and while advocates of practitioner ethnography have generally departed from the idea of intellectuals providing a perspective that frees practitioners from ideology, they have often retained some of the substantive Marxist ideas characteristic of critical theory about what enlightenment and emancipation amount to (see Carr and Kemmis 1986). But these ideas are highly problematic.[16] In short, what I am suggesting is that there is a danger of various substantive values being smuggled in under the disguise of the formal value of reflection. I would not wish to imply that all outcomes of reflection are necessarily good (any more than implying that all the results of research are necessarily good), but I think we must be careful not to adopt a conception of reflexivity that effectively prejudges what the nature of those outcomes should be.[17]

In terms of the scheme I presented above, reflection of this kind typically produces knowledge that is of direct but general relevance. In this respect it is distinct both from research and from what I called problem-solving inquiry. Furthermore, in my view, none of these forms of inquiry can substitute for any of the others, though each may draw selectively on the others' products and methods.

In this section I have argued that while all research ought to be directed towards the production of findings that have practical relevance, such relevance can take indirect as well as direct, general as well as specific forms. I outlined a model of specialist research which, for good reasons, tended to produce findings having indirect and general relevance. At the same time, I argued that such research is not the only useful form of inquiry, and I sketched two kinds of practical inquiry (problem-solving investigations and reflection). These tend to produce findings of more specific and/or direct relevance than research, though they are not (on the average) as reliable as research findings.[18] I argued that it is important for these forms of practical inquiry to be regarded as distinct in character from specialist ethnographic research. While they might usefully draw on the techniques of the latter, these techniques are not always appropriate. It is also worth emphasising that these forms of practical inquiry are not isomorphic with practice, and (as in the case of research) there are limits to the information they can provide. They too will often not be able to meet the informational demands of practice.[19]

INVALIDITY

It is sometimes suggested that the findings of non-practitioner ethnography are likely to be invalid because it is impossible for an outsider to a situation to understand it. Only those actually involved can truly understand. This argument is founded on the idea that direct experience of, or closeness to, a phenomenon gives one valid knowledge of it. Ironically, this is an argument that has often been used by conventional ethnographers themselves in claiming the superiority of their approach over other kinds of social research (see, for example, Blumer 1969). But in doing so, of course, they open themselves up to the criticism that because they are not as close to the phenomena they study as full participants, their knowledge is less likely to be valid than participants' knowledge.

In my view, however, while closeness to and involvement with the phenomena being investigated have some relevance for the validity of findings, the epistemological assumption that sometimes underlies this argument – that knowledge comes from contact with reality – is unsound. This is because all knowledge is a construction; we have no direct knowledge of the world (see Chapter 3). There are, though, some more specific and defensible methodological arguments on which the claim that practitioners are best able to understand their activities and situations could be based:

(a) that practitioners have access to their own intentions and motives in a way that an observer does not, and so have a deeper understanding of their own behaviour than an outsider could ever have;

(b) that the practitioner will usually have long-term experience of the setting being studied, and will therefore know its history at first hand, as well as other information that may be required to understand what is going on. It would take an outsider a long time to acquire such knowledge, indeed this may never be possible;

(c) that the practitioner already has relationships with others in the setting and can use these in order to collect further data. Once again, an outsider would need to spend a considerable time in the field building up such relationships;

(d) that because practitioners are key actors in the setting, they are in a position to test theoretical ideas in a way that a mere observer can never do.

Each of these arguments points to an advantage that insiders may have in the sources of information available to them. And, as they stand, I think they have some plausibility. However, for each of these advantages, there is a countervailing disadvantage.[20]

(a) People can be wrong even about their own intentions and motives; self-knowledge is not immediately given and therefore valid. Furthermore, people can deceive themselves about their intentions, motives etc. Indeed, they may often have an interest in such self-deception, where an outsider might have less reason to prefer one account over another. Also, understanding often requires seeing a phenomenon in its wider context, and this may be particularly difficult for those closely involved in it. It is for this reason that ethnographers stress the importance of maintaining some (at least intellectual) distance from the activities they observe.

(b) The information that practitioners have about the situations they operate in is a product of experience deriving from a particular role (or a limited number of roles) that will have given access to some sorts of information but not to others. In particular, their understanding of the perspectives of other categories and groups of people involved in the setting may be superficial or distorted. Furthermore, the knowledge they have will have been processed implicitly and to a large extent on the basis of practitioner concerns, and may involve misconceptions that serve those concerns. A researcher, on the other hand, may be able to tap a wider range of sources of information and will be able to process that information for the specific purposes of inquiry and (to some extent at least) in an explicit way that allows for checking by others.

(c) Again, the relationships available to the practitioner will exclude as well as include, and may not include what is necessary for research purposes. Furthermore, some of those relationships may place constraints on the inquiry (for example on what can be observed, what questions can be asked, what conclusions can be published etc.) that an outside researcher would be able to avoid.

(d) What is required to test theoretical ideas may well conflict with what is needed for good practice. The practitioner may therefore be faced with a dilemma, and as a result may not be able to test her or his ideas. In any case, quasi-experimentation is only one possible research strategy, one with characteristic disadvantages (notably potentially high reactivity) as well as advantages.

In short, I do not believe that being a participant in a situation provides access to valid knowledge that is not available to an outside researcher. In general, I think that the chances of the findings being valid can be enhanced by a judicious combination of involvement and estrangement. However, no position, not even a marginal one, *guarantees* valid knowledge; and no position prevents it either. There are no overwhelming advantages to being an insider or an outsider. Each position has advantages *and* disadvantages, though these will take on slightly different weights, depending on the particular circumstances and purposes of the research.[21]

Before leaving the issue of validity, I want to reiterate the point I made in the previous section: that an essential feature of research is the role of the research community in assessing the findings of particular studies. There is an ambiguity on the part of some who espouse practitioner ethnography: on the one hand, they argue that research is not a specialised activity at all, it is something practitioners of all kinds routinely engage in; on the other hand, they portray practitioner ethnography as requiring practitioners to become more systematic, rigorous and explicit in their inquiries. In my view, systematicity, rigour and explicitness are not exclusive to research. They are a variable feature of all activities. Nor can research ever be fully systematic, rigorous and explicit; it too shows legitimate variation in these features. The difference between research and practice is that the variation is governed by somewhat different considerations. Researchers are as systematic, rigorous and explicit as they need to be to satisfy themselves and their colleagues. Practitioners are as systematic, rigorous and explicit as they need to be to satisfy themselves and *their* colleagues (and perhaps also their superiors and clients). But, given the different activities in which these categories of actor are engaged, what is appropriate will vary. I have argued that because the research community operates (or at least should operate) on the basis of a routine scepticism, the results of research will, other things being equal, be less likely to be invalid than those of other kinds of inquiry. However, as I pointed out, this is bought at the expense of the sort of relevance research findings can have. And it does not mean that conclusions extrapolated from research about any particular situation will be superior to the relevant practitioners' local knowledge. They may or may not be; this is a matter for judgement in particular cases.

EXPLOITATION

The final argument for practitioner ethnography that I shall address is a political and ethical one to the effect that conventional research is exploitative, either because it involves the exercise of power by researchers over practitioners (or at least serves the interests of researchers rather than those of the people studied), and/or because it aids powerful social groups in controlling others. I shall deal with each version of this argument.[22]

One aspect of the first argument is the idea that the sole function of research is to serve the careers of researchers:

> For many people, the word 'research' is associated with voluminous and abstract scientific work which is presented frequently in esoteric language, by specialists who deal with narrow subjects. These long-term research projects are usually carried out under the aegis of a university, where they often represent nothing more than the fulfilment of

academic rules and conditions for obtaining honours and degrees. In spite of all the knowledge which these works supposedly represent, it is not infrequent that, having been solemnly presented, they go quietly to rest on the shelves of university libraries.

(de Oliveira and de Oliveira 1982: 41)

There is no doubt that many researchers may be motivated by careerism, to one degree or another; but it does not follow from this that what they produce is of no value. Fortunately or unfortunately, what is of value does not always spring from good intentions; nor do the latter guarantee beneficial results. There is an important difference between the motives that individuals may have for becoming researchers and the function of research as an institution.[23] Furthermore, the fact that the products of research terminate on library shelves does not imply that they are 'useless' (de Oliveira and de Oliveira 1982: 41–2). Libraries are not simply storage facilities; their contents are used to one degree or another. Nor does the fact that many research publications are little used imply that they are of no value. Among some advocates of practitioner ethnography there is a hankering after the sort of direct relationship between research and practice that is assumed by both the model of applied science and the emancipatory model of critical theorists, but which in my view is simply not possible (see Chapter 7). Political action may bring about change (though it will not always be of the kind intended or desired), but research is not an effective way of changing the world (not in any direct and immediate way at least).[24]

A different point concerns the question of the degree to which it is true that researchers exercise power over the people they study. In one sense, at least, this power seems to be minimal. Ethnographers typically have to request and negotiate access to the settings and groups they study, and this may be blocked at any point. Of course, the extent to which the people studied are able to block access will depend on their position in society generally, and in the particular setting, and on who (if anybody) is sponsoring the ethnographer. Thus, when (as is common) an ethnographer negotiates access to a setting via a gatekeeper who is at the top of an authority hierarchy within the setting, people lower down that hierarchy may feel pressure to cooperate, lest they suffer sanctions from the gatekeeper. However, it is rare, I suspect, for participants to be forced into cooperation in this way; there are usually ways in which they can be less than cooperative without incurring the wrath of their superiors (and it is unusual for superiors to be very strongly committed to research). In any event, most ethnographers would probably respect the wishes of subordinates to refuse access. More often than not, I would suggest, ethnographers are in a relatively weak position *vis-a-vis* most of the people they study, in terms of gaining access.

A more obvious way in which researchers may be said to exercise power over participants is that they are more able to publish, and thereby perhaps to gain a wide readership for, their accounts. And in this way they may significantly shape the situation and fortunes of the people studied, and others:

> The worker in a Latin American factory or the landless Asian labourer or the poor African peasant is not among those who are authorised to create knowledge. Their ideas will never be read in the journals or discussed in the conferences, let alone in the economic planning ministeries where government policies are being set. And yet the papers and reports of researchers from national universities or even from other countries will be read and perhaps influence others even if they are written about the same Latin American factory or African/Asian villages.
>
> (Hall *et al.* 1982: 7)

It is true that researchers may be able to publish their accounts more easily than (at least some) practitioners. However, neither the ease of publication of research reports nor their influence on policy-making should be exaggerated. Furthermore, there is a hint in some versions of this criticism of the belief that democracy requires that everyone should have an equal voice in the public realm, that there are no sources of intellectual authority that would give the researcher more justification for publication than others. Thus, Hall declares that the fundamental question is 'who has the right to create knowledge?' (Hall 1982: 15). He argues that to claim intellectual authority for social science is to deny 'the knowledge-generating abilities innate to every human being in the world' (p.24). Rudduck (1987: 5), an advocate of the teacher-as-researcher, hints at the same point:

there is an urgent need to analyse the structures that govern the production and distribution of research knowledge and the right to engage in research acts. Teacher research is, at one level, a means of countering the hegemony of academic research which teachers are often distanced by.

What seems to be involved here is some model of participatory democracy as the basis for knowledge generation.[25] But in everyday life we do not treat all opinions as of equal value, and with good reason. We judge the likely validity of views on a variety of grounds, and among these we certainly take account of their source. We assign certain sources of information a degree of intellectual authority on particular sorts of topic. This does not mean that we simply accept what they say at face value, simply that we are more likely to turn to them, or to listen to them, when we require valid information about some topic to which their authority is relevant. This is not a 'dependence' relationship (de Oliveira and de Oliveira 1982: 58), but simply a reasonable adaptation to circumstances; and a justifiable one. Research has intellectual authority in this sense. Its authority relies, as I suggested earlier, on the role of the research community in exercising a higher level of routine scepticism towards knowledge claims and engaging in the pursuit of findings that satisfy that scepticism. It is this which justifies the publication of research results; indeed the scrutiny of these results by the research community *requires* their publication.[26] However, I noted earlier that research is not the only form of inquiry. And this indicates that there are other sources of intellectual authority besides research. Practical experience and first-hand observation on the part of practitioners are amongst these.

In summary, then, research is not intrinsically exploitative. Some research may be; but it need not be.[27] Let me turn now to the other aspect of the argument about exploitation, the claim that research serves powerful groups in society and aids their exploitation of the oppressed. The answer to this, once again, is that some research may do this, but that it need not do so. The argument that conventional research necessarily serves powerful groups sometimes relies on the idea that implicit in the very character of such research is a technical interest in social control (Fay 1975; Popkewitz 1984). This criticism has usually been directed at quantitative rather than qualitative research. More common in relation to the latter is the claim that it serves the ideological function of legitimation, for example suggesting that all conflict is the result of miscommunication. But this notion of trans-cendental, constitutive interests underlying research is highly questionable (Overend 1978). It implies, once again, an overly direct and powerful relationship between research and practice. More straightforward is the argument that ethnography is funded by, and therefore serves the interests of, powerful groups in society; and that this is revealed by the fact that in general it involves 'studying down' rather than 'studying up'. But, while it is true that the sponsoring of research sometimes does affect what is investigated and perhaps even the findings, much ethnographic research does not suffer from such sponsorship constraint to any significant degree. At least, the critics have not shown this to be the case. Similarly, to suggest that research on people of low power and status within society necessarily serves the interests of those at the top, or that research on those at the top serves the interests of those at the bottom, is not convincing. Much depends on the nature of the research and its effects. Furthermore, deciding what is in whose interests is not always straightforward.

The complement to this critique of the exploitative character of conventional ethnographic research is the argument that research could and should be directed towards emancipation, and that the most effective means of achieving this is by practitioner ethno-graphy:

> The object of research, like the object of education, should be the *liberation of human creative potential and the mobilization of human resources* for the solution of social problems.
>
> (Hall 1982: 23)

> In short, rather than using science as a simple technique for making society function better, we want to show its usefulness as a tool for unmasking and criticising any situation which negates the human being.
>
> (de Oliveira and de Oliveira 1982: 47)

What seems to be involved here is a notion of humanity indepen-dent of society, which the latter constrains and from which it must be set free; or the more sophisticated (but equally implaus-ible) teleological view of history that is characteristic of Marxism (on which see Chapter 6). In my judgement it is a mistake to

150

assume that any research can bring about emancipation; here again we have an over-estimation of the potential contribution of research to practice. Equally, though, the political framework implied by such an unrestricted interpretation of the concepts of oppression and emancipation is misconceived. Emancipation or liberation is always from some particular constraint, it can never be from all constraints.[28] Assumed here, it seems to me, are excessive expectations regarding what research can do and a naïve politics, effectively aiming at the achievement of participatory democracy through the research process. Furthermore, there is no reason to believe that practitioner ethnography is *necessarily* in the interests of those engaging in it. Even less can we assume, as some versions of the emancipatory model do, that it is in the interests of others too.

In my view, then, there is little ground for the belief that conventional ethnographic research is exploitative, either in itself or because it serves the interests of power groups in society. It can be, but it need not be. And there has been little or no documentation of the extent to which this is the case. Conversely, there is no guarantee that practitioner ethnography is emancipatory; indeed, there are good reasons to believe that no form of inquiry can be emancipatory, both because this assumes too large a potential contribution of research to practice and because the concept of emancipation employed by many advocates of practitioner ethnography is simplistic.

CONCLUSION

In this chapter I have examined the case for practitioner ethnography. I outlined the contexts out of which this proposal has arisen and the arguments used to support it. I identified three such arguments: that conventional ethnographic research is irrelevant to practice; that it is invalid because it lacks the insider perspective; and that it is exploitative.

In addressing the first of these issues I began by looking at the assumption that research must be relevant to practitioners. I accepted this assumption, but argued that relevance could be indirect and general, as well as direct and specific. I then distinguished between specialist research directed towards the production of findings having indirect and general relevance, on the one hand; and problem-solving and reflective inquiry on the other, these producing information that is of more specific and/ or direct relevance to practice. I emphasised the distinct functions served by these types of inquiry and at the same time the limits to the contribution that any of them can make to practice. In these terms the criticisms of conventional ethnographic research made by advocates of practitioner ethnography are about the *sort* of relevance that it has for practice, they do not establish its irrelevance. Nor do they show that direct and specific relevance is superior to indirect and general relevance.

As regards the second argument, that outsider research is likely to be invalid because only those involved in activities can understand them, I suggested that this was often based on a naïve realism. And where it is not, what it points to are simply the relative advantages of insider research, these often being counterbalanced by various disadvantages. Furthermore, it ignores the distinctive claim to validity that is built into specialist research.

Finally, in relation to the third argument, I rejected both the charge that conventional ethnography involves, and the suggestion that it serves, exploitation. In neither respect is there any necessary connection between conventional ethnography and exploitation, nor has an empirical connection been established. And I suggested that there are good reasons for doubting that practitioner ethnography can be emancipatory (in the unrestricted sense of that term used by its advocates). Indeed, there is no reason to assume that such research is necessarily in the interests of the practitioners involved, and even less of others as well.

My conclusion, then, is that while there are forms of inquiry that are closely related to practical activities, and while these may usefully draw on ethnographic ideas, it is important to distinguish them from ethnography. In my view, the latter should conform to the model of specialist research that I outlined, in which research is the activity of a research community oriented to discovering errors and producing knowledge of general, rather than specific, relevance to practice.

NOTES

1 On the attitude of Chicago sociologists towards this issue, see Harvey (1987). Of course, the terms 'pure' and 'applied' cover a complex field; see below for a discussion of the various ways in which research may be relevant to practice.

2 Eddy (1985) gives some reasons why this has occurred in the case of educational anthropology in the US, and these may also apply elsewhere. See also the current debates within anthropology about advocacy: Paine (ed.) (1985) and Hastrup and Elsass (1990).

3 I am using the term 'practitioner' here in a general sense to refer to anyone engaging in some form of practice other than research. And I am including under the heading of practitioner ethnography forms of collaborative research that retain a distinction, albeit minimal, between researcher and researched. For discussions of the role of the researcher in collaborative research see, for example, de Oliveira and de Oliveira (1982) and Gibson (1985).

4 Stenhouse (1979) distinguishes case study from ethnography, appealing to history rather than anthropology as a model; but for my purposes here this is not significant.

5 See Hall *et al.* (1982); Latapi (1988). See also the journal *Convergence*, issues VIII, 2, 1975; XIV, 3, 1981; and XXI, 2 and 3, 1988. Illich 1981 provides an unusual discussion based on the work of the twelfth-century philosopher Hugh of St Victor.

6 At one extreme, some see collaborative research as serving the same function as more conventional research, without necessarily replacing it; for example, Kelly (1985). At the other, there are those who reject what they regard as the oppressive functions served by conventional research and recommend practitioner ethnography directed towards the solution of practical social problems and/or the emancipation of the oppressed.

7 Here I am rejecting both the idea that all knowledge is of value and the claim that the goal of research is simply to document reality (or even its deep structure). In my view the structure of reality under-determines research, so that decisions about what to research, what findings are of value etc. rely on other values as well as that of truth (see Chapter 1).

8 This is not, of course, to deny that the views of researchers are affected by *their* circumstances. It is simply to argue that they may have a valuable perspective too.

9 For the argument that conventional ethnographic research is often irrelevant to practice, coming from well-known exponents of such research in the field of education, see Burgess (1978 and 1980) and Woods (1986: ch.1). For an exchange of views on this issue: Mac-Namara (1980) and Hammersley (1981b).

10 For a more detailed account of this model of the research community, see Hammersley (1991a: ch.3).

11 The conventional model of research is often assumed to be necessarily based on one or other of these positions, see for example Elliott (1988). It is important to stress, perhaps, that I am not defending the status quo of social, or even ethnographic, research. In my view such research is currently not only under-resourced but also badly organised. The degree of coordination among ethnographic studies is extremely low (see Hammersley 1987a and 1991a: ch.5).

12 Indeed, the more diverse the backgrounds of researchers the more

effective the research community is likely to be as a check on the validity of research findings. There are, however, practical constraints on practitioners of other kinds engaging in research. At the moment, those who work in higher education often have research included in their job descriptions, and may be provided with some resources to engage in that activity. And while the pressures of teaching and administration are growing in such a way as to threaten their participation in research, teachers in higher education still generally enjoy conditions that are more conducive to this activity than practitioners of most other kinds.

13 I recognise that 'research' is a status-loaded word and that to deny problem-solving inquiry that designation may be interpeted as denying it value. All I can say is that for my part there is no such implication. Indeed, I am following a distinction proposed by Rudduck (1987: 3–4), one of the advocates of practitioner ethnography.

14 See Burgess (1978 and 1980) and Woods (1986) for examples of the argument that such canons should be applied to teacher research.

15 Note how this is justified by the fact that practitioners operate in local circumstances that for the most part they will know very well. Researchers, on the other hand, are aiming at general knowledge. Also, the latter usually need to make their assumptions more explicit: their aim is knowledge that will be judged valid, not action that will be judged reasonable or successful.

16 For a discussion of some of the problems surrounding the concept of emancipation, see Chapter 6.

17 Perhaps we should even ask whether reflexivity is so much a good thing that more of it is always desirable. Might not reflection on our activities sometimes result in incapacity rather than improvement? And even if more reflection on one's life is always desirable in principle, it is not always desirable in practice. This is because it always takes place at the expense of engagement in some other activity, including (perhaps) the form of practice on which reflection is to occur. A trade-off is necessarily involved, then, between reflection and other activities. Advocates of reflexivity do not always seem to recognise this: see, for example, Carr and Kemmis (1986) and Pollard and Tann (1987). There is a tendency to identify reflection with practice itself, for example via the notion of 'reflective practice'. This is not to deny that there can be reflection-in-action, simply to deny that it exhausts action.

18 Note that by this I mean that research findings are more reliable in themselves, not that their application to particular situations will necessarily be more reliable than the local knowledge and judgements of practitioners.

19 The typology of the sorts of inquiry I have outlined here is not intended to be exhaustive. For instance, I recognise that there are those who are employed as researchers (and are therefore specialists) whose primary responsibility and orientation is towards the provision of directly and specifically relevant information; much market research is of this kind.

20 See Burgess (1980) for a discussion of some of these problems in the context of teachers-as-researchers.

21 For an extended discussion of 'insider arguments', see Merton (1972).

22 An issue I shall not address here is whether the exercise of power is always exploitative; in other words whether power is always zero-sum. This seems to be assumed by the critics. At the very least, however, this is not a foregone conclusion (Parsons 1967). For a discussion of this and other issues surrounding the concept of power, see Philp (1985).

23 It is worth adding that this variety of motives, good and bad, and the distinction between motives and functions applies just as much to practitioners as to researchers.

24 Some will reject the distinction I have drawn here between political action and research. However, I am not making a general claim that research is not political. The distinction hinges on the fact that research, on the model I outlined earlier, is concerned most immediately with producing knowledge (albeit knowledge that is relevant to practice); whereas political action is immediately concerned with preserving or changing social arrangements.

25 See, for example, Carr and Kemmis (1986) and Pollard and Tann (1987). Also, Roth's discussion of 'ethnographic democracy' in the literature on anthropological rhetoric (Roth 1989).

26 This also points to the limited circulation publication that most research reports enjoy.

27 Of course, deciding whether a study falls into this category will require the exercise of judgement and must take into account its purposes and circumstances. Moreover, such judgements are often likely to be open to some degree of reasonable disagreement.

28 See the useful discussion in Cranston (1967: ch.1).

Part III

QUALITATIVE VERSUS QUANTITATIVE METHOD

9

DECONSTRUCTING THE QUALITATIVE–QUANTITATIVE DIVIDE[1]

In this chapter I want to challenge the widely held idea that there are two methodological paradigms in social research: the quantitative and the qualitative. This idea seems to have become a matter of consensus over the past few years among many who see themselves on one side of this divide or the other (and even amongst those who wish to sit astride it). I shall argue, however, that the distinction between qualitative and quantitative is of limited use and, indeed, carries some danger.

It is striking how prone we are to the use of dichotomies, and how these often come to represent distillations of all that is good and bad. 'Qualitative' and 'quantitative' are sometimes used to represent fundamentally opposed approaches to the study of the social world, one representing the true way, the other the work of the devil (see, for example, Filstead 1970). But even where the evaluative overtones are absent and the two approaches are given parity, the distinction is still misleading in my view because it obscures the breadth of issues and arguments involved in the methodology of social research.

In one form or another the debate about quantitative and qualitative research has been taking place since at least the mid-nineteenth century. At that time there was much argument about the scientific status of history and the social sciences, with quantification often being seen as one of the key features of natural science.[2] Similarly, in US sociology in the 1920s and 1930s there was a dispute between advocates of case study and statistical method. Many of the claims made about quantitative and qualitative method today have their origins in these earlier debates (see Hammersley 1989a). By the 1940s and 1950s, in sociology, psychology and some other fields, quantitative method (in the

159

form of survey and experimental research) had become the dominant approach. However, since the 1960s, there has been a revival in the fortunes of qualitative types of research in these disciplines, to the point where their legitimacy is widely accepted.[3] In some areas this has led to a *détente* (Rist 1977; Smith and Heshusius 1986) and to increased interest in the combination or even integration of quantitative and qualitative. But such talk still preserves the dichotomy. And it seems to me that in some respects *détente* is worse than cold war. In learning to live and let live there is the danger that we will all quietly forget the methodological disagreements that we should be tackling.[4]

What I am recommending, then, is not that we should revert from two paradigms to one, in such a way as to deny the variety of ideas, strategies and techniques to be found in social research. Quite the reverse. My aim is to show that this diversity cannot be encapsulated within two (or, for that matter, three, four or more) paradigms. Nor should the variety of approach be regarded as stemming simply from fundamental philosophical or political commitments. Arguments about the latter are, and should be, important in methodology. However, they are not the only considerations that are significant; the particular purposes of the research and the practicality of various strategies given the circumstances in which the inquiry is to be carried out are others. Nor do philosophical and political assumptions have the sort of determinate implications for method that they are sometimes assumed to have.[5]

What I want to do in this chapter is to identify the various component meanings of the qualitative–quantitative distinction, particularly as used by advocates of qualitative research. I shall argue that these issues are not as simple or as closely related as is sometimes believed. I have identified seven such issues here. There may be others, but these are probably the main ones:

1 qualitative versus quantitative data;
2 the investigation of natural versus artificial settings;
3 a focus on meanings rather than behaviour;
4 adoption or rejection of natural science as a model;
5 an inductive versus a deductive approach;
6 identifying cultural patterns as against seeking scientific laws;
7 idealism versus realism.

1 QUALITATIVE VERSUS QUANTITATIVE DATA

In their book on qualitative analysis Miles and Huberman characterise the distinction between qualitative and quantitative research in terms of the use of words rather than numbers (Miles and Huberman 1984: 15). While it is rare to find such an interpretation spelled out so clearly, it seems to underlie much talk of qualitative method. And it is true that research reports do differ sharply in the extent to which tables and statistical analysis, on the one hand, and verbal descriptions and explanations, on the other, predominate. At the same time, a large proportion of research reports (including many that are regarded as qualitative) combine the two, to varying degrees. More importantly, though, the fact that this is not a very satisfactory basis for the distinction between qualitative and quantitative is illustrated by an exchange that took place in US sociology in the 1930s, between Znaniecki (an advocate of case study) and Lundberg (a positivistic supporter of statistical method). Znaniecki had written a book in which he largely dismissed the use of statistical techniques in sociology. Here is how Lundberg replies to him:

> The current idea seems to be that if one uses pencil and paper, especially squared paper, and if one uses numerical symbols, especially Arabic notation, one is using quantitative methods. If, however, one discusses masses of data with concepts of 'more' or 'less' instead of formal numbers, and if one indulges in the most complicated correlations but without algebraic symbols, then one is *not* using quantitative methods.
>
> A striking illustration from a recent book by a prominent sociologist will make the point clear. After a discussion of the lamentable limitations of statistical methods, the author appends this remarkable footnote: 'Wherever the statistical method definitely gains the ascendancy, the number of students of a high intellectual level who are attracted to sociology tends to fall off considerably' (Znaniecki 1934: 235). In short, this author finally reverts to a statistical proof of the deplorable effects of statistics.
>
> (Lundberg 1964: 59–60)

It has frequently been pointed out that ethnographers regularly make quantitative claims in verbal form, using formulations like

161

'regularly', 'frequently', 'often', 'sometimes', 'generally', 'in the main', 'typically', 'not atypically' etc. And it is fairly obvious, I think, that (as Lundberg indicates) the form in which such claims are made makes no difference to their character.

The contrast between words and numbers does not get us very far, then. But there is an important sort of variation in the nature of data that is not unrelated to the word/number contrast. When quantitative researchers criticise ethnographers' use of words rather than numbers, what is usually at issue is precision. They are arguing that ethnographers are insufficiently precise in their claims, and that the necessary precision requires quantification.

Still, we must ask what precision is, and whether the most precise formulations are always the best; or, indeed, whether they are always necessary. Also I think it is clear that precision does not necessarily mean numbers. For example, where we are concerned with the presence or absence of a particular type of feature in a situation, this can be described quite precisely without the use of numbers. It is also important to remember that precision is not the only virtue in description and measurement. Accuracy is usually even more important; and it is widely recognised that we should not express our findings in terms that imply a greater degree of precision than their likely accuracy warrants. For instance, to report findings to six figures of decimals is rarely if ever justified in social research. It follows from this that sometimes it may not be legitimate to use terms that are more precise than 'sometimes', 'often', 'generally' etc.[6] Handlin (1979: 11–12) provides an illustration of this from history:

> I cannot wholly agree that historical problems that hinge on the question 'how many?' are always better solved by numeri-cal answers. The more precise statement is not always the more accurate one. In 1813 John Adams tried to estimate how many colonists were for independence and hazarded various guesses – nearly equally divided; a third; five to two. It would no doubt be more precise to be able to say 39 percent were for, 31 percent against, and 30 percent neutral, or to plant a good solid decimal point with a long series of digits behind it. But it would be less accurate to do so, for the data does not support that degree of refinement.

Furthermore, while increased precision may often be of value, it is not always so. It may not be of value because the level of precision already achieved is sufficient for our purposes, or because the likely costs of achieving greater precision are greater than the probable benefits. The latter is an especially important point in the context of case study research, where a relatively wide focus is adopted. Given fixed resources, the attempt to make any part of the picture more precise will necessarily tend to reduce the width of focus that is possible. The researcher must judge whether the benefits of this outweigh the costs, and sometimes they will not. Equally, though, on other occasions they will; and more precise, even numerical, descriptions will be appropriate.[7]

We are not faced, then, with a stark choice between words and numbers, or even between precise and imprecise data; but rather with a range from more to less precise data. Furthermore, our decisions about what level of precision is appropriate in relation to any particular claim should depend on the nature of what we are trying to describe, on the likely accuracy of our descriptions, on our purposes, and on the resources available to us; not on ideological commitment to one methodological paradigm or another.

2 INVESTIGATION OF 'NATURAL' VERSUS 'ARTIFICIAL' SETTINGS

A second interpretation of the qualitative–quantitative distinction focuses on the nature of the phenomenon investigated: whether it is 'naturally occurring' or has been created by the researcher. The sharpest contrast here is between experiments and ethnographic research. The former involves study of a situation especially established by the researcher, probably using volunteer subjects, and designed to capture different values of some theoretical variables while controlling relevant extraneous variables. Ethnographic research, on the other hand, requires the study of situations that would have occurred without the ethnogapher's presence, and the adoption of a role in that situation designed to minimise the researcher's impact on what occurs. In common parlance, experimenters study 'artificial' settings, while ethnographers study 'natural' settings; and the implication is that only the latter is worth while because it is 'natural' behaviour we are concerned to understand.

The charge of artificiality may also be directed at formal, structured interviews of the kind used by survey researchers. These may be contrasted with unstructured and/or informal interviews, where the interviewer plays a less dominant role. While the latter do not represent an entirely 'natural' setting, it is often argued that their closeness to ordinary conversation renders them approximations to the natural.

In my view this distinction between natural and artificial settings is spurious. What happens in a school class or in a court of law, for example, is no more natural (or artificial) than what goes on in a social psychological laboratory. To treat classrooms or courtrooms as natural and experiments as artificial is to forget that social research is itself part of the social world, something that should never be forgotten.

Once again, though, there is an important issue implicit in this distinction: variation in the degree to which the researcher shapes the data. There is a trade-off between, on the one hand, trying to make sure that one gets the relevant data (in the most efficient manner possible) and, on the other hand, the danger of reactivity, of influencing the people studied in such a way that error is introduced into the data. It has long been a criticism of experiments that their findings do not generalise to the 'real world' (that is, to non-experimental situations) because people's behaviour is shaped by their awareness of the experimental situation, and by the personal characteristics of the experimenter (or her/his assistants). Similarly, structured interviews have been criticised because we cannot generalise from what is said in them to what is said and done elsewhere.[8] However, while there is some truth in these arguments, they by no means render the results of research using 'artificial' methods of no value. Much depends on whether the reactivity affects the results in ways that are relevant to the research topic and in ways that cannot be allowed for. All research is subject to potential error of one kind or another. Indeed, even ethnographic research in 'natural' settings is not immune to reactivity. While the ethnographer may strive to minimise her or his effects on the situation studied, no one can guarantee this; and sometimes the effects can be significant despite the researcher's best efforts. Also, we must remember what the significance of reactivity is: it makes the setting investigated unrepresentative of those about which the researcher wishes to generalise, an issue sometimes referred to as ecological invalidity. But reactivity is not the only source of ecological invalidity. Even without reactivity, a natural setting can be unrepresentative because it differs in important ways from most other cases in the same category. Simply choosing to investigate natural settings, and seeking to adopt a low profile in them, does not ensure ecological validity.[9]

For these reasons the distinction between natural and artificial settings does not provide a sound basis for the qualitative–quantitative distinction. The terms 'natural' and 'artificial' have misleading connotations. And, while the issue of ecological validity is important, it is not the only important methodological issue. Nor does research in 'natural' settings guarantee ecological validity, any more than research in 'artificial' settings automatically debars us from it.

3 A FOCUS ON MEANINGS VERSUS A FOCUS ON BEHAVIOUR

This component of the qualitative–quantitative distinction emphasises the interpretative or hermeneutic character of qualitative research. Of all the issues discussed in this chapter, this one links most obviously back to nineteenth-century debates about the difference between natural science and history, as well as to twentieth-century disputes such as that surrounding behaviourism.

It is sometimes suggested that the central goal of qualitative research is to document the world from the point of view of the people studied (from the native point of view, in Malinowski's terms), rather than presenting it from the perspective of the researcher. And it is true that qualitative research does seek to understand the perspectives of the people studied, on the grounds that this is essential if we are to describe and explain their behaviour effectively. However, it is very rare for qualitative research to restrict itself to documenting the native point of view. And there are good reasons for not doing this; not the least of which is that the people studied can often do this for themselves! Even those approaches that restrict the research focus to participants' perspectives do not simply reproduce these, but seek to analyse their structure and/or production in ways that are likely to be alien to the people studied. This is true, for example, of both ethnosemantics and ethnomethodology. But, as I have said, most qualitative research does not restrict its focus this narrowly. It seeks to describe and explain both perspectives *and* behaviour, recognising that the latter does not merely flow from the former, and may even be discrepant with it. Indeed, such ironic discrepancies have been a major focus for qualitative research (see, for example, Keddie 1971, Sharp and Green 1975, and Willis 1977).

Conversely, much quantitative research is concerned with attitudes rather than simply with behaviour. Advocates of an interpretative approach may argue that attitude research effectively studies attitudes as behaviour displayed in response to interview questions. Yet, critiques of behaviourism emphasise that it is not possible to study human behaviour without attributing meanings to it, and that behaviourists routinely do this despite themselves. Given this fact, it seems that attitude researchers cannot but be studying 'meanings'. Moreover, most attitude researchers do not operate on the basis of a strict behaviourism.

It is still true of course that there are differences between attitude researchers and qualitative sociologists, both in how they conceptualise the meanings held to underlie behaviour, and in how they seek to identify those meanings. Even here, though, the differences are not as great as is sometimes suggested. It is common for ethnographers to ascribe perspectives or definitions of the situation to the people they study, and it is not clear how these differ in character from attitudes. Ethnographers may stress that they do not assume a mechanical relationship between attitude and behaviour. However, the more contingent is the relationship between perspective and behaviour, the less value perspectives have as explanatory factors. So this is not an argument that ethnographers can pursue very far without undercutting the rationale for their own hermeneutic approach.

As regards differences in the approach that attitude researchers and ethnographers employ in identifying attitudes/perspectives, the contrast is between the use of attitude scales and more unstructured approaches. As such, it reduces to the two distinctions I have already discussed, and to the distinction between inductive and deductive approaches that I shall deal with below. Here again, though, we do not have a clear-cut distinction between two contrasting approaches.

4 NATURAL SCIENCE AS A MODEL

It is common for quantitative method to be criticised for taking natural science as its model. It is worth noting, however, that advocates of qualitative method have sometimes themselves regarded the natural sciences as exemplary. Thomas and Znaniecki, two of the most influential advocates of case study and life history methods in the 1920s and 1930s, make the following comment at the beginning of their study of *The Polish Peasant in Poland and America*:

> The marvellous results attained by rational technique (that is, by science and technology) in the sphere of material reality invite us to apply some analogous procedure to social reality. Our success in controlling nature gives us confidence that we shall eventually be able to control the social world in the same measure.
>
> (Thomas and Znaniecki 1927: 1)

Nor were Thomas and Znaniecki unusual in holding this view. While he was uncertain about the chances of its achievement, Herbert Blumer was also committed, at least in the 1920s and early 1930s, to the pursuit of a science of society modelled on the natural sciences. Much the same was true in social anthropology. Boas, Malinowski and Radcliffe-Brown all took the natural sciences as a paradigm for their approach to the study of 'primitive' societies; though as in the case of Blumer and other Chicago sociologists this was tempered with ideas about the distinctiveness of social phenomena (Hammersley 1989a).

From a historical point of view, then, differences in attitude to natural science do not seem to map on to the distinction between quantitative and qualitative research in a straightforward way. And, even today, there are advocates of qualitative method who justify their approach precisely on the basis of its similarity to that of natural scientists.[10]

What this highlights is that the issue of whether natural science is an appropriate model for social research is not a simple one. There are at least three complications.

(a) We must consider *which* natural science we are taking as the model, and during which period of its development. There are significant differences, for example, between physics and biology; and, indeed, *within* each natural science discipline over time.

(b) Which *interpretation* of the methods of natural science is to be adopted? Keat and Urry (1975) identify positivist, conventionalist and realist interpretations of physics; and even these distinctions do not exhaust the variety of views to be found among philosophers of science.

(c) What aspects of natural science method are to be treated as generic? Not even the most extreme positivist would argue that the methods of physics should be applied lock, stock and barrel to the study of the social world. And there are few who would insist that there is no aspect of natural science method that is relevant to social research. What is involved here is a matter of degree.

Once again, we have a complex set of considerations that resist reduction to a simple contrast.

5 INDUCTIVE VERSUS DEDUCTIVE APPROACHES

It is common for qualitative researchers to contrast their own inductive approach with the deductive, or hypothetico-deductive, method of quantitative research. Here too, though, we have an over-simplification. Not all quantitative research is concerned with hypothesis-testing. Many surveys are straightforwardly descriptive, and some quantitative research is explicitly concerned with theory-generation. Equally, by no means all ethnographers reject the hypothetico-deductive method.[11] Indeed, it seems to me that all research involves both deduction and induction in the broad senses of those terms; in all research we move from ideas to data as well as from data to ideas. What *is* true is that one can distinguish between studies that are primarily exploratory, being concerned with generating theoretical ideas, and those which are more concerned with testing hypotheses. But these types of research are not alternatives; we need both. Nor need the former be quantitative and the latter qualitative.

A common version of the inductive versus deductive contrast is built into advocacy of *Verstehen* or understanding, as opposed to forms of explanation that rely on observation of the external features of human behaviour. Here again we have a link back to nineteenth-century debates.[12] In its most extreme formulation, *Verstehen* involves some kind of direct contact with the experience of others, or a re-living of it on the basis of one's own experience. Some versions place great importance on the nature of the relationship between researcher and researched, perhaps regarding equality as essential if understanding is to occur (Reinharz 1983).

But while there is no doubt that it is important in research to take account of one's own cultural assumptions and to open them up to possible disconfirmation, the idea that *Verstehen* involves direct contact with social reality or with other people must be rejected. We can never entirely escape our own assumptions about the world.[13] And even in face-to-face contact with people with whom we share a lot, we are not given knowledge that is necessarily beyond reasonable doubt. As has often been stressed in the ethnographic literature, there are advantages and disadvantages to closeness. On the one hand, it may provide us with inside information that we would otherwise not gain, both about what happens and about people's experiences of events. On the other hand, through a process of over-rapport we may come to take over false assumptions held by the people we are studying, and become unable to see the world in any other way than that in which it appears to them. Only if we assume that the perspectives of those we are studying necessarily embody genuine knowledge about the world is over-rapport not a danger. And in my view no individual or group has such a monopoly on truth.

From this point of view, then, we cannot but rely on constructing hypotheses, assessing them against experience and modifying them where necessary. This is true whether we engage in hypothesis-testing in a formal, explicit and narrow way that involves subjecting hypotheses to crucial tests; or whether we adopt a more informal and broader approach in which we sacrifice some of the sharpness of the test in order to allow more of our assumptions to be thrown open to challenge. Furthermore, which of these approaches is most appropriate should depend on our purposes, and the stage that our research has reached, not on paradigmatic commitments.

6 IDENTIFYING CULTURAL PATTERNS VERSUS SEEKING SCIENTIFIC LAWS

Following on from the contrast between qualitative and quantitative approaches in terms of a commitment to the model of natural science is the idea that these approaches differ in their goals. Quantitative research is often believed to be committed to the discovery of scientific laws; whereas qualitative research is concerned with identifying cultural patterns. However, as I pointed out in the previous section, much quantitative research is concerned with description rather than with theory development and testing. And, indeed, rather more survey research may *appear* to be concerned with discovering theoretical laws than is actually the case because survey researchers sometimes fail to distinguish between this goal and that of explaining particular events or relationships.[14]

Similarly, while it is common these days for qualitative researchers to deny the possibility of scientific laws, this was not always so. In the early decades of the twentieth century case study researchers often justified their approach on the grounds that it could produce laws, whereas statistical method could produce only probabilistic generalisations (Blumer 1928; Znaniecki 1934). Even today qualitative researchers often claim that their goal is theory rather than the mere description of cultural patterns. And sometimes the concept of theory involved seems to be not far removed from that characteristic of survey research; though it should be said that there is considerable uncertainty about the precise nature of ethnographic theory (see Chapters 1 and 2).

7 IDEALISM VERSUS REALISM

At the most abstract philosophical level it has been claimed that qualitative and quantitative researchers are committed to different epistemological positions. A clear example of this argument is to be found in the writings of John K. Smith (Smith 1984 and 1989a; Smith and Heshusius 1986). He argues that quantitative research is wedded to a realist epistemology in the sense of assuming that true accounts correspond to how things really are and that competing accounts must be judged in terms of whether the procedures adopted ensure accurate representation of reality. By contrast, qualitative method is idealist, he claims, in that it rejects any possibility of representing reality. It recognises that there may be 'as many realities as there are persons' (Smith 1984: 386).

I think it can be shown with little difficulty that this characterisation is inaccurate empirically. First, not all quantitative researchers are realists. Take the following quotation:

> In any valid epistemological or scientific sense we must say that the substitution of a Copernican for the Ptolemaic theory of the universe represented a major change in the universe. To say that it was not the universe but our concep-

tion of it which changed is merely a verbal trick designed to lead the unwary into the philosophical quagmires of Platonic realism, for obviously the only universe with which science can deal is 'our conception' of it.

What we have here is an idealist account of natural science knowledge in which there is a denial that it can represent some independent reality. But it does not come from a qualitative researcher. It comes from George Lundberg again, positivist advocate of quantitative method in the 1930s, 1940s and 1950s (Lundberg 1933: 309). There was a strong element of phenomenalism in late nineteenth- and twentieth-century positivism, and Lundberg's anti-realism reflects this. By contrast Herbert Blumer's influential concept of naturalistic method is quite clearly realist in character: he talks of research being concerned with discovering the nature of social reality, of tearing away the veil of our preconceptions so that we may see it (Hammersley 1989a). In more recent times Harré has based his advocacy and practice of qualitative research in social psychology on an explicit realism.[15] And, indeed, the reliance of ethnography on realism has come under increasing criticism, for example from those influenced by post-structuralism (Tyler 1985; Clifford and Marcus 1986; Plummer 1990; and Denzin 1990).

More important than the empirical question of whether it is true that quantitative researchers are realists and qualitative researchers idealists, though, is the philosophical issue of whether there is any necessary connection between qualitative method and a particular epistemological position. Smith does not offer any support for this argument beyond his claim that qualitative research is founded on a relativistic idealism. He accepts the self-refuting character of relativism and that relativists' defences against this criticism are inadequate. What he fails to do, above all, however, is to recognise that in dealing with the philosophical issues that underlie social research we are not faced with a stark choice between naïve realism or empiricism on the one hand and idealism or relativism on the other. Indeed, some of the literature he cites, such as the work of Putnam (1981), is precisely concerned with constructing a more subtle form of realism that is immune to the criticisms of anti-realists. In epistemology, as in methodology, dichotomies obscure the range of options open to us.

CONCLUSION

In this chapter I have looked at some of the components of the conventional distinction between qualitative and quantitative method. In each case I have argued that what is involved is not a simple contrast between two opposed standpoints, but a range of positions sometimes located on more than one dimension. It should also be clear, I think, that there is no necessary relationship between adopting a particular position on one issue and specific positions on the others. Many combinations are quite reasonable. Furthermore, I emphasised that selection among these positions ought often to depend on the purposes and circumstances of the research, rather than being derived from methodological or philosophical commitments. This is because there are trade-offs involved. For instance, if we seek greater precision we are likely to sacrifice some breadth of description; and vice versa. And the costs and benefits of various trade-off positions will vary according to the particular goals and circumstances of the research being pursued.

What all this implies is that the distinction between quantitative and qualitative approaches does not capture the full range of options that we face; and that it misrepresents the basis on which decisions should be made. What is involved is not a cross-roads where we have to go left or right. A better analogy is a complex maze where we are repeatedly faced with decisions, and where paths wind back on one another. The prevalence of the distinction between qualitative and quantitative method tends to obscure the complexity of the problems that face us and threatens to render our decisions less effective than they might otherwise be.

NOTES

1 My use of the term 'deconstructing' in the title of this chapter is no more than a rhetorical flourish; my philosophical assumptions are very different from those of deconstructionists. However, given their views about meaning, they can have no justifiable complaint against my theft of this term! For an excellent discussion of Derrida see Dews (1987); and for a sustained critique of deconstructionism see Ellis (1989).

2 This debate has persisted within history, indeed it has intensified in recent years as a result of the growth of 'cliometrics'. For contrasting perspectives on this development see Fogel and Elton (1983).

3 For a useful discussion of the current state of this debate in sociology, see Bryman (1988).

4 To this extent I am in agreement with Smith and Heshusius, but I disagree with much of the rest of what they say. In my view the commitment to paradigms, in whatever form, tends to close down the debate rather than keep it open. See Chapter 9.

5 This is illustrated by the debates about methodology among Marxists and feminists. See, for example, the debate about Marxism and method in *Berkeley Journal of Sociology* XXXIV 1989, especially the articles by Wright and Burawoy. On feminism and method, see the very different views expressed by Mies, Jayaratne, Reinharz, and Stanley and Wise in Bowles and Klein (1983).

6 My own use of imprecise formulations will not be lost on the reader!

7 There is also the practical question of how much precision is possible. While I would not want to suggest any insuperable barriers to increased precision of measurement of social phenomena, there is no doubt that as things presently stand there are severe practical limits to the level of combined precision and accuracy that can be achieved in many areas of social science.

8 In some respects this is a misleading argument since it fails to draw the necessary distinction between, on the one hand, inferring from what people do in interviews to what they do elsewhere, and, on the other, the question of the truth of what people say in interviews about what they and others do elsewhere. See the discussion of this in Chapter 3.

9 Equally, it is worth noting that some quantitative researchers carry out their research in natural settings, notably in the form of systematic observational research: see McCall (1984) and Croll (1986).

10 See, for example, the work of Harré: Harré (1970), Harré and Secord (1972).

11 On exploratory quantitative analysis, see Baldamus (1979) for an example; Erickson and Nosanchuk (1979) for techniques. Some practitioners of analytic induction (such as Lindesmith 1968) and of grounded theorising (Strauss 1987) explicitly equate their approach with the hypothetico-deductive method.

12 Platt (1985) points out that Weber's discussion of *Verstehen* seems to have had little influence on early qualitative researchers. However, Weber drew the concept from earlier nineteenth-century discussions, notably those of Dilthey, and these did have an influence on Chicago sociologists; both directly, and indirectly through Windelband, Rickert and Simmel for example. It also seems likely that Cooley, who was quite influential on the Chicagoans, drew his concept of sympathetic introspection from the German Romantics.

13 This is the conclusion of more sophisticated versions of hermeneutics, notably that of Gadamer.

14 On this distinction, see Chapters 2 and 10.

15 See note 7, above.

10

THE LOGIC OF
THEORY-TESTING
IN CASE STUDY RESEARCH

In an influential article entitled 'Case study and situational analysis', Clyde Mitchell has argued that since the early 1950s there have been major developments in survey research techniques, but that there has been little parallel development in 'the epistemology of the case study' (Mitchell 1983: 188). His article is an attempt to remedy this, by outlining the nature of case study analysis and showing that it constitutes a 'reliable and respectable' procedure (p.207). Mitchell argues that much criticism of case study research, and in particular the claim that it is invalid because it seeks to generalise from a single case, is based on the misconception that case study and survey research use the same basis for extrapolating from data to theory. This is a misconception, Mitchell claims, because while survey research uses two types of inference, statistical inference from sample to population and logical inference about necessary or logical relationships among features within a case, case study research relies entirely upon logical inference:

> The validity of the extrapolation (in case study analysis) depends not on the typicality or representativeness of the case but on the cogency of the theoretical reasoning.
>
> (Mitchell 1983: 207)

I want to challenge this argument by suggesting that there is no difference between case study and survey research in what is required to test theoretical claims, and that in *neither* type of research does either statistical or logical inference provide a basis for extrapolation from the case(s) studied to conclusions about the validity of a theory. I shall begin by discussing the role of statistical inference in theory development and testing, before turning to logical inference and sketching an alternative view of the process of theoretical inquiry.

STATISTICAL INFERENCE

It seems to me that Mitchell seriously over-estimates the extent to which developments in statistical techniques have facilitated the process of theory testing in survey research. He claims that:

> Hand in hand with the steady strides in the sophistication of statistical techniques a theory of sampling soundly based on probability mathematics has grown up so that the survey analyst has available an extensive armamentarium of procedures and techniques all resting on firm epistemological grounds.
>
> (Mitchell 1983: 188)

Mitchell himself notes that correlations do not prove causality, and this obviously limits the role of statistical techniques, especially when applied to non-experimental data. But over and above this, probability sampling is inapplicable to the problem of selecting cases for study so as to test theory. While the latter *is* a sampling problem, it is *not* one to which statistical sampling techniques can be applied. This is because the population concerned is infinite: it consists of all past, present and future instances to which the theory claims to apply (Camilleri 1962; Willer 1967; Freese 1980). Probability theory is only applicable where we are generalising from samples to finite populations.

As a result of this, the role of statistical sampling techniques in survey research is limited to generalisation *within* cases, since then the population is likely to be finite. For example, if we were testing a theory about the political culture of a particular type of nation, we could use probability methods to draw samples from the adult populations of each of the countries selected as cases. Even then we might want to question whether the attitudes of individuals are the constituents of political cultures and/or whether all individuals are of equal weight in representing the political culture of a nation (Galtung 1967). But putting these theoretical issues aside, it is possible in principle to apply statistical sampling techniques to this kind of generalisation within cases. However, one should not use these techniques to select the nations to be studied since the theory relates to *all* nations of the type concerned, not just those that have existed and currently exist, and, therefore, to an infinite population.

At the same time, it is important to notice that sampling theory is applicable in precisely the same limited way to case study research. If one is studying a single school or a local community in order to test a theory about school or community processes, and one wishes to generalise about, say, all pupils in the school or all adults in the community, then one could use statistical sampling techniques to generalise from an appropriately drawn sample to the relevant population. This is an area where case studies are sometimes weak, making generalisations within cases of this kind without either studying all the individuals involved or drawing a sample in such a way that there is a reasonable chance of it being representative.[1] Here also, though, statistical techniques cannot be used in selecting the case, or cases, for study.

My first point, then, is that statistical sampling theory is not applicable to the problem of generalising from cases studied to cases relevant to a theory, *in either survey or case study research.* While the problem *is* one of empirical inference or generalisation, it cannot be dealt with by statistical techniques. It is, in fact, the problem of induction and has exercised philosophers for centuries, but no generally accepted solution to it has yet been found (Chalmers 1978; Black 1967). On the other hand, statistical sampling techniques can and should be used, wherever appropriate, for generalising *within* cases, in both survey and case study research.

LOGICAL INFERENCE

I want now to turn to the role of logical inference. It is not entirely clear what Mitchell means by this term, but he seems to have in mind some process whereby theoretical relationships among phenomena can be induced from detailed investigation of a single or a small number of cases:

the process of inference from case studies is only logical or causal and cannot be statistical .... We infer that the features present in the case study will be related in a wider population not because the case is representative but because our analy-

sis is unassailable. The emphasis [is] on case studies used to
relate theoretically relevant characteristics reflected in the
case to one another in a logically coherent way.

(Mitchell 1983: 200)

It seems to be assumed here that necessary relationships among
phenomena can be inferred in some determinate way from the
observation of temporal relationships among events in a setting:

The extended case study enables the analyst to trace how
events chain on to one another and how therefore events are
necessarily linked to one another through time.

(Mitchell 1983: 194)

This is a strong interpretation of 'logical inference' in which it is a
process of induction from particulars to universals. However,
Mitchell sometimes uses the term in a weaker sense to refer merely
to the identification of *plausible* relationships:

The inference about the *logical* relationship between the two
characteristics is not based upon the representativeness of
the sample and therefore upon its typicality, but rather upon
the plausibility or upon the logicality of the nexus between
the two characteristics.

(Mitchell 1983: 198)

The strong interpretation of 'logical inference', if it were legitimate, would provide a basis for sound extrapolation. The weak
interpretation does not. Judging a theory plausible is not a test of
it, since there may be many competing plausible explanations. We
need evidence to show that it is the *most* plausible of those available
and that it is sufficiently plausible to be accepted.

Mitchell bases his distinction between logical and statistical
inference on Znaniecki's contrast between enumerative and
analytic induction (Znaniecki 1934). Znaniecki's argument for the
importance of analytic induction seems to involve the following
steps:

(a) all concrete objects are descriptively inexhaustible, so selective
description of their characteristics is essential;
(b) the criteria for this selection are provided by the participation
of these objects in semi-closed systems of various kinds, and the
sociologist is interested in social, and more generally, cultural
systems;

(c) the essential characteristics of the class or classes of phenomena involved in a particular closed system can be identified neither by deductive processes (through identifying the class *a priori*), nor by enumerative induction (studying the superficial characteristics of objects belonging to a predefined class). They can only be discovered by analytic induction. This involves in-depth study of one or a small number of cases, and identification of the functional relationships among the characteristics of each case.

Znaniecki seeks to justify the need for in-depth study of cases on the grounds that physical scientists typically study a small number of individual cases in detail, rather than trying to derive theory from multi-variate analysis of a large number of cases. And he regards analytic induction as the method of science *par excellence*.

A similar view of the research process has been put forward by Lindesmith (1968) and Cressey (1950 and 1953), and there has been much debate about the relative status of analytic and enumerative induction. Some have argued that the distinction between these two forms of induction is false (Robinson 1951); others that it is correct and important, but that the two approaches are equally valid (Lindesmith 1968), or that they are complementary (Turner 1953). Mitchell's position represents a further variant. As we have seen, he treats survey and case study research as equally valid approaches, but regards survey research as combining both types of inference whereas case study relies on analytic induction alone. In other words, the two forms of inference are complementary in survey research but analytic induction is sufficient in case study. However, Mitchell does not explain why survey research needs both types of inference to test a theory, while case study can succeed with analytic induction alone. Nor does he clarify what analytic induction involves.

The argument that analytic induction allows us to extrapolate from the case studied to all cases of the same type hinges on the cogency of the argument that necessary relationships can be inferred from the patterning of events observed within a case. Mitchell provides no justification for this assumption other than that such a process of inference must be possible since 'most social anthropological and a good deal of sociological theorising has been founded upon case studies' (Mitchell 1983: 197). But this point begs precisely the point it is intended to establish: on what grounds do we assume that this theorising is sound?

Znaniecki discusses the issue at greater length, but he too fails to provide a convincing justification. Curiously, both these authors recognise the key problem with the idea of logical induction: that the process of inference does not have a determinate outcome, that many theoretical principles can be inferred from the same case. Yet they do not offer solutions to the problem.

Znaniecki argues that the identification of the essential features of a case must be on the basis of knowledge of a closed system:

> Thus, when a particular concrete case is being analysed as typical or eidetic, we assume that those traits are essential to it, which determine what it is, are common to and distinctive of all the cases of a class. The essential traits of a given animal are assumed to be common and distinctive of all the animals of a species; those of a physical process, to all processes of a given kind. There are no formal logical difficulties in the way of such an assumption. We are always free to constitute a logical class composed of all the data and only the data possessing the same essential characters of any given particular datum. But there are obvious methodological problems. What is essential about a particular datum? What characters deserve to be abstracted from its concrete complexity and generalised as common to and distinctive of a whole class?
>
> There would be no answer to these questions possible at all, abstraction and consequent generalisation would be entirely arbitrary, if we had to deal with the concreteness of pure empirical reality as given in unprejudiced observation. The existence of relatively closed systems limits this arbitrariness, and makes possible the first and most important step towards analytic induction. Once we have selected a system as object-matter, we know that everything that characterises it, belongs to it, and goes on within it is relatively essential as compared with all the accidental data which, while accompanying its actual existence, are not included or are explicitly excluded from it as irrelevant. While a thermodynamic experiment is going on in a laboratory room, we know which of the objects and processes in this room are relatively essential as belonging to the experiment, and which accidental in the sense of irrelevant; and in describing it we are sure to omit such

179

contemporary phenomena as the chairs and pictures, or a flirtation between ... experimenter and ... secretary. When studying a military regiment as a social group, that which concerns its composition and structure must be regarded as relatively essential as against everything the officers and soldiers are thinking, saying, and doing as private persons without reference to regimental affairs.

(Znaniecki 1934: 252–3)

In much the same way, Mitchell argues that it is theory which provides us with the structure which is essential to induction:

The single case becomes significant only when set against the accumulated experience and knowledge that the analyst brings to it. In other words the extent to which generalisation may be made from case studies depends upon the adequacy of the underlying theory and the whole corpus of related knowledge of which the case is analysed rather than on the particular instance itself.

(Mitchell 1983: 203)

This proposed solution to the problem of the inexhaustibility of description is circular. It will work where we have a well-established theory and are using it to explain a particular event, but we must ask how the validity of that theory was established in the first place. Analytic induction is advocated as a strategy for developing and testing theory, but on this account it presupposes precisely what is supposed to be the goal of the enterprise: a valid theory. The rabbit has been put into the hat.

It seems unlikely that there is a logical solution to the problem of induction (Popper 1968), and neither Znaniecki nor Mitchell provide any reason for thinking otherwise. If this is correct, we cannot extrapolate on logical grounds from the study of a single case, or from the study of a small or a large number of cases, to necessary truths about all cases of a given type.

CONCLUSION

If neither statistical nor logical inference can provide us with a basis for extrapolation from cases studied to all cases relevant to a theory, both survey and case study researchers are left with a problem. In my view it is a problem of generalisation, but not one to which any algorithmic solution is available. There is no basis for demonstrating the certainty of any such generalisation. However, there *are* ways in which we can maximise the confidence we can legitimately have in the truth of a theory. We can do this by subjecting the theory to the severest possible tests, through the way in which we select cases for study. Popper (1968) has outlined the nature of such crucial tests, and Eckstein (1975) briefly applies and elaborates what this implies for case study research in social science. For example, he suggests that:

> in a crucial case it must be extremely difficult, or clearly petulant, to dismiss any finding contrary to theory as simply 'deviant' (due to chance, or the operation of unconsidered factors, or whatever 'deviance' might refer to other than the fact of deviation from theory *per se*), and equally difficult to hold that any finding confirming theory might just as well express quite different regularities.
>
> (Eckstein 1975: 118)

He argues that investigation of both most favourable and least favourable cases for a theory can provide powerful evidence.

The distinction between enumerative and analytic induction has been used to distinguish between different approaches to social research, either to present one as correct and others as inadequate, or to identify them as differentially appropriate or complementary strategies. Mitchell declares that his own argument is that 'in the end the oppositions are more apparent than real' (Mitchell 1983: 208). However, this does not seem to be the implication of his argument. While he treats survey and case study research as equally valid approaches and argues that both use logical inference, he claims that statistical inference is crucial to survey research but unnecessary for case study. This might be taken to imply that case study is a more efficient way of generating and testing theory. Indeed, a superficial reading of his article might lead to the conclusion that while survey research can only produce correlations, case study can provide knowledge of causal relationships. At the very least, though, Mitchell's argument does suggest that the criteria by which the products of the two research strategies are judged should be different.

Against this, I have argued that the process of scientific inquiry, in so far as it is concerned with theory-building, is the same for both survey and case study research, and that neither statistical nor logical inference provides a basis for extrapolation from the cases studied to all cases relevant to a theory. Indeed, there is no source of deterministic inference of this kind available. On the other hand, by selecting cases in such a way as to open the theory up to maximal threat we can provide a basis for increased confidence in the theory if it survives such a test or a series of such tests. Unfortunately, little survey or case study research has taken the problem of testing theory seriously, and as a result there have been few attempts at systematic falsification of this kind. What Eckstein says of the practitioners of macro-politics applies equally to sociology and to case study researchers:

> One may consider it reprehensible that so many comparativists are willing to stop where only that much (i.e. plausibility), or little more, has been accomplished, and then go on to new, still merely plausible, ideas on new subject matter. We certainly have no right to bewail the fact that others do not take up our ideas if we ourselves drop them far short of the point to which they could be taken.
>
> (Eckstein 1975: 110)[2]

There is a tendency to regard survey and case study research as competing research paradigms, with their own standards and strategies, and despite his intentions it seems to me that this is an implication of Mitchell's argument. In my view this is a fundamental error. I believe that the process of inquiry in science is the same whatever method is used, and that the retreat into paradigms effectively stultifies debate and hampers progress.

NOTES

1 Mitchell (1967) and Colson (1967) provide excellent discussions of this issue. It should be remembered, though, that statistical sampling techniques are not the only means by which we may generalise. I address this issue in relation to generalising to larger populations in Chapters 5 and 11.

2 There are, however, some problems facing those who set about the task of systematic theory testing: see Chapter 2. Elsewhere, in Chapter 4, I treat plausibility as one of the means by which we assess the validity of claims. But I agree with Eckstein that judgement of the relative plausibility of a claim in relation to its competitors is only a first step, we must also assess whether the claim is sufficiently plausible or credible for us not to require evidence before treating it as probably valid.

11

SO, WHAT ARE CASE STUDIES?

One of the problems that face us when we try to understand what 'case study' means is that, like a number of other terms used by social scientists ('theory' and 'ideology' are others), it is employed in a wide variety of ways that are often only vaguely characterised. Another, and more difficult, problem arises from the widespread tendency to see research method in terms of contrasting approaches or paradigms involving different epistemological assumptions. A variety of terms are used to make such contrasts: most commonly, 'quantitative' versus 'qualitative' method. The term 'case study' is sometimes implicated in this, being used as a partial synonym for 'qualitative research'. Thus, one of the earliest uses of the term, in US sociology in the 1920s and 1930s, contrasted it with the newly emerging statistical method. There was much debate about which of these two methods was scientific (that is, which was closest to the methods of natural science); though many argued that *both* were legitimate and necessary (Platt 1981; Hammersley 1989a). This was a forerunner of more recent debates about qualitative and quantitative method. Yet, in my view, such simple contrasts are unproductive; even when the different approaches are regarded as complementary. Distinctions between comprehensive alternative research paradigms do not capture the variety of strategies that one finds deployed in social research. Nor are they reasonable philosophically. Epistemological debate among philosophers has not been, and is not today, a dialogue between only two positions; the arguments are more diverse and complex. What this means is that in doing research we are not faced with a fork in the road, with two well-defined alternative routes between which to choose. The research process is more like finding one's way through a maze. And it is a rather badly kept and complex maze; where paths are not always clearly distinct, and also wind back on one another; and where one can never be entirely certain that one has reached the centre. If this is right, then we need a methodological language that gives us rather more guidance about the range of routes that is available at each point in our journey than the conventional dichotomies between alternative approaches provide.[1]

Despite these problems, as currently used the concept of case study captures an important aspect of the decisions we face in research. It highlights, in particular, the choices that we have to make about how many cases to investigate and how these are to be selected. What I mean by the term 'case' here is the phenomenon (located in space/time) about which data are collected and/or analysed, and that corresponds to the type of phenomena to which the main claims of a study relate. Examples of cases can range from micro to macro, all the way from an individual person through a particular event, social situation, organisation or institution, to a national society or international social system.

What I shall recommend is that 'case study' be defined as one case selection strategy among others; the others being experiment and survey.[2] The selection of cases can be distinguished from at least four other general aspects of research design: problem formulation; data collection; data analysis; and reporting the findings.[3] Figure 11.1 summarises these distinctions.

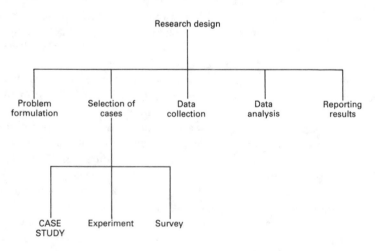

Figure 11.1 Case study as one case selection strategy

What I am proposing, then, is a narrower definition of the term 'case study' than is conventional. There is no implication here that case studies always involve the use of participant observation, the collection and analysis of qualitative rather than quantitative data, that they focus on meaning rather than behaviour, or that case study inquiry is inductive or idiographic rather than deductive or nomothetic etc.[4] Nor do I believe that case studies display a distinctive logic that sets them apart from surveys and experiments.[5] As I shall try to show, the same methodological issues apply to all three; the different strategies simply vary in how they deal with these issues. From this point of view, each of these strategies might often be usable to pursue the same research problem, though they would have varying advantages and disadvantages, depending on the purposes and circumstances of the research.[6]

Given that I have identified 'case study' as one of three case selection strategies, a good way to set the stage for defining it is to clarify what I mean by 'experiment' and 'survey'. What is distinctive about an experiment, in my view, is that the researcher creates the cases to be studied through the manipulation of the research situation, thereby controlling theoretical and at least some relevant extraneous variables. The distinctiveness of surveys is that they involve the simultaneous selection for study of a relatively large number of naturally occurring cases. From this perspective, case study combines some features of these other two strategies. It involves the investigation of a *relatively small* number of *naturally occurring* (rather than researcher-created) cases.[7]

A number of implications follow from defining case study in this way, and I shall be concerned with these in the remainder of this chapter. They underline the problems that we face in doing case study research and the strategies open to us in dealing with these. They can be discussed most usefully, I think, by pursuing a little further the contrast between case study and the other two case selection strategies. My discussion will be based on the assumption that in selecting one rather than another of these strategies we are usually faced with trade-offs. We can never have everything we want, and usually we can only get more of one thing at the expense of getting less of something else. Given this, it seems to me that our choice of case selection strategy should be determined by our judgement of the resulting gains and losses in the light of the particular goals and circumstances of our research, including the resources available.

185

CASE STUDIES AND SURVEYS

Let me begin, then, by comparing case study with the survey. Here, I suggest, the choice of case study involves buying greater detail and likely accuracy of information about particular cases at the cost of being less able to make effective generalisations to a larger population of cases.[8] I can illustrate the relationship between the case study and the survey with a diagram (see Figure 11.2).

It is worth noting two things about Figure 11.2. First, the difference between case studies and surveys is a matter of degree. We have a gradient or dimension here, not a dichotomy. As the number of cases investigated is reduced, the amount of detail that can be collected on each case is increased, and the chances of there being error in the information probably reduces too. As this happens, we shift imperceptibly from survey to case study.[9]

Of course, this trade-off is relative to the relationship between resource demands and the resources available. An investigation focusing on relatively small and easily accessible cases and/or having a relatively high level of resources (more researchers, more

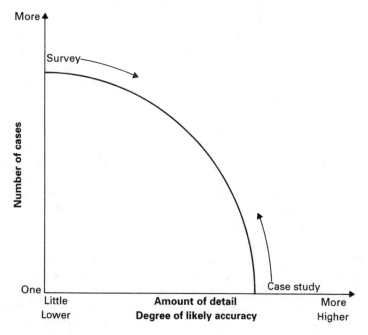

Figure 11.2 Relationship between survey and case study

186

time etc.) would be able to study more cases in more detail than one focusing on geographically and/or temporally large cases and/or having less resources.[10] The effect of these factors in terms of the diagram is to move the curve outwards or inwards, but not to change its shape. The trade-off remains whatever the level of resource demands and resources available.

This leads me to the second point I want to make. It might be thought that with lavish resources we would be able to maximise both the number of cases studied and the detail and accuracy of the information available. This would only be true, however, if there were finite end-points to the two dimensions in the diagram. As we shall see, at best this is likely to be true only under certain conditions.

Let me deal with the possibility of a maximum amount of detail first. It is sometimes thought that case study involves the representation of a case in unique and concrete terms; perhaps involving its reproduction or evocation. The assumption is that the phenomenon is a coherent entity with its own inner logic.[11] However, this is misleading. All description is selective. Descriptions never *reproduce* the phenomena described. We can always in principle provide more detail (see Chapter 1). Of course, practically speaking, we can usually resolve the problem of how much detail is required with little trouble. Our purposes generally dictate fairly clearly the degree of detail that is necessary. However, because our conception of the research problem may change over the course of the research early on we may have to err on the side of maximising detail.

The same sort of argument applies to accuracy. The accuracy of information can always be subjected to further checks, in principle at least: for instance, we may ask not just for evidence in support of claims made, but also for evidence of the validity of the evidence provided, and so on *ad infinitum*. There is no foundation for us to reach that would stop this process. Practically speaking, though, we usually soon reach the point at which we decide that it is not reasonable to search for or to ask for further evidence. What is the appropriate point at which to stop is impossible to specify in the abstract: it will depend considerably on the nature of the claim and evidence involved, and the purpose which that information is intended to serve. And while, in my view, researchers should exercise a higher level of routine scepticism than others, even they can never base their claims on some indubitable bedrock.[12]

Let me turn now to the other dimension highlighted in Figure 11.2: number of cases. Here, there is an obvious possible end-point. If we were trying to represent a population the maximum number of cases would be reached when we had included all of that population as cases to be researched. But this assumes that the population of cases in which we are interested is finite. Sometimes this is true. But there are situations where the population of interest is not finite. This is the case, for example, where we are interested in testing a theory, where the term 'theory' implies universal or probabilistic relationships among categories of phenomena. Such theories refer to all possible instances that meet their conditions: those that have occurred and those that could occur. While even here (other things being equal) the more cases we study the better, there is no possibility of us studying all the cases.

It is worth emphasising that not only are there often no end-points to these two dimensions in principle, for most practical purposes the dimensions are likely to extend beyond our trade-off point: so that in most studies we could always usefully have pursued more detail or done more checking for accuracy or collected information on more cases. So, the distinction between case study and survey is a matter of degree, and it involves a trade-off between the likely generalisability of the information obtained on the one hand and the detail and likely accuracy of data about particular cases on the other. And the position along this dimension that we select should depend on our goals and the resources available to us.

This immediately points to a potential weakness of case study: that its findings may be unrepresentative of a larger population in which we are interested. A common reaction of case study advocates to this criticism is to deny that case studies are intended to be representative or typical in the sense that is true of the findings of surveys. Thus, Yin distinguishes between the logic of what he calls statistical and analytical generalisation, arguing that only the latter is relevant to case studies (Yin 1984). Similarly, Mitchell (1983) argues that case study research involves logical but not statistical inference. In both cases generalisation from sample to population is defined as statistical and irrelevant to case study research. There are some good reasons for this reaction, but as it stands it is misleading. It is true that, as I pointed out earlier, where we are concerned with theory development and testing the issue is not generalisation to a finite population, and that where the population is infinite statistical techniques are of no help (Morrison and

Henkel 1970), so that other case selection strategies than the survey may be more appropriate.[13] Also, sometimes the population that we are interested in is not very large. Indeed, it may be a population of one, consisting entirely of the case we are studying. A study of the National Front, such as that by Nigel Fielding (1981), can be concerned simply with describing that organisation; so that the issue of generalisability does not arise.[14] And even if the population we are interested in is larger than this but still relatively small, it may be reasonable to treat the few cases studied as likely to be representative of the remainder. (The proportion of the population that our sample represents is more important than the absolute magnitude of the sample.)

However, often the issue of generalisability to a relatively large, finite population *is* relevant to case study work. It is quite common for such research to make this type of claim. For instance, Punch seeks to base general statements about policing in the inner city areas of modern Western societies on the basis of his study of police officers in the Warmoestraat area of Amsterdam; and Woods treats the option system at the secondary school he studied as typical of those at other English secondary schools (Punch 1979; Woods 1979).[15] Empirical generalisation is just as legitimate a goal for case study research as is theoretical inference, and in some respects it is more straightforward (see Chapter 5). But where empirical generalisation is the goal there is no doubt that, whatever its advantages in terms of detail and accuracy, case study is usually weaker than the survey in the generalisability of its findings.

However, to say that case study offers a weaker basis for generalisation to large, finite populations compared with the survey is not to say that it provides no basis for such generalisation, or that we cannot improve and assess the generalisability of its findings. It is very important not to think of generalisability as synonymous with the use of statistical sampling. The latter is one useful way of providing for generalisability to a finite population; but it is neither perfect nor the only way. If we cannot use it, as we usually cannot in case study research, we should not assume that our findings are therefore not generalisable, or that we cannot know whether they are representative.

A variety of strategies for improving and/or checking the generalisability of the findings of case study research is available. It may be possible to draw on relevant information in published statistics about the aggregate to which generalisation is being made. So, for example, in their study of two juvenile courts Parker *et al.* used statistics about the proportions of different sorts of disposal in such courts in England and Wales and in the Merseyside area to show the atypicality of one of the courts they studied in this respect and the relative typicality of the other (Parker *et al.* 1981: 79). Equally, it may be possible to select cases for study that cover some of the main dimensions of suspected heterogeneity in the population in which we are interested. For instance, in studying the degree of choice given to pupils by option choice schemes in secondary schools, if we were studying more than one school we might select these to cover dimensions which could be expected to affect this phenomenon: such as large/small number of pupils, predominantly working-class/substantially middle-class catchment area etc. Even where we are carrying out an intensive study of one case, we may be able to make brief investigations of one or more other cases in order to assess the ways in which our primary case is or is not representative of the larger population that is of concern. Skolnick's study of law enforcement processes in US cities is an example of this strategy. The bulk of his research took place in one city, but he made a brief investigation of another to assess the likely generalisability of his findings (Skolnick 1966).

Similarly, where studies have been carried out by others on other cases in the same population in the same time period comparison may allow some judgement of typicality to be made. This strategy is illustrated by Strong's study of paediatric consultations (Strong 1979). Even though he adopts a survey approach in my terms, he seeks to generalise from the cases he studied to a larger population in part by comparing his data with that from other studies.[16] He argues that the bureaucratic format he identified as characteristic of those consultations is not typical only of them, but also that (with minor modifications) it predominates in all medical consultations in the British health service. In order to establish this he first considers the extent to which the fact that children were the patients in the paediatric consultations he studied shaped the ceremonial order characteristic of them, arguing that it made little difference. Second, he draws on other studies of medical consultation involving adults as patients to assess how far these conformed to the bureaucratic mode.

It is worth noting that where the case study strategy is adopted cases are sometimes selected for investigation on the basis of their atypicality. In the early 1970s Cicourel and Kitsuse studied Lakeside High, a school which they point out was unrepresentative of US high schools at the time, particularly in having a professionalised counselling service (Cicourel and Kitsuse 1963). But the authors argue that in this respect the school was in advance of changes that were taking place among US high schools generally, so that more and more schools would become similar to Lakeside High in this respect. On this basis, Cicourel and Kitsuse claim that their findings will be generalisable to many other schools in the future. This sort of generalisation requires different kinds of support to the more conventional process of generalisation to an already existing population of cases. In assessing Cicourel and Kitsuse's claims we need to be sure that their assumptions about the trend in the development of US high schools are accurate. In fact, they do not provide much evidence for this, although as readers now we may be in a better position than they were to assess whether they were right.[17]

I am not suggesting that these various strategies are always able to give us a very sound basis for generalisation, but they can provide some evidence, and we should not scorn that evidence simply because it is not statistical. By means of these strategies we can moderate the relative weakness of case study in providing for the generalisability of findings to a large, finite population of cases. And often this is necessary if the findings of case study research are to be of value (see Chapter 5).

So, the first implication of my definition of case study is that in relation to the survey it involves a trade-off between empirical generalisability on the one hand, and accuracy and detail on the other. However, I have emphasised that these are tendencies not guarantees, and that generalisability to large, finite populations is not always a goal of research. Furthermore, there are ways in which case study researchers can improve and assess the representativeness (in this sense) of the cases they study.

CASE STUDIES AND EXPERIMENTS

If we turn now to the contrast between case study and experiment, this highlights a complementary dimension of strength and weakness on the part of case studies. This is one that is primarily relevant to theory development and testing. Here the trade-off is between more and less researcher control of variables on the one hand and the level of likely reactivity on the other. The advantage of the experiment is that by creating the cases we need we can vary theoretical and extraneous variables fairly easily in such a way as to maximise our chances of coming to sound conclusions about whether the causal relationship we are investigating does or does not hold. The disadvantage of the experiment is that the exercise of control by the researcher may render the research situation artificial in that it cannot give us information about the naturally occurring situations in which we are interested.

It might seem that here we have a dichotomous rather than a continuous or quantitative contrast: we either create cases or study existing ones. This is not so. The difference here is quantitative too. Quasi and field experiments involve less control over variables than do true experiments but more than case studies, and therefore constitute mid-points on a scale. Once again I can illustrate the relationship with a diagram (see Figure 11.3).

The advantage and disadvantage of the case study in this respect are the mirror image of those of the experiment. The case study provides us with information that is less likely to be affected by reactivity and therefore is more likely to be ecologically valid; but it does so at the cost of making it more difficult to come to convincing conclusions about the existence of the causal relationships in which we are interested.[18]

Here again, I think that we ought to be honest about the limitations of case study. We should not pretend that they do not exist. It is sometimes argued that case studies can identify causal relationships in a relatively direct manner. This argument has quite a long history. In the 1930s we find it in an article by Willard Waller, a Chicago-trained sociologist and advocate of case study. He draws on Gestalt psychology to claim that 'there is in some cases a direct perception of the causal interdependence of events'; though later he recognises that such insight can be mistaken (Waller 1934: 285 and 297). More recently, Glaser and Strauss have claimed that 'in field work ... general relations are often discovered *in vivo*, that is, the field worker literally sees them occur' (Glaser and Strauss 1967: 40). Something of this kind also seems to be implicit in Mitchell's defence of case study (Mitchell 1983; see Chapter 10). However, one does not have to accept all of David Hume's views about causality to recognise the cogency of his

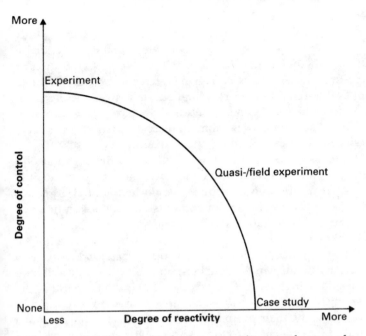

Figure 11.3 Relationship between experiment and case study

argument that we cannot *see* causality in some immediate fashion, that the ascription of causal power always relies on assumptions. Indeed, it is widely accepted by philosophers today that we cannot see anything directly or immediately. All perception and observation depend on assumptions, even though most of the time we are not aware of those assumptions.

Given this, we must ask: how are we to identify causal relationships? The classic solution is the hypothetico-deductive method. This involves comparing situations where the causal variable is different in value but other relevant variables remain the same. And the experiment is the most effective means of making such comparisons.

Once again, though, we must not conclude that because case study is not as well suited to the identification of causes as the experiment, it cannot be used for this task. It is possible to approximate the hypothetico-deductive method using a case study strategy through the appropriate selection of cases for study; and we should remember that even laboratory experiments are only approximations to this method, they do not guarantee control of all relevant extraneous variables. An example of case study research that conforms quite closely to the hypothetico-deductive method is a sequence of studies in the sociology of education by Hargreaves, Lacey and Ball. This research involved the development and testing of differentiation-polarisation theory: the claim that differentiation of pupils on academic-behavioural grounds (in the form of streaming or banding in secondary schools) produces polarisation in their attitudes towards school.

The first of these studies published was an investigation of a secondary modern school, where the researcher can have had little doubt that polarisation of attitudes would be found (Hargreaves 1967). What Hargreaves's study amounts to is the description of a case where differentiation was high and so too was polarisation. Useful though this is, it is obviously rather weak evidence for the validity of the theory. After all, many other factors were likely to have been operative in the situation, some of which may well have produced the high level of polarisation. For instance, perhaps the streaming system in the school Hargreaves studied sorted pupils on the basis of their attitudes to school, these being largely a product of extra-school factors. This could have occurred both directly because this was judged by teachers to be an important consideration, and indirectly because these attitudes affected academic performance. Differences in pupil attitude produced by factors outside the school could therefore explain the correlation between stream and orientation to school that Hargreaves found.

If we turn now to Lacey's study of a grammar school, we can see how it contributes to the process of testing the theory (Lacey 1970). Not only does he document much the same correlation between stream and attitude as Hargreaves, but:

1 the case he studied involved some control over the factor of differences between pupils in attitude on entry to the school. This is because since Hightown was a selective school most of the pupils who were recruited to it had been successful and highly motivated in their primary schools,

2 he shows that the polarisation increased over time from the point of initial differentiation in the first year through to the fourth year of secondary schooling.

These features add considerably to the plausibility of the theory, in my judgement; even if they do not render it absolutely convincing. There are always potential doubts. For instance, in relation to the first point above, we must remember that differences in attitude are a matter of degree. Despite relative homogeneity in comparison with differences in attitude across the whole age group, there will still have been differences in attitude among the new recruits to Hightown, and the streaming system may simply have allocated pupils to streams on that basis. Similarly, we could explain the growing polarisation over time not as the product of differentiation but as the result of external factors operating on existing differences in attitude. After all, a lot of things happen to children outside of school during their secondary-school careers, both changes in relationships at home and in peer groups; and some of these are likely to be systematically related to attitude towards school.[19]

In the third of this sequence of studies, Ball investigated a comprehensive school (Ball 1981). As a result of this choice of school type he was not able to control for pupils' attitude on entry in the way that Lacey did. However, he did look at change in pupils' attitudes over time, confirming Lacey's findings. Furthermore, he documented a change in the level of differentiation in the institution (the abandonment of banding in favour of mixed ability grouping), looking at the effects of this on the level of polarisation. Given that this involved a change within a single institution over a relatively short period of time we can assume that much (though not everything) remained the same between the two situations, before and after. Ball shows that the level of polarisation was much lower after mixed ability grouping had been adopted.

This is further important evidence in support of differentiation-polarisation theory, but once again it is not beyond reasonable question. It does not rule out all the other relevant possibilities. For example, the data produced by these studies could be explained by a kind of imitation theory whereby the attitudes of members of a school class are affected by the balance of extant pro and antischool attitudes to be found within it, a theory that some teachers hold. This would explain the reduction of polarisation following the abolition of banding independently of level of differentiation.

However, whatever the remaining questions, this sequence of studies is one of the clearest examples of systematic theory development and testing in ethnographic research, and indeed in sociology generally. And it illustrates that while case studies do not involve manipulation of variables, it is possible to use the comparison of existing cases to make reasonable judgements about causal relationships. Furthermore, it is often not feasible or ethical to carry out experiments in social research; and (as I noted earlier) the findings of case study research are likely to suffer less from reactivity and therefore may involve higher ecological validity than experimental research.[20]

CONCLUSION

In this chapter I have tried to clarify the concept of case study in such a way as to contribute to a more effective language for understanding social research methodology. I started out from the position that it is not fruitful to think of social research method in terms of contrasting approaches, each involving a comprehensive and harmoniously integrated range of components all the way from epistemological assumptions right through to specific research techniques. The methodological decisions that we face in social research are more complex than this, allowing for more variation than such dichotomous models assume. I identified five aspects of research design, and defined case study as one means of tackling the problem of case selection. I contrasted it with two other case selection strategies, surveys and experiments; emphasising the trade-offs involved in selecting one rather than another of these strategies. Compared with the survey, there is a trade-off between generalisability of findings to finite populations on the one hand and detail and accuracy of information on the other. Compared with the experiment, case study involves a trade-off between control of variables and level of reactivity. I noted that the significance of these trade-offs varies according to the goals and circumstances of the research. And I emphasised that we must be honest about the relative weakness of case study in the above respects (while denying that it is weaker in any general sense). At the same time, I argued that there are various strategies we can use to overcome these weaknesses at least partially. Furthermore, when we broaden our focus from single studies to look at the development of research in particular fields, we can see that it may be possible to maximise the advantages of two or more case selection strategies by combining them.

196

So, in my view, we must not see research methodology in terms of competing traditions, but rather as involving a complex of assumptions and arguments, some of them in conflict, and a range of strategies and techniques that have advantages and disadvantages for particular goals and in particular circumstances. Moreover, the disadvantages of adopting one strategy or technique rather than another may be tempered through ameliorative modifications and perhaps even overcome through combination with other strategies and techniques. In this chapter I have outlined a conception of 'case study' that is compatible with this viewpoint.

NOTES

1 For a more detailed assessment of the qualitative–quantitative divide, see Chapter 9.
2 Terminologically, this is a little confusing since all research involves the selective study of cases, but not all research adopts the case study strategy. However, the only way to avoid this problem would be to abandon conventional usage of the terms 'case' and/or 'case study' completely; and in my view the likely costs of this would be greater than the danger of terminological confusion associated with the definitional approach I have adopted.
3 These are aspects of the research process, rather than stages of it. To one degree or another, we need to have outline plans of all of them at the start, and detailed planning or replanning in each area may become necessary at any stage. Furthermore, any changes in one might lead us to reconsider our thinking about the others.
4 Case study may involve no primary data collection at all, it can be based on secondary analysis. For a definition of case study that is much closer to the more conventional usage, see Becker (1968).
5 See Znaniecki (1934) and Lindesmith (1968) for the argument that the logic of case study (analytic induction) is distinct from that of statistical method (enumerative induction). See Chapter 10. For a detailed assessment of analytic induction, see Hammersley (1989a).
6 One of the implications of my rejection of the paradigms perspective is a recognition that research may be designed to serve a variety of purposes and that these purposes place different requirements on the research. We can identify a number of different products of social research (description, explanation, prediction, evaluation, prescription and theory), and the three case selection strategies may have differential suitability for research pursuing these products; in particular the appropriateness of the experiment seems to be limited to theory development and testing. I have argued elsewhere that one of the problems with qualitative research is an endemic lack of clarity about goals, see Chapter 1.

7 It may involve the study of only one case, but where more than one is studied these are likely to be selected consecutively rather than simultaneously, and analysis of data from the first case will influence the choice of subsequent cases for investigation. The latter is what Glaser and Strauss (1967) refer to as theoretical sampling. It is worth noting that more than one case selection strategy can be combined in the same research project. Also, embedded designs are possible: for example where a survey is used to provide information about a single case selected for study that is relatively large, such as an organisation with many members or a national population. Here the survey provides a basis for generalisation within the case rather than generalisation across cases.

8 It must be emphasised that what I am identifying here are potentials: there is no guarantee that the findings of case study research will be more detailed and more accurate or that those of surveys will be more generalisable. As such I think that the assumptions I am making here about the two strategies are reasonable. Perhaps the most questionable is the argument that case studies are likely to produce more accurate information. This obviously depends on the sort of information involved, but where accuracy depends on understanding in context and/or on penetrating false fronts, I think it is clear that case study has the greater capacity for accuracy. Also, more often than with survey work, it allows the use of multiple sources and types of data to check the accuracy of major factual claims.

9 I should add a warning here that while it is true that most of what we would normally regard as ethnographic or qualitative research employs a case study strategy (or at least it is at the case study end of the spectrum), this is not true of all such research. For example Strong's book *The Ceremonial Order of the Clinic* involved the investigation of over 1000 cases of paediatric consultation (Strong 1979). As far as data collection is concerned, his case selection strategy was a survey, though in other respects his research is more conventionally ethnographic. In fact, in selecting cases for analysis he adopts a version of analytic induction. This is a useful illustration of the sort of variation in research practice that global contrasts between comprehensive research paradigms miss.

10 Strong's focus on the relatively small-scale case of the paediatric consultation and his collaboration with another researcher in collecting the data explains how he was able to collect information on such a large number of cases.

11 Znaniecki's notion of the 'closed system' (Znaniecki 1934) and Becker's use of the concept of social system (Becker 1971: 33) are relatively clear illustrations of this point. The concern with capturing cases in their own terms also seems to be implied when Platt defines case studies as retaining the individuality of each case (Platt 1988: 2). Similarly, Bromley talks of dealing with cases in their 'actual context' (Bromley 1986: xii). And, while early on in his book he recognises the necessarily selective character of description, he later argues that case

198

studies must 'preserve the wholeness of the phenomenon studied' (Bromley 1986: 288).

12 For this argument, see Chapter 4.

13 I shall address this issue below in drawing the contrast between case studies and experiments.

14 The problem of generalisation *within* the case may arise, but not that of generalisation across cases, which is my concern here.

15 Though it is true that in these and other instances the authors of case study research are not always very clear about whether they intend their findings to be generalisable to some finite population (what I shall call 'empirical generalisation') or to all the instances falling under a particular theoretical category ('theoretical inference'). For a discussion of this in relation to Woods's research, see Hammersley (1991c).

16 This illustrates that the strategies for dealing with the problem of generalisation sketched here are not limited to case study research.

17 For an excellent discussion of selecting cases to investigate what may or could happen, see Schofield (1990).

18 'Ecological validity' in the sense I am using the term here is concerned with the generalisability of findings, but it is generalisability to an infinite not a finite population: to all those cases, actual and possible, that meet the conditions of the theory. The strategy of studying 'natural' rather than experimental cases is based on the assumption that the latter are likely to be significantly different to 'natural situations', because of reactivity, and hence are a potentially unreliable basis for generalisation. It is worth noting that case studies may involve reactivity, for instance where the researcher plays an influential role within the setting, either intentionally (as in action research) or inadvertently. Also, reactivity is not the only source of ecological invalidity: natural cases can be unrepresentative in relevant respects of other cases falling under the theoretical category simply because there is variability within that class. This is especially likely where classes are defined in terms of family resemblances or prototypes rather than in terms of necessary and sufficient conditions.

19 Lacey was, of course, aware of these factors and incorporated them into his account, but as subordinate factors to differentiation. His analysis of differentiation within school classes, which I have not discussed here, adds further support to his general argument.

20 For a more detailed discussion of the work of Hargreaves, Lacey and Ball from this point of view, see Hammersley (1985a). See also the recent work of Abraham (1989). I must add a qualification to this argument about the role of experiments and case studies in testing theories. The hypothetico-deductive method is only applicable in this way where we are dealing with theory in the form of precisely defined universal laws. If the laws are probabilistic or the conditions of their application are not definable in precise terms, then reliance on a small number of cases to test the theory (whether via case study or experiment) is not justified (see Chapter 2). We would need a large number of cases to pick up the probabilistic trend and to avoid

marginal peculiarities distorting our conclusions. Under these circumstances (other things being equal), surveys may be best suited to the task of theory-testing; though of course other things are rarely equal, and the problem might be dealt with by carrying out multiple experiments or case studies, or by complementing case study or experiment with survey research.

Rejection of the idea of deterministic sociological laws is quite common among advocates of qualitative and case study research. But the implications of this position have not been fully explored. Bromley touches on the problem in suggesting that the similarities between cases consist of family resemblances, and in describing cases as prototypical and as providing a basis for 'case-law' rather than more precise and determinate forms of scientific law (Bromley 1986: 2–3, 9, 276–82). However, in other places he effectively treats case-law as similar in character to scientific laws.

POSTSCRIPT

In this *Postscript* I want to try to summarise the implications of the essays collected in this volume. In the *Introduction* I outlined what I see as the crisis facing ethnography and the main issues that must be dealt with if that crisis is to be resolved. The essays have covered many of those issues. The positions I have taken are, I hope, consistent with one another, and thereby point to a general conception of the purpose and nature of social research. That conception probably does not fall into any conventional category. At the same time, it does not pretend to be a radical new approach. It retains much of the current conceptualisation and practice of ethnography, while abandoning some of what are currently regarded as its central features.

In response to the arguments of anti-realist critics of ethnographic methodology, I have argued for retention of the commitment to realism and thus to a correspondence theory of truth. The anti-realist case seems to me to collapse into relativism and as a result to be internally inconsistent, as well as carrying unacceptable practical implications, notably the loss of any possibility of rational discourse. Similarly, in response to the advocates of critical and applied ethnography I tried to show that their proposals are not convincing, that there is a role for specialised research that is not aimed directly at a practitioner audience.

At the same time, I have sought to modify current methodological thinking about ethnographic research in a variety of ways. The sort of subtle realism that I advocate as an epistemological basis for social research implies some changes in the way in which ethnographers think about and do their research. It certainly makes the task of assessing the validity of ethnographic findings more difficult than it seemed before. It also makes justifying social science to a sceptical public more troublesome than it would be if we could appeal to naïve realism. If we accept that even scientific conclusions can rest only on judgements about plausibility and credibility, their superiority and thus their value is more difficult to establish than if we could present those conclusions as the product of a method that guaranteed valid results.

Similarly, while rejecting arguments for making ethnography more directly relevant to, or even integrating it with, practice, I argued that it is essential that relevance be treated as a criterion for the assessment of ethnographic research, along with validity. But assessing ethnographic studies in terms of this criterion is even more problematic than assessing their validity on the basis of subtle realism. Judgements of relevance rely on factual and value assumptions that are themselves likely to be contestable. Furthermore, it is an implication of my arguments that relevance is a matter of degree, and I have suggested that what is appropriate in general is a more limited and remote relationship between research and other forms of practice than advocates of applied or practitioner ethnography demand. Once again, though, this makes the public justification of research more difficult than it would be if we could assume a more substantial and direct contribution.

Perhaps the most dramatic conclusion that might be drawn from the arguments in this book concerns the very identity of ethnography. When I began my research career I regarded ethnography as a distinct paradigm quite different in assumption and orientation from quantitative method. Over time, however, I came to revise that view, increasingly seeing ethnography as one method amongst others, and the methodological ideas associated with it as relevant to all research. The articles included in the last section of this book point to a third position: the deconstruction of quantitative and qualitative method into a much more complex array of options: in terms of the formulation of research topics, the selection of cases for study, the choice of types of data and forms of analysis etc. Ethnography disappears here, even as a method. I think this is as it should be. The meaning of 'ethnography' is not specific enough to form part of a typology that would capture one set of options available to the social researcher. And viewed as a general approach it not only misleads about the range of options available but also about the basis on which choice between options should be made. It implies that decisions should flow from commitment to general methodological principles, instead of being made on the basis of those epistemological, methodological and practical assumptions that are most reasonable in the particular research context (including the capabilities of the researcher). My argument here is an application of the point I made in Chapters 6 and 7, about the limited contribution that general ideas and information can make to practice, and in this case, to research itself as a form of practice.

This line of thinking gives what is perhaps the most striking answer to the question posed in the title of this book, since it effectively undercuts the rationale for ethnography, not only as a separate paradigm but even as a distinct method. I no longer believe 'ethnography' to be a useful category with which to think about social research methodology. While this judgement concerns more than mere terminology, it is not a simple rejection of ethnographic thinking and practice. Rather, it is an attempt to integrate both the methodological ideas and methods that the term 'ethnography' normally refers to into a more appropriate methodological framework for the social sciences. The nature of that framework remains to be discovered. In my view its development is one of the most important methodological tasks that face social scientists in the future.

BIBLIOGRAPHY

ABRAHAM, J. (1989) 'Testing Hargreaves' and Lacey's differentiation-polarization theory in a setted comprehensive', *British Journal of Sociology*, 40, 1, pp.46–81.

ADLER, P. (1985) *Wheeling and Dealing: an ethnography of an upper-level drug dealing and smuggling community*. New York: Columbia University Press.

ADORNO, T. (ed.) (1976) *The Positivist Dispute in German Sociology*. London: Heinemann.

ALBERT, H. (1985) *Treatise on Critical Reason*. Princeton: Princeton University Press.

ANDERSON, G. (1989) 'Critical ethnography in education: origins, current status and new directions', *Review of Educational Research*, 59, 3, pp.249–70.

ANDERSON, R. , HUGHES, J. and SHARROCK, W. (1985) *The Sociology Game*. London: Longman.

ANGUS, L. (1986a) 'Developments in ethnographic research in education: from interpretive to critical ethnography', *Journal of Research and Development in Education*, 20, pp.59–67.

—— (1986b) 'Research traditions, ideology and critical ethnography', *Discourse*, 7, 1, pp.61–77.

ARONSON, J. (1984) *A Realist Philosophy of Science*. London: Macmillan.

ASAD, T. (1973) 'Two European images of Non-European rule', in T. Asad (ed.) *Anthropology and the Colonial Encounter*. London: Ithaca.

ATHENS, L. (1984) 'Scientific criteria for evaluating qualitative studies', in N. K. Denzin (ed.) *Studies in Symbolic Interaction*, vol.5. Greenwich: JAI Press.

ATKINSON, P. (1982) 'Writing ethnography', in H.J. Helle (ed.) *Kultur und Institution*. Berlin: Dunker und Humblot, pp.77–105.

—— (1988) 'Ethnomethodology: a critical review', *Annual Review of Sociology*, 14, pp.441–65.

—— (1990) *The Ethnographic Imagination*. London: Routledge.

ATKINSON, P. and DELAMONT, S. (1985) 'Bread and dreams or bread and circuses: a critique of "case study" research in education', in M. Shipman (ed.) *Educational Research*. Lewes: Falmer.

ATKINSON, P., DELAMONT, S. and HAMMERSLEY, M. (1988)

'Qualitative research traditions: a British response to Jacob', *Review of Educational Research*, 58, 2, pp.231–50.

BALDAMUS, W. (1979) 'Alienation, anomie and industrial accidents' in M. Wilson (ed.) *Social and Educational Research in Action*. London: Longman.

BALL, S. J. (1981) *Beachside Comprehensive*. Cambridge: Cambridge University Press.

—— (1982) 'Competition and conflict in the teaching of English: a socio-historical analysis', *Journal of Curriculum Studies*, 15, 1, pp.1–28.

—— (1983a) 'Case study research in education: some notes and problems', in M. Hammersley (ed.) *The Ethnography of Schooling*. Driffield: Nafferton.

—— (1983b) 'A subject of privilege: English and the school curriculum 1906–35', in M. Hammersley and A. Hargreaves (eds) *Curriculum Practice: some sociological case-studies*. Lewes: Falmer Press.

BALL, T. (1977) 'Plato and Aristotle: the unity versus the autonomy of theory and practice', in T. Ball (ed.) *Political Theory and Praxis*. Minneapolis: University of Minnesota Press.

BECKER, H. S. (1952) 'Social-class variations in teacher–pupil relationships', *Journal of Educational Sociology*, 25, pp.451–65.

—— (1963) *Outsiders*. New York: Free Press.

—— (1966) 'Introduction' to C. Shaw, *The Jack Roller*. Chicago: University of Chicago Press.

—— (1968) 'Social observation and case studies', in D. Sills (ed.) *International Encyclopaedia of Social Sciences*. vol. 11. New York: Macmillan.

—— (1971) *Sociological Work: method and substance*. London: Allen Lane.

—— (1990) 'Generalizing from case studies', in E. Eisner and A. Peshkin (eds) *Qualitative Inquiry in Education: the continuing debate*. New York: Teacher College Press.

BECKER, H.S., GEER, B., HUGHES, E.L. and STRAUSS, A.L. (1961) *Boys in White*. Chicago: Chicago University Press.

BELL, D. (1990) *Husserl*. London: Routledge.

BERGER, P. and LUCKMANN, T. (1966) *The Social Construction of Reality*. Harmondsworth: Penguin.

BERK, R. (1974) 'Qualitative methodology', unpublished manuscript.

BERLIN, I. (1976) *Vico and Herder*. London: Hogarth.

BERNSTEIN, R. (1983) *Beyond Objectivism and Relativism*. Philadelphia: University of Pennsylvania Press.

BERTAUX, D. (ed.) (1981) *Biography and Society: the life history approach in the social sciences*. Beverly Hills, Calif., Sage.

BHASKAR, R. (1978) *A Realist Theory of Science*. Brighton: Harvester (2nd edn).

BITTNER, E. (1973) 'Objectivity and realism in sociology', in G. Psathas (ed.) *Phenomenological Sociology*. New York: Wiley.

BLACK, M. (1967) 'Induction', in P. Edwards (ed.) *The Encyclopedia of Philosophy*. New York: Macmillan.

BLOOR, M. (1978) 'On the analysis of observational data: a discussion of the worth and uses of inductive techniques and respondent validation', *Sociology*, 12, 3, pp.545–62.

BLUMER, H. (1928) 'Method in social psychology', unpublished Ph.D. dissertation, University of Chicago.

—— (1939) *Critiques of Research in the Social Sciences: I An Appraisal of Thomas and Znaniecki's 'The Polish Peasant in Europe and America'*, New York: Social Science Research Council.

—— (1969) 'The methodological position of Symbolic Interactionism', in H. Blumer *Symbolic Interactionism*. Englewood Cliffs: Prentice Hall.

BOGDAN, R. and TAYLOR, S. (1975) *Introduction to Qualitative Research Method*. New York: Wiley (2nd edn: Taylor and Bogdan 1984).

BOOTH, W.C. (1974) *Modern Dogma and the Rhetoric of Assent*. Chicago: University of Chicago Press.

BOWLES, G. and KLEIN, R. D. (1983) *Theories of Women's Studies*. London: Routledge and Kegan Paul.

BRODKEY, L. (1987) 'Writing critical ethnographic narratives', *Anthropology and Education Quarterly*, 18, pp.67–75.

BROMLEY, D. (1986) *The Case Study Method in Psychology and Related Disciplines*. Chichester: Wiley.

BROWN, R.H. (1977) *A Poetic for Sociology*. Cambridge: Cambridge University Press.

BRUUN, H.H. (1972) *Science, Values and Politics in Max Weber's Methodology*. Copenhagen: Munksgaard.

BRYMAN, A. (1988) *Quality and Quantity in Social Research*. London: Unwin Hyman.

BUCK-MORSS, S. (1979) 'Adorno', in D. Sills (ed.) *International Encyclopedia of the Social Sciences*, Biographical Supplement, vol.18. New York: Free Press.

BULMER, M. (1980) 'Why don't sociologists make more use of official statistics?', *Sociology*, 14, 4, pp.505–23.

—— (1984) *The Chicago School of Sociology*. Chicago: University of Chicago Press.

BURAWOY, M. (1987) 'The limits of Wright's analytical Marxism and an alternative', *Berkeley Journal of Sociology*, 32, pp.51–72.

BURGER, T. (1976) *Max Weber's Theory of Concept Formation: history, laws and ideal types*. Durham, North Carolina: Duke University Press.

BURGESS, E.W. (1927) 'Statistics and case studies as methods of sociological research', *Sociology and Social Research*, 12, pp.103–20.

—— (1930) 'Discussion', in C. Shaw (1966) *The Jack Roller: a delinquent boy's own story*. Chicago: Chicago University Press.

BURGESS, R.G. (1978) 'Preparations for teacher-based research: a report from an in-service course', *British Journal of In-Service Education*, 5, pp.14–19.

—— (1980) 'Some fieldwork problems in teacher-based research', *British Educational Research Journal*, 6, 2, pp.165–73.

BURKE, P. (1985) *Vico*. Oxford: Oxford University Press.

CAMILLERI, S. F. (1962) 'Theory, probability, and induction in social research', *American Sociological Review*, 27, pp.170–8. Reprinted in J.E.

Morrison and R.E. Henkel (1970) *The Significance Test Controversy.* Chicago: Aldine.

CAMPBELL, D. (1957) 'Factors relevant to the validity of experiments in social settings', *Psychological Bulletin,* 54, 4, pp.297–312.

CAMPBELL, D. and STANLEY, J. C. (1963) 'Experimental and quasi-experimental designs for research on teaching', in N. Gage (ed.) *Handbook of Research on Teaching.* Chicago: Rand McNally.

CARBY, H. (1982) 'White women listen! Black feminism and the boundaries of sisterhood', in Centre for Contemporary Cultural Studies *The Empire Strikes Back.* London: Hutchinson.

CAREY, J. (1975) *Sociology and Public Affairs: the Chicago school.* Beverley Hills: Sage.

CARR, W. (1987) 'What is an educational practice?', *Journal of the Philosophy of Education,* 21, 2, pp.163–75.

CARR, W. and KEMMIS, S. (1986) *Becoming Critical: education, knowledge and action research.* Lewes: Falmer.

CHALMERS, N. (1978) *What is This Thing Called Science?* Milton Keynes: Open University Press.

CHISHOLM, R. (1973) *The Problem of the Criterion.* Milwaukee: Marquette University Press.

CHURCHLAND, P. and HOOKER, C. (1986) *Images of Science: essays on realism and empiricism,* Chicago, University of Chicago Press.

CICOUREL, A.V. and KITSUSE, J.I. (1963) *The Educational Decision-makers.* New York: Bobbs-Merrill.

CLIFFORD, J. (1986a) 'Introduction: partial truths', in J. Clifford and G. Marcus (eds) *Writing Culture: the poetics and politics of ethnogaphy.* Berkeley: University of California Press.

—— (1986b) 'On ethnographic allegory' in J. Clifford and G. Marcus (eds) *Writing Culture: the poetics and politics of ethnography.* Berkeley: University of California Press.

—— (1988) *The Predicament of Culture.* Cambridge, Mass.: Harvard University Press.

CLIFFORD, J. and MARCUS, G. (eds) (1986) *Writing Culture: the poetics and politics of ethnography.* Berkeley: University of California Press.

COLLINGWOOD, R. (1940) *An Essay in Metaphysics.* Oxford: Oxford University Press.

COLSON, E. (1967) 'The intensive study of small sample communities', in A.L. Epstein (ed.) *The Craft of Social Anthropology.* London: Tavistock.

CONNERTON, P. (1980) *The Tragedy of Enlightenment: an essay on the Frankfurt School.* Cambridge: Cambridge University Press.

COOK, T. and CAMPBELL, D. (1979) *Quasi-Experimentation.* Chicago: Rand McNally.

CRANSTON, M. (1967) *Freedom.* London: Longman (3rd edn).

CRAPANZANO, V. (1986) 'Hermes' dilemma: the masking of subversion in ethnographic description', in J. Clifford and G. Marcus (eds) *Writing Culture: the poetics and politics of ethnogrophy.* Berkeley: University of California Press.

CRESSEY, D. (1950) 'The criminal violation of financial trust', *American Sociological Review,* 15: 738–43.

—— (1953) *Other People's Money*. Glencoe, Ill. : Free Press.

CROLL, P. (1986) *Systematic Classroom Observation*. Lewes: Falmer.

DANCY, J. (1985) *An Introduction to Contemporary Epistemology*. Oxford: Blackwell.

DENZIN, N.K. (1978) *The Research Act*. New York: McGraw Hill (2nd edn).

—— (1989) *Interpretive Interactionism*. Newbury Park: Sage.

—— (1990) 'The spaces of postmodernism: reading Plummer on Blumer', *Symbolic Interaction*, 13, 2, pp.145–54.

DEVITT, M. (1984) *Realism and Truth*. Oxford: Blackwell.

DEWS, P. (1987) *Logics of Disintegration: post-structuralist thought and the claims of critical theory*. London: Verso.

DICKENS, D. (1983) 'The critical project of Jurgen Habermas', in D.R. Sabia and J. Wallulis (eds) *Changing Social Science: critical theory and other critical perspectives*. Albany: State University of New York Press.

DOBBERT, M.L. (1982) *Ethnographic Research: theory and application for modern schools and societies*. New York: Praeger.

DONMOYER, R. (1990) 'Generalizing and the single case study', in E. Eisner and A. Peshkin (eds) *Qualitative Inquiry in Education: the continuing debate*. New York: Teacher College Press

DOUGLAS, J.D. and RASMUSSEN, P.K. with FLANAGAN, C. A. (1977) *The Nude Beach*. Beverley Hills: Sage.

DRAY, W. (1957) *Laws and Explanation in History*. Oxford: Oxford University Press.

—— (1964) *Philosophy of History*, Englewood Cliffs, N.J.: Prentice Hall.

—— (1967) 'History and value judgments', in P. Edwards (ed.) *The Encyclopedia of Philosophy*. New York: Macmillan.

—— (1979) 'New departures in the theory of historiography', *Philosophy of the Social Sciences*, 9, pp.499–507.

ECKSTEIN, H. (1975) 'Case study and theory in political science' in F. Greenstein and N. Polsby (eds) *Strategies of Inquiry, Handbook of Political Science*, vol. 7. Menlo Park, California: Addison-Wesley.

EDDY, E.M. (1985) 'Theory, research and application in educational anthropology', *Anthropology and Education Quarterly*, 16, pp.83–194.

EDDY, E.M. and PARTRIDGE, W.L. (eds) (1978) *Applied Anthropology in America*. New York: Columbia University Press.

EDMONDSON, R. (1984) *Rhetoric in Sociology*. London: Macmillan.

EISNER E. and PESHKIN A. (1990) *Qualitative Inquiry in Education: the continuing debate*. New York: Teacher College Press

ELLIOTT, J. (1988) 'Educational research and outsider–insider relations', *Qualitative Studies in Education*, 1, 2, pp.155–66.

ELLIS, J. (1989) *Against Deconstruction*. Princeton: Princeton University Press.

EPSTEIN, A.L. (ed.) (1967) *The Craft of Social Anthropology*. London: Tavistock.

ERICKSON, B. and NOSANCHUK, T. (1979) *Understanding Data: an introduction to exploratory and confirmatory data analysis for students in the social sciences*. Milton Keynes: Open University Press.

ERMARTH, M. (1978) *Wilhelm Dilthey: the critique of historical reason*. Chicago: University of Chicago Press.

EVANS, J. (1983) 'Criteria of validity in social research: exploring the relationship between ethnographic and quantitative approaches', in M. Hammersley (ed.) *The Ethnography of Schooling.* Driffield: Nafferton.

FAY, B. (1975) *Social Theory and Political Practice.* London: Allen and Unwin.

—— (1987) *Critical Social Science: liberation and its limits.* Cambridge: Polity Press.

FETTERMAN, D. (1984) *Ethnography in Educational Evaluation.* Beverly Hills: Sage.

FETTERMAN, D. and PITMAN, M. (1986) *Educational Evaluation: ethnography in theory, practice and politics.* Beverly Hills: Sage.

FEYERABEND, P. (1975) *Against Method.* London: Verso.

FIELDING, N. (1981) *The National Front.* London: Routledge and Kegan Paul.

FILSTEAD, W. J. (1970) *Qualitative Methodology.* Chicago: Markham.

FINCH, J. (1986) *Research and Policy,* Lewes, Falmer.

FINE, B. (1977) 'Labelling theory: an investigation into the sociological critique of deviance', *Economy and Society,* 6, pp.166–93.

FOGEL, R.W. and ELTON, G.R. (1983) *Which Road to the Past?* New Haven: Yale University Press.

FREESE, L. (ed.) (1980) *Theoretical Methods in Sociology.* Pittsburgh: University of Pittsburgh Press.

FREIRE, P. (1972) *Pedagogy of the Oppressed.* Harmondsworth: Penguin.

—— (1982) 'Creating alternative research methods', in B. Hall, A Gillett and R. Tandon (eds) *Creating Knowledge: a monopoly?* New Delhi: Society for Participatory Research in Asia.

GADAMER, H.-G. (1979) *Truth and Method.* London: Sheed and Ward (2nd edn).

GALTUNG, J. (1967) *Theory and Methods of Social Research.* London: Allen and Unwin.

GARDINER, P. (1967) 'Vico, Giambattista', in P. Edwards (ed.) *The Encyclopedia of Philosophy.* New York: Macmillan.

GARFINKEL, A. (1981) *Forms of Explanation.* New Haven: Yale University Press.

GEERTZ, C. (1975) 'Thick description', in C. Geertz, *The Interpretation of Cultures.* London: Hutchinson.

—— (1984) 'Anti anti-relativism', *American Anthropologist,* 86, pp.263–78.

—— (1988) *Works and Lives: the anthropologist as author.* Stanford: Stanford University Press.

GEUSS, R. (1981) *The Idea of Critical Theory.* Cambridge: Cambridge University Press.

GIBSON, M (1985) 'Collaborative educational ethnography: problems and profits', *Anthropology and Education Quarterly,* 16, 2, pp.124–48.

GITLIN, A.D. (1990) 'Educative research, voice and school change', *Harvard Educational Review,* 60, 4, pp.443–66.

GITLIN, A.D., SIEGEL, M. and BORU, K. (1989) 'The politics of method: from leftist ethnography to educative research', *Qualitative Studies in Education,* 2, 3, pp.237–53.

GLASER, B.G. (1978) *Theoretical Sensitivity*. Mill Valley, CA: Sociology Press.

GLASER, B.G. and STRAUSS, A. (1967) *The Discovery of Grounded Theory*. Chicago: Aldine.

GOETZ, J.P. and LECOMPTE, M.D. (1984) *Ethnography and Qualitative Design in Educational Research*. Orlando: Academic Press.

GOFFMAN, E. (1961) *Asylums*. New York: Doubleday Anchor.

GOLDTHORPE, J.H., LOCKWOOD, D., BECHHOFER, F. and PLATT, J. (1969) *The Affluent Worker in the Class Structure*. Cambridge: Cambridge University Press.

GOODSON, I. (1981) 'Becoming an academic subject', *British Journal of Sociology of Education*, 2, 2, pp.163–80.

—— (1983a) 'The use of life histories in the study of teaching', in M. Hammersley (ed.) *The Ethnography of Schooling*. Driffield: Nafferton.

—— (1983b) *School Subjects and Curriculum Change*. London: Croom Helm.

—— (1983c) 'Defending the subject: geography and environmental studies', in M. Hammersley and A. Hargreaves (eds) *Curriculum Practice: sociological case-studies*. Lewes: Falmer Press.

GUBA, E.G. (1981) 'Criteria for assessing the trustworthiness of naturalistic inquiries', *Educational Communication and Technology Journal*, 29, 2, pp.75–92.

GUBA, E.G. and LINCOLN, Y.S. (1982) 'Epistemological and methodological bases of naturalistic inquiry', *Educational Communication and Technology Journal*, 30, 4, pp.233–52.

GUSTAVSEN, B. (1986) 'Social research as participative dialogue', in F. Heller (ed.) *The Use and Abuse of Social Science*. London: Sage.

HAAN, N., BELLAH, R., RABINOW, P. and SULLIVAN, W. (1983) *Social Science as Moral Inquiry*. New York: Columbia University Press.

HABERMAS, J. (1987) *Knowledge and Human Interests*. Cambridge: Polity Press.

—— (1988) *Theory and Practice*. Cambridge: Polity Press.

HALL, B. (1982) 'Breaking the monopoly of knowledge: research methods, participation and development', in B. Hall, A. Gillett and R. Tandon (eds) *Creating Knowledge: a monopoly?* New Delhi: Society for Participatory Research in Asia.

HALL, B., GILLETT, A. and TANDON, R. (eds) (1982) *Creating Knowledge: a monopoly?* New Delhi: Society for Participatory Research in Asia.

HAMMERSLEY, M. (1980) 'On interactionist empiricism', in P. Woods (ed.) *Pupil Strategies*. London: Croom Helm.

—— (1981a) 'Ideology in the staffroom? A critique of false consciousness', in L. Barton and S. Walker (eds) *Schools, Teachers and Teaching*. Lewes: Falmer.

—— (1981b) 'The outsider's advantage: a reply to MacNamara', *British Educational Research Journal*, 7, 2, pp.167–71.

—— (1984) 'The paradigmatic mentality: a diagnosis', in L. Barton and S. Walker (eds) *Social Crisis and Educational Research*. London: Croom Helm.

—— (1985a) 'From ethnography to theory', *Sociology*, 19, 244–59.
—— (1985b) 'The good, the bad and the gullible', *British Journal of Sociology of Education*, 6, 2, pp.243–8.
—— (1986) 'Ethnography and measurement', in M. Hammersley (ed.) *Case Studies in Classroom Research*. Milton Keynes: Open University Press.
—— (1987a) 'Ethnography and the cumulative development of theory', *British Educational Research Journal*, 13, 3, 283–96.
—— (1987b) 'Ethnography for survival? A reply to Woods', *British Educational Research Journal*, 13, 3, 309–17.
—— (1987c) 'Some notes on the terms "validity" and "reliability"', *British Educational Research Journal*, 13, 1, pp.73–81.
—— (1989a) *The Dilemma of Qualitative Method: Herbert Blumer and the Chicago tradition*. London: Routledge.
—— (1989b) 'The problem of the concept: Herbert Blumer on the relationship between concepts and data', *Journal of Contemporary Ethnography*, 18, pp.133–159.
—— (1989c) 'The methodology of ethnomethodology', unpublished paper.
—— (1990a) 'An assessment of two studies of gender imbalance in the classroom', *British Educational Research Journal*, 16, 2, pp.125–43.
—— (1990b) 'On feminist methodology', *Sociology*, forthcoming.
—— (1990c) 'Keeping the conversation open: a response to Smith and Heshusius', unpublished paper.
—— (1991a) *Reading Ethnographic Research*. London: Longman.
—— (1991b) 'A note on Campbell's distinction between internal and external validity', *Quality and Quantity*, forthcoming.
—— (1991c) 'A myth of a myth? An assessment of two studies of option choice in secondary schools', *British Journal of Sociology*, 42, 1, pp.61–94.
—— (1991d) 'Review of P. Atkinson, *The Ethnographic Imagination*', *Reviewing Sociology*, forthcoming.
—— (1991e) 'Some reflections on ethnography and validity', forthcoming in *International Journal of Qualitative Studies in Education*.
HAMMERSLEY, M. and ATKINSON, P. (1983) *Ethnography: principles in practice*. London: Tavistock.
HAMMERSLEY, M. and SCARTH, J. (1990) 'On the concept of the teacher as researcher', unpublished paper.
HAMMERSLEY, M., SCARTH, J. and WEBB, S. (1984) 'Developing and testing theory: the case of research on student learning and examinations', in R. Burgess, (ed.) *Issues in Educational Research: Qualitative Methods*. Lewes: Falmer Press.
HANDLIN, O. (1979) *Truth in History*. Cambridge, Mass.: Harvard University Press.
HARGREAVES, A. (1984) 'Marxism and relative autonomy', unit 22, Open University course *E205 Conflict and Change in Education*. Milton Keynes: Open University Press.
HARGREAVES, D. H. (1967) *Social Relations in a Secondary School*. London: Routledge.
—— (1978) 'Whatever happened to symbolic interactionism?', in L.

Barton and R. Meighan (eds) *Sociological Interpretation of Schooling and Classrooms*. Driffield: Nafferton.
HARRÉ, R. (1970) *The Principles of Scientific Thinking*. London: Macmillan.
HARRÉ, R. and SECORD, P. (1972) *The Explanation of Social Behaviour*. Oxford: Blackwell.
HART, H.L.A. and HONORÉ, T. (1985) *Causation and the Law*. Oxford: Oxford University Press (2nd edn).
HARVEY, L. (1987) *Myths of the Chicago School*. Aldershot: Gower.
—— (1990) *Critical Social Research*. London: Unwin Hyman.
HASTRUP, K. and ELSASS, P. (1990) 'Anthropological advocacy: a contradiction in terms?', *Current Anthropology*, 31, 3, pp.301–11.
HAYEK, F.A. (1955) *The Counter-Revolution of Science: studies in the abuse of reason*. New York: Free Press.
HEMPEL, C.G. (1959) 'The function of general laws in history', in P. Gardiner (ed.) *Theories of History*. New York: Free Press.
—— (1963) 'Reasons and covering laws in historical explanations', in S. Hook (ed.) *Philosophy and History*. New York: New York University Press.
HERSKOVITS, M. (1972) *Cultural Relativism*. New York: Random House.
HERZFELD, M. (1987) *Anthropology Through the Looking Glass: critical ethnography in the margins of Europe*. Cambridge: Cambridge University Press.
HINDESS, B. and HIRST, P.Q. (1975) *Pre-Capitalist Modes of Production*. London: Routledge and Kegan Paul.
HODGES, H.A. (1952) *The Philosophy of Wilhelm Dilthey*. London: Routledge and Kegan Paul.
HUFF, T.E. (1984) *Max Weber and the Methodology of the Social Sciences*. New Brunswick: Transaction Books.
HUGHES, E. (1971) *The Sociological Eye*. Chicago: Aldine/Atherton.
IGGERS, G.G. (1968) *The German Conception of History*. Middletown, Connecticut: Wesleyan University Press.
ILLICH, I. (1981) *Shadow Work*. London: Marion Boyars.
INGRAM, D. (1987) *Habermas and the Dialectic of Reason*. New Haven: Yale University Press.
JACOB, E. (1987) 'Qualitative research traditions: a review', *Review of Educational Research*, 57, 1, pp.1–50.
JAMES, W. (1902) *The Varieties of Religious Experience*. New York: Longman, Green and Co.
—— (1909) *The Meaning of Truth*. New York: Longman, Green and Co.
JARVIE, I.C. (1964) *The Revolution in Anthropology*. London: Routledge and Kegan Paul.
—— (1975) 'Cultural relativism again', *Philosophy of the Social Sciences*, 5, pp.343–53.
—— (1983) *Rationality and Relativism*. London: Routledge and Kegan Paul.
JAY, M. (1973) *The Dialectical Imagination: a history of the Frankfurt School and the Institute for Social Research 1923–1950*. Boston: Little, Brown.
JOHNSON, J.M. (1975) *Doing Field Research*. New York: Free Press.

KATZ, J. (1983) 'A theory of qualitative methodology: the social system of analytic fieldwork', in R.M. Emerson (ed.) *Contemporary Field Research*. Boston: Little, Brown.

KEAT, R. (1981) *The Politics of Social Theory*. Oxford: Blackwell.

KEAT, R. and URRY, J. (1975) *Social Theory as Science*. London: Routledge and Kegan Paul.

KEDDIE, N. (1971) 'Classroom knowledge', in M. F. D. Young (ed.) *Knowledge and Control*. New York: Collier Macmillan.

KELLNER, D. (1975) 'The Frankfurt School revisited: a critique of Martin Jay's "The Dialectical Imagination"', *New German Critique*, 4, pp.131–52.

KELLY, A. (1985) 'Action research: what it is and what it can do', in R.G. Burgess (ed.) *Issues in Educational Research: qualitative methods*. Lewes: Falmer.

KENNEDY, M.M. (1979) 'Generalizing from single case studies', *Evaluation Quarterly*, 3, pp.661–78.

KIRK, J. and MILLER, M. (1986) *Reliability and Validity in Qualitative Research*. Beverly Hills: Sage.

KOLAKOWSKI, L. (1975) *Husserl and the Search for Certitude*. New Haven: Yale University Press.

—— (1978) *Main Currents of Marxism*, vol. 3. Oxford: Oxford University Press.

KORNHAUSER, R. R. (1978) *Social Sources of Delinquency*. Chicago: University of Chicago Press.

KORTIAN, G. (1980) *Metacritique: the philosophical argument of Jurgen Habermas*. Cambridge: Cambridge University Press.

KRIEGER, L. (1977) *Ranke: the meaning of history*. Chicago: University of Chicago Press.

KRIEGER, S. (1983) *The Mirror Dance: identity in a women's community*. Philadelphia: Temple University Press.

—— (1984) 'Fiction and social science', in N.K. Denzin (ed.) *Studies in Symbolic Interactionism*, vol. 5. Greenwich, Connecticut: JAI Press.

KRONER, R. (1914) *Kant's 'Weltanschauung'*. English translation, Chicago, University of Chicago Press (1956).

KUHN, T. S. (1962) *The Structure of Scientific Revolutions*. Chicago: University of Chicago Press (2nd edn 1970).

LACEY, C. (1970) *Hightown Grammar*. Manchester: Manchester University Press.

LATAPI, P. (1988) 'Participatory research: a new research paradigm?', *Alberta Journal of Education*, 34, 1, pp.310–19.

LATHER, P. (1984) 'Critical theory, curricular transformation and feminist mainstreaming', *Journal of Education*, 166, pp.49–62.

—— (1986a) 'Issues of validity in openly ideological research', *Interchange*, 17, 4, pp.63–84.

—— (1986b) 'Research as praxis', *Harvard Education Review*, 56, 3, pp.257–76.

LAYTON, D. (1973) *Science for the People*. London: Allen and Unwin.

LE ROY LADURIE, E. (1978) *Montaillou*. Aldershot: Scolar Press.

LECOMPTE, M.D. and GOETZ, J.P. (1982) 'Problems of reliability and validity in ethnographic research', *Review of Educational Research*, 52, 1, pp.31–60.

LEFF, G. (1969) *History and Social Theory*. London: Allen and Unwin.

LIAZOS, A. (1972) 'The poverty of the sociology of deviance: nuts, sluts and perverts', *Social Problems*, 20, pp.102–20.

LINCOLN, Y.S. and GUBA, E.G. (1985) *Naturalistic Inquiry*, Beverly Hills: Sage.

LINDESMITH, A. (1937) *The Nature of Opiate Addiction*. Chicago: University of Chicago Libraries.

—— (1968) *Addiction and Opiates*. Chicago: Aldine.

LOBKOWICZ, N. (1967) *Theory and Practice*. Notre Dame: University of Notre Dame Press.

—— (1977) 'On the history of theory and practice', in T. Ball (ed.) *Political Theory and Praxis*. Minneapolis: University of Minnesota Press.

LOFLAND, J. (1966) *Doomsday Cult: a study of conversion, proselytization and maintenance of faith*. Englewood Cliffs, N.J.: Prentice Hall.

—— (1967) 'Notes on naturalism', *Kansas Journal of Sociology*, 3, 2, pp.45–61.

—— (1972) *Analyzing Social Settings*. Belmont, CA: Wadsworth. (2nd edn, Lofland and Lofland 1984).

—— (1974) 'Styles of reporting qualitative field research'. *American Sociologist*, 9, pp.101–11.

—— (1976) *Doing Social Life*. New York: Wiley.

—— (1988) 'Interactionism as anarchism', *Society for the Study of Symbolic Interaction Notes*, 14, 3, pp.5–6.

LOFLAND, J. and LOFLAND L.H. (1984) *Analyzing Social Settings*. Belmont, CA: Wadsworth (2nd edn).

LOWITH, K. (1949) *Meaning in History: the theological implications of the philosophy of history*. Chicago: University of Chicago Press.

LUNDBERG, G. (1929) *Social research*. New York: Longman, Green and Co.

—— (1933) 'Is sociology too scientific?', *Sociologus*, 9, pp.298–322.

—— (1964) *Foundations of Sociology*. New York: McKay.

LUTZ, F. (1981) 'Ethnography: the holistic approach to understanding schooling', in J. Green and C. Wallat (eds) *Ethnography and Language in Educational Settings*. Norwood, N.J.: Ablex.

LYNCH, F.R. (1977) 'Field research and future history: problems posed for ethnographic sociologists by the "Domesday Cult" making good', *American Sociologist*, 12, April, pp.80–8.

LYND, R.S. and LYND H.M. (1929) *Middletown: a study in American culture*. New York: Harcourt and Brace.

McCALL, G. (1984) 'Systematic field observation', *Annual Review of Sociology*, 10, pp.262–82.

McCALL, G. and SIMMONS, J.L. (1969) *Issues in Participant Observation*. Reading, Mass.: Addison-Wesley.

McCARTHY, T. (1978) *The Critical Theory of Jurgen Habermas*. London: Hutchinson.

McCLAREN, P. (1986) *Schooling as a Ritual Performance*. London: Routledge and Kegan Paul.

—— (1987) 'Schooling for salvation: a review of Peshkin's "God's Choice"', *Journal of Education*, 169, 2, pp.132–9.

McDERMOTT R.P. (1982) 'Rigor and respect as standards in ethnographic description', *Harvard Educational Review*, 52, 3, pp.321–8.

MacINTYRE, A. (1981) *After Virtue*. London: Duckworth.

—— (1988) *Whose Justice, Which Rationality?* Notre Dame: University of Notre Dame Press.

MacNAMARA, D. (1980) 'The outsider's arrogance: the failure of participant observers to understand classroom events', *British Educational Research Journal*, 6, 2, pp.113–25.

van MAANEN, J. (1988) *Tales of the Field*. Chicago: University of Chicago Press.

MANDELBAUM, M. (1977) *The Anatomy of Historical Knowledge*. Baltimore, Md.: Johns Hopkins University Press.

MANNING, P.K. (1982) 'Analytic induction', in R.B. Smith and P.K. Manning (eds) *Handbook of Social Science Methods, volume II: Qualitative methods*. Cambridge, Mass.: Ballinger.

MARCUS, G. and CUSHMAN, D. (1982) 'Ethnographies as texts', *Annual Review of Anthropology*, 11, pp.25–69.

MARCUS, G. and FISCHER, M. (1986) *Anthropology as Cultural Critique*. Chicago: University of Chicago Press.

MARSHALL, C. (1985) 'Appropriate criteria of trustworthiness and goodness for qualitative research on educational organizations', *Quality and Quantity*, 19, pp.353–73.

MASEMANN, V.L. (1982) 'Critical ethnography in the study of comparative education', *Comparative Education Review*, 26, 1, pp.1–15.

MATZA, D. (1964) *Delinquency and Drift*. New York: Wiley.

—— (1969) *Becoming Deviant*. Englewood Cliffs: Prentice Hall.

MEASOR, L. (1983) 'Gender and the sciences', in M. Hammersley and A. Hargreaves (eds) *Curriculum Practice: Some Sociological Case-Studies*. Lewes: Falmer.

MERTON, R.K. (1972) 'Insiders and outsiders', *American Journal of Sociology*, 78, pp.9–47.

MIES, M. (1983) 'Toward a methodology for feminist research', in G. Bowles and R.D. Klein (eds) *Theories of Women's Studies*. London: Routledge and Kegan Paul.

MILES, M.B. and HUBERMAN, M. (1984) *Qualitative Data Analysis*. Beverly Hills: Sage.

MILLER, R.W. (1987) *Fact and Method: explanation, confirmation and reality*. Princeton: Princeton University Press.

MILLHAM, S., BULLOCK, R., HOSIE, K. and HAAK, M. (1986) *Lost in Care: the problem of maintaining links between children in care and their families*. Aldershot: Gower.

MISHLER, E.G. (1990) 'Validation in inquiry-guided research: the role of exemplars in narrative studies', *Harvard Educational Review*, 60, 4, pp.415–42.

MITCHELL, J.C. (1967) 'On Quantification in Social Anthropology', in A.L. Epstein (ed.) *The Craft of Social Anthropology*. London: Tavistock.

—— (1983) 'Case study and situational analysis', *Sociological Review*, 31, 2, pp.187–211.

MOON, J.D. (1983) 'Political ethics and critical theory', in D.R. Sabia and J. Wallulis (eds) *Changing Social Science: critical theory and other critical perspectives*. Albany: State University of New York Press.

MORRISON, J.E. and HENKEL, R.E. (eds) (1970) *The Significance Test Controversy*. Chicago: Aldine.

NEWTON-SMITH, W.H. (1981) *The Rationality of Science*. London: Routledge and Kegan Paul.

NISBET, R.A. (1962) 'Sociology as an art form', *Pacific Sociological Review*, 5, 2, pp.67–74. Reprinted in M. Stein and A. Vidich (eds) (1963) *Sociology on Trial*. Englewood Cliffs: Prentice Hall.

OAKES, G. (1988) *Weber and Rickert: concept formation in the cultural sciences*. Cambridge, Mass.: Massachusetts Institute of Technology Press.

OAKESHOTT, M. (1933) *Experience and its Modes*. Cambridge: Cambridge University Press.

OLESEN, V.L. and WHITTAKER, E.W. (1968) *The Silent Dialogue: a study in the social psychology of professional socialization*. San Francisco: Jossey Bass.

de OLIVEIRA, R. and de OLIVEIRA, M. (1982) 'The militant observer: a sociological alternative', in B. Hall, A. Gillett and R. Tandon (eds) *Creating Knowledge: a monopoly?* New Delhi: Society for Participatory Research in Asia.

OVEREND, T. (1978) 'Enquiry and ideology: Habermas's trichotomous conception of science', *Philosophy of the Social Sciences*, 8, pp.1–13.

OWENS, R. G. (1982) 'Methodological rigor in naturalistic inquiry', *Educational Administration Quarterly*, 18, 2, pp.1–21.

PAINE, R. (ed.) (1985) *Advocacy and Anthropology*. Newfoundland: Institute for Economic and Social Research, Memorial University.

PAPINEAU, D. (1987) *Reality and Representation*. Oxford: Blackwell.

PARKER, H., CASBURN, M. and TURNBULL, D. (1981) *Receiving Juvenile Justice*. Oxford: Blackwell.

PARRY, O. (1987) 'Uncovering the ethnographer', in N. McKeganey and S. Cunningham-Burley (eds) *Enter the Sociologist*. Aldershot: Avebury.

PARSONS, T. (1967) 'On the concept of political power', in R. Bendix and S.M. Lipset (eds) *Class, Status and Power*. London: Routledge and Kegan Paul (2nd edn).

PESHKIN, A. (1986) *God's Choice: the total world of a fundamentalist Christian school*. Chicago: University of Chicago Press.

PHILP, M. (1985) 'Power', in A. Kuper and J. Kuper (eds) *The Social Science Encyclopedia*. London: Routledge and Kegan Paul.

PILCHER, W. (1972) *The Portland Longshoreman: a dispersed urban community*. New York: Holt, Rinehart and Winston.

PLATT, J. (1971) *Social Research in Bethnal Green: an evaluation of the work of the Institute of Community Studies*. London: Macmillan.

—— (1981) 'Whatever happened to the case study', unpublished.

—— (1985) 'Weber's *Verstehen* and the history of qualitative research: the missing link', *British Journal of Sociology*, XXXVI, 3, pp.448–66.

—— (1988) 'What can case studies do?', *Studies in Qualitative Sociology*, vol.1. Greenwich, Connecticut: JAI Press, pp.1–23.

PLUMMER, K. (1983) *Documents of Life*. London; Allen and Unwin.

—— (1990) 'Herbert Blumer and the life history tradition', *Symbolic Interaction*, 13, 2, pp.125–44.

POLIER, N. and ROSEBERRY, W. (1989) 'Tristes tropes: post-modern anthropologists encounter the other and discover themselves', *Economy and Society*, 18, 2, pp.245–64.

POLLARD, A. (1982) 'A model of classroom coping strategies', *British Journal of Sociology of Education*, 3, 1.

—— (1984a) 'Ethnography and social policy for classroom practice', in L. Barton and S. Walker (eds) *Social Crisis and Educational Research*. London: Croom Helm.

—— (1984b) 'Coping strategies and the multiplication of differentiation in infant classrooms', *British Educational Research Review*, 10, 1, pp.33–48.

POLLARD, A. and TANN, S. (1987) *Reflective Teaching in the Primary School: a handbook for the classroom*. London: Cassell.

POLLOCK, J. (1987) *Contemporary Theories of Knowledge*. London: Hutchinson.

POPKEWITZ, T. (1984) *Paradigm and Ideology in Educational Research*. Lewes: Falmer.

POPPER, K.R. (1957) *The Poverty of Historicism*. London: Routledge and Kegan Paul.

—— (1968) *The Logic of Scientific Discovery*. London: Hutchinson (3rd edn).

—— (1979) *Objective Knowledge*. Oxford: Oxford University Press (2nd edn).

PROKOPCZYK, C. (1980) *Truth and Reality in Marx and Hegel: a reassessment*. Amherst, Mass.: University of Massachusetts Press.

PRUS, R. (1987) 'Generic social processes: maximizing conceptual development in ethnographic research', *Journal of Contemporary Ethnography*, 16, 3, pp.250–93.

PUNCH, M. (1979) *Policing in the Inner City*. London: Macmillan.

PUTNAM, H. (1981) *Reason, Truth and History*. Cambridge: Cambridge University Press.

QUANTZ, R. and O'CONNOR, T. (1988) 'Writing critical ethnography: multi-voicedness and carnival in cultural contexts', *Educational Theory*, 38, pp.95–109.

RADCLIFFE-BROWN, A.R. (1922) *The Andaman Islanders*. Cambridge: Cambridge University Press.

REASON, P. and ROWAN, J. (1981) *Inquiry: source book of New Paradigm research*. Chichester: Wiley.

REINHARZ, S. (1983) 'Experiential analysis: a contribution to feminist research', in G. Bowles and R. Duelli-Klein (eds) *Theories of Women's Studies*. London: Routledge and Kegan Paul.

—— (1985) 'Feminist distrust: problems of context and content in sociological work', in D. Berg and K. Smith (eds) *Clinical Demands of Social Research*. Beverly Hills: Sage.

RESCHER, N. (1984) *The Limits of Science*. Berkeley: University of California Press.

RICKERT, H. (1962) *Science and History*. Princeton: Van Nostrand. (First published in German in 1914.)

—— (1986) *The Limits of Concept Formation in Natural Science*. Cambridge: Cambridge University Press. (First published in German in 1902.)

RIST, R. (1970) 'Student social class and teacher expectations: the self-fulfilling prophecy in ghetto education', *Harvard Educational Review*, 40, pp.411–51.

—— (1977) 'On the relations among educational research paradigms: from disdain to *détente*', *Anthropology and Education Quarterly*, 8, 2, pp.42–9.

—— (1980) '*Blitzkrieg* ethnography: on the transformation of a method into a movement', *Educational Researcher*, 9, 2, pp.8–10.

—— (1984) 'On the application of qualitative research to the policy process: an emergent linkage', in L. Barton and S. Walker (eds) *Social Crisis and Educational Research*. London: Croom Helm.

ROBINSON, W.S. (1951) 'The logical structure of analytic induction', *American Sociological Review*, 16, 6, pp.812–18. Reprinted in McCall and Simmons (1969).

ROCK, P. (1973) 'Phenomenalism and essentialism in the sociology of deviance', *Sociology*, 7, 1, pp.17–29.

ROMAN, L. and APPLE, M. (1990) 'Is naturalism a move away from positivism? Materialist and feminist approaches to subjectivity in ethnographic research', in E. Eisner and A. Peshkin (eds) *Qualitative Inquiry in Education: the continuing debate*. New York: Teacher College Press.

RORTY, R. (1984) 'Solidarity or objectivity?', in J. Rajchman and C. West (eds) *Post-Analytic Philosophy*. New York: Columbia University Press.

ROSALDO, R. (1986) 'From the door of his tent: the fieldworker and the inquisitor', in J. Clifford and G. Marcus (eds) *Writing Culture: the poetics and politics of ethnography*. Berkeley: University of California Press.

ROTH, P.A. (1989) 'Ethnography without tears', *Current Anthropology*, 30, 5, pp.555–69.

RUDDUCK, J. (1987) 'Teacher research, action research, teacher inquiry: what's in a name?', in J. Rudduck, D. Hopkins, J. Sanger and P. Lincoln, *Collaborative Inquiry and Information Skills*, British Library research paper 16. Boston Spa: British Library.

SABIA, D.R. and WALLULIS, J. (eds) (1983) *Changing Social Science: critical theory and other critical perspectives*. Albany: State University of New York Press.

SANGREN, P.S. (1988) 'Rhetoric and the authority of ethnography: "postmodernism" and the social reproduction of texts', *Current Anthropology*, 29, pp.405–35.

SCARTH, J. (1983) 'Teachers' school-based experiences of examining', in M. Hammersley and A. Hargreaves (eds) *Curriculum Practice: some sociological case-studies.* Lewes: Falmer Press.

SCHATZMAN, L. and STRAUSS, A. (1973) *Field Research: strategies for a natural sociology.* Englewood Cliffs: Prentice Hall.

SCHEFF, T. (1986) 'Towards resolving the controversy over "thick description"', *Current Anthropology*, 24, 4, pp.408–9.

SCHEFFLER, I. (1967) *Science and Subjectivity.* New York: Bobbs-Merrill.

—— (1974) *Four Pragmatists.* London: Routledge and Kegan Paul.

SCHOFIELD, J.W. (1990) 'Increasing the generalizability of qualitative research', in E. Eisner and A. Peshkin (eds) *Qualitative Inquiry in Education: the continuing debate.* New York: Teacher College Press.

SCHON, D. (1986) *Educating the Reflective Practitioner.* San Francisco: Jossey Bass.

SCHUTZ, A. (1970) *Reflections on the Problem of Relevance.* New Haven: Yale University Press.

SCHUTZ, A. and LUCKMANN, T. (1974) *The Structures of the Life-World.* London: Heinemann.

SCHWAB, J. (1969) 'The practical: a language for curriculum', *School Review*, 78, pp.1–24.

SCRIVEN, M. (1959) 'Truisms as the grounds for historical explanations', in P. Gardiner (ed.) *Theories of History.* New York: Free Press.

SEWELL, W.H. (1967) 'Marc Bloch and the logic of comparative history', *History and Theory: studies in the philosophy of history*, VI, 2.

SHANKMAN, P. (1984) 'The thick and the thin: on the interpretive theoretical program of Clifford Geertz', *Current Anthropology*, 24, 4, pp.261–70 (See also the discussions of Shankman's article that appear in the same issue.)

SHARP, R. (1982) 'Self-contained ethnography or a science of phenomenal forms and inner relations', *Boston University Journal of Education*, 164, 1, pp.48–63.

SHARP, R. and GREEN, A. (1975) *Education and Social Control.* London: Routledge and Kegan Paul.

SHAW, C. (1931) 'Case study method', *Publications of the American Sociological Society*, 21, pp.149–57.

—— (1966) *The Jack Roller: a delinquent boy's own story.* Chicago: Chicago University Press.

SHAYER, D. (1970) *The Teaching of English in Schools.* London: Routledge and Kegan Paul.

SIEBER, S.D. (1973) 'The integration of fieldwork and survey methods', *American Journal of Sociology*, 78, pp.1335–59.

SIMMEL, G. (1977) *The Problems of the Philosophy of History.* New York: Free Press.

SIMON, R. and DIPPO, D. (1986) 'On critical ethnographic work', *Anthropology and Education Quarterly*, 17, pp.195–202.

SKOLNICK, J. (1966) *Justice Without Trial: law enforcement in democratic society.* New York: Wiley.

SMITH, J.K. (1984) 'The problem of criteria for judging interpretive inquiry', *Educational Evaluation and Policy Analysis*, 6, 4, pp.379–91.

—— (1989a) *The Nature of Social and Educational Inquiry: empiricism versus interpretation.* Norwood, N. J.: Ablex.

—— (1989b) 'Alternative research paradigms and the problem of criteria', paper given at International Conference on Alternative Paradigms for Inquiry, San Francisco.

SMITH, J.K. and HESHUSIUS, L. (1986) 'Closing down the conversation: the end of the quantitative–qualitative debate among educational inquirers', *Educational Researcher*, 15, 1, pp.4–12.

SMITH, P. (1981) *Realism and the Progress of Science.* Cambridge: Cambridge University Press.

STAKE, R.E. (1978) 'The case study method in social inquiry', *Educational Researcher*, Feb., pp.5–8.

STENHOUSE, L. (1975) *An Introduction to Curriculum Research and Development.* London: Heinemann.

—— (1979) 'The problem of standards in illuminative research', *Scottish Educational Review*, 11, 1, pp.5–10.

STOCKMAN, N. (1978) 'Habermas, Marcuse and the Aufhebung of science and technology', *Philosophy of the Social Sciences*, 8, pp.15–35.

STONE, L. (1981) *The Past and the Present.* London: Routledge and Kegan Paul.

STORING, H.J. (ed.) (1962) *Essays on the Scientific Study of Politics.* New York: Holt, Rinehart and Winston.

STRAUSS, A. (1987) *Qualitative Analysis for Social Scientists.* Cambridge: Cambridge University Press.

STRONG, P.M. (1979) *The Ceremonial Order of the Clinic.* London: Routledge and Kegan Paul.

STRONG, P.M. (1988) 'Minor courtesies and macro structures', in P. Drew and A. Wootton (eds) *Erving Goffman: exploring the interaction order.* Cambridge: Polity Press.

SUDNOW, D. (1967) *Passing On: the social organization of dying.* Englewood Cliffs, N.J.: Prentice Hall.

SUPPE, F. (ed.) (1974) *The Structure of Scientific Theories.* Chicago: University of Chicago Press.

TENNEKES, J. (1971) *Anthropology, Relativism and Method.* Assen: Van Gorcum.

THOMAS, J. (1983) 'Toward a critical ethnography: a reexamination of the Chicago legacy', *Urban Life*, 11, 4, pp.477–90.

THOMAS, W.I. and ZNANIECKI, F. (1927) *The Polish Peasant in Europe and America*, five volumes. Chicago: University of Chicago Press/ Boston: Badger Press.

TORBERT, W.R. (1983) 'Initiating collaborative inquiry', in G. Morgan (ed.) *Beyond Method: strategies for social research*, Beverly Hills: Sage.

TRIGG, R. (1980) *Reality at Risk.* Brighton: Harvester.

TRIPP, D.H. (1985) 'Case study generalisation: An agenda for action', *British Educational Research Journal*, 11, 1, pp.33–43.

TURNBULL, C. (1973) *The Mountain People.* London: Jonathan Cape.

TURNER, R.H. (1953) 'The quest for universals in sociological research', *American Sociological Review*, 18, pp.604–11. Reprinted in McCall and Simmons (1969).

TURNER, S. and FACTOR, R. (1981) 'Objective possibility and adequate causation in Weber's methodological writings', *Sociological Review*, 29, 1, pp.5–28.

TYLER, S.A. (1985) 'Ethnography, intertextuality, and the end of description', *American Journal of Semiotics*, 3, 4, pp.83–98.

—— (1986) 'Post-modern ethnography: from document of the occult to occult document', in J. Clifford and G. Marcus (eds) *Writing Culture: the poetics and politics of ethnography*. Berkeley: University of California Press.

VISION, G. (1988) *Modern Anti-Realism and Manufactured Truth*. London: Routledge.

WALKER, R. (1978) 'The conduct of educational case studies', in B. Dockerill and D. Hamilton (eds) *Rethinking Educational Research*. London: Hodder and Stoughton.

WALLER, W. (1934) 'Insight and scientific method', *American Journal of Sociology*, 40, 3, pp.285–97.

WALTERS, R.G. (1980) 'Signs of the times: Clifford Geertz and the historian', *Social Research*, 47, 3.

WEBER, M. (1949) *The Methodology of the Social Sciences*. New York: Free Press.

—— (1975) *Roscher and Knies: the logical problems of historical economics*. New York: Free Press.

WEINBERG, M. (1973) 'The nudist management of respectability' and 'Becoming a nudist', in E. Rubington and M.S. Weinberg (eds) *Deviance: the interactionist perspective*. New York: Macmillan.

WEINSHEIMER, J. C. (1985) *Gadamer's Hermeneutics*, New Haven: Yale University Press.

WEST, W.G. (1984) 'Phenomenon and form in interactionist and neo-Marxist qualitative educational research', in L. Barton and S. Walker (eds) *Social Crisis and Educational Research*. London: Croom Helm.

WHITE, S. (1983) 'Habermas on the foundations of ethics and political theory', in D.R. Sabia and J. Wallulis (eds) *Changing Social Science: critical theory and other critical perspectives*. Albany: State University of New York Press

—— (1988) *The Recent Work of Jurgen Habermas*. Cambridge: Cambridge University Press.

WHYTE, W.F. (1943) *Street Corner Society*. Chicago: Chicago University Press.

WIEDER, D.L. (1974) *Language and Social Reality: the case of telling the convict code*. The Hague: Mouton.

WILLER, D. (1967) *Scientific Sociology: theory and method*. Englewood Cliffs, N.J.: Prentice Hall.

WILLIAMS, R. (1976) 'Symbolic interactionism: fusion of theory and research', in D.C. Thorns (ed.) *New Directions in Sociology*. Newton Abbott: David and Charles.

—— (1988) 'Understanding Goffman's methods', in P. Drew and A. Wootton (eds) *Erving Goffman: exploring the interaction order*. Cambridge: Polity Press.

van WILLIGEN, J. (1986) *Applied Anthropology: an introduction.* Massachusetts: Bergin and Garvey.

WILLIS, P. (1977) *Learning to Labour.* Farnborough: Saxon House.

WINCH, P. (1958) *The Idea of a Social Science and its Relation to Philosophy.* London: Routledge and Kegan Paul.

—— (1964) 'Understanding a primitive society', *American Philosophical Quarterly*, 1, pp.307–24.

WOLCOTT, H. F. (1973) *The Man in the Principal's Office: an ethnography.* New York: Holt, Rinehart and Winston.

—— (1975) 'Criteria for an ethnographic approach to research in schools', *Human Organization*, 34, pp.111–27.

—— (1980) 'How to look like an anthropologist without really being one', *Practising Anthropology*, 3, 2, pp.56–9.

—— (1982) 'Mirrors, models and monitors: educator adaptations of the ethnographic "innovation"', in G. Spindler (ed.) *Doing the Ethnography of Schooling.* New York: Holt, Rinehart and Winston.

—— (1990) 'On seeking – and rejecting – validity in qualitative research', in E. Eisner and A. Peshkin (eds) *Qualitative Inquiry in Education: the continuing debate.* New York: Teacher College Press.

WOODS, P. (1979) *The Divided School.* London: Routledge and Kegan Paul.

—— (1985) 'Ethnography and theory construction in educational research', in R.G. Burgess (ed.) *Field Methods in the Study of Education.* Lewes: Falmer Press.

—— (1986) *Inside Schools.* London: Routledge and Kegan Paul.

—— (1987) 'Ethnography at the crossroads: a reply to Hammersley', *British Educational Research Journal*, 13, pp.297–307.

YIN, R. (1984) *Case Study Research.* Beverly Hills: Sage.

ZELDITCH, M. (1962) 'Some methodological problems of field studies', *American Journal of Sociology*, 67, pp.566–76.

ZNANIECKI, F. (1934) *The Method of Sociology.* New York: Farrar and Rinehart.

ZORBAUGH, H. (1929) *The Gold Coast and the Slum.* Chicago: University of Chicago Press.

NAME INDEX

223

SUBJECT INDEX